The Forger's Tale

NEW AFRICAN HISTORIES SERIES

Series editors: Jean Allman and Allen Isaacman

David William Cohen and E. S. Atieno Odhiambo, *The Risks of Knowledge: Investigations into the Death of the Hon. Minister John Robert Ouko in Kenya, 1990*

Belinda Bozzoli, *Theatres of Struggle and the End of Apartheid*

Gary Kynoch, *We Are Fighting the World: A History of Marashea Gangs in South Africa, 1947–1999*

Stephanie Newell, *The Forger's Tale: The Search for Odeziaku*

Jacob A. Tropp, *Natures of Colonial Change: Environmental Relations in the Making of the Transkei*

The Forger's Tale

The Search for Odeziaku

∽

Stephanie Newell

OHIO UNIVERSITY PRESS
ATHENS

Ohio University Press, Athens, Ohio 45701
www.ohio.edu/oupress
© 2006 by Ohio University Press

Printed in the United States of America
All rights reserved

Ohio University Press books are printed on acid-free paper ∞ ™

13 12 11 10 09 08 07 06   5 4 3 2 1

Library of Congress Cataloging-in-Publication Data

Newell, Stephanie, 1968–
  The forger's tale : the search for Odeziaku / Stephanie Newell.
    p. cm. — (New African histories series)
  Includes bibliographical references and index.
  ISBN-13: 978-0-8214-1709-6 (hardcover : acid-free paper)
  ISBN-10: 0-8214-1709-6 (hardcover : acid-free paper)
  ISBN-13: 978-0-8214-1710-2 (pbk. : acid-free paper)
  ISBN-10: 0-8214-1710-X (pbk. : acid-free paper)
  1. Stuart-Young, John Moray, 1881–1939. 2. Authors, English—20th century—Biography. 3. Gay authors—Great Britain—Biography. 4. Gay men—Great Britain—Identity. 5. Gay men—Africa—Identity. 6. Great Britain--Colonies—Africa—History—20th century. 7. Forgers—Great Britain—Biography. I. Title.
  PR6037.T915Z79 2006
  828'.91209--dc22

2006021296

Contents

List of Figures ix
Acknowledgments vii

Introduction   Buried beneath Imperial History
                The Search for "Odeziaku"   1

Chapter 1   Forging Ahead
           The Secret Gentleman of Ardwick Green   21

Chapter 2   The Palm Oil Trader's View   33

Chapter 3   Fragments of Oscar Wilde in Colonial Nigeria   56

Chapter 4   "Uranian" Love in West Africa   75

Chapter 5   The Politics of Naming
           Igbo Perspectives on Stuart-Young   89

Chapter 6   The Strange Toleration of Stuart-Young in the African-Owned Press of Nigeria   108

Chapter 7   A Class Apart
           "Johnny Jones" of Back Kay Street   119

Chapter 8   The Production of a Poet
           Stuart-Young's Verse and Its Readers   138

Conclusion   "Tales That Lie Awake"   159

Notes   171
Bibliography   213
Index   227

Figures

Front cover. Stuart-Young in Onitsha.

Fig. 1. Conviction of "John Mount Stewart Young" at the City of Manchester Court of Summary Jurisdiction, 8 February 1899 — 22

Fig. 2. Photograph of Stuart-Young taken in the year of his conviction — 31

Fig. 3. Photograph of Stuart-Young taken in 1904 or 1905 — 58

Fig. 4. Photograph of Stuart-Young taken in 1895 — 59

Fig. 5. "My Own Jack": letter purportedly from Oscar Wilde to Stuart-Young — 60

Fig. 6. "My Dear Jack": letter purportedly from Oscar Wilde to Stuart-Young — 60

Fig. 7. "My Dear Mahaffy": authentic letter in Wilde's handwriting — 61

Fig. 8. "'Ibrahim the Unkissed' and J. M. Stuart-Young" — 79

Fig. 9. Photograph of Onwuije Hayford Bosah taken during his tour of Britain with Stuart-Young in 1911–12 — 81

Fig. 10. "The Admirer" — 85

Fig. 11. "The Hearer" — 85

Fig. 12. Letter from Stuart-Young to Frank Harris, dated 11 April 1925 — 95

Fig. 13. Carved staff in the form of the python as foreigner — 99

Fig. 14. Map of Back Kay Street drawn by Stuart-Young — 121

Fig. 15. Ardwick and Back Kay Street in 1932 — 121

Fig. 16. Typical dwellings in Ardwick, Manchester: Back John Street, 1902 — 122

Fig. 17.	Street scene from Ardwick, Manchester: 4–8 Union Place, 1902	122
Fig. 18.	A view of Stuart-Young's neighborhood as it is today: Kale Street, which replaced Kay Street	123
Fig. 19.	Buildings on the site of Back Kay Street in 2005	123
Fig. 20.	St. Thomas's School, Ardwick	124
Fig. 21.	Photograph of the boys' entrance, St. Thomas's School, Ardwick	125
Fig. 22.	The Little House of No Regrets in 2005	168
Fig. 23.	Contemporary uses for gravestones from the old cemetery, where Stuart-Young was buried	169

Acknowledgments

THIS BOOK IS DEDICATED to Douglas Killam, who generously gave me his entire collection of research materials on Stuart-Young, gathered over many years. A great intellectual debt is also owed to Timothy d'Arch Smith, who provided many fascinating leads on Stuart-Young's place in an English literary subculture.

In Nigeria, Professor Akachi Ezeigbo and Professor Chinyere Stella Okunna provided enormous practical and academic support over a four-year period. Anayo Andy Adibemma, Gab Okpaleze, and Victor Agusiobo were first-class research assistants, translators, and friends in Onitsha. Thanks are due to the many senior men and women of Onitsha who agreed to be interviewed for this project. Staff at the National Archives of Nigeria in Ibadan and Enugu provided a friendly and efficient service.

Anna Kerr's sensitive advice on how to rethink and restructure the story kept me working at the manuscript, and Jonathan Wild's willingness to share ideas about "middle-brow" British culture in the early twentieth century helped open my mind to Stuart-Young's social position in Manchester. I am indebted to Jean Allman, Allen Isaacman, and Gillian Berchowitz for their assistance in guiding the manuscript through its final stages. The comments of members of the English Department at the University of Lagos also helped to shape my ideas about the Igbo names for Stuart-Young.

Grahame Smith and Angela Smith provided useful guidance on Edwardian poetry. Donald H. Mader kindly shared his copy of Stuart-Young's *Impressions*, and the ever-inspiring Misty Bastian offered many ideas about Mami Wata in Onitsha. Karen Chiarodit's comments on Stuart-Young's forgeries helped me to appreciate his complex personality, as did Kathryn Thorndycraft's report comparing Stuart-Young's and Oscar Wilde's handwriting samples. Research trips to West Africa and an extended period of writing were generously funded by a Leverhulme Research Fellowship in 2004–2005. Research funding also came from Trinity College Dublin in 2002 and the Research Fund of the School of Humanities, University of Sussex.

A version of chapter 3 appeared as "Fragments of Oscar Wilde in Colonial Nigeria: the Story of J. M. Stuart-Young," *English Literature in Transition* 47, no. 1 (2004): 3–27; an earlier version of chapter 5 appeared as "Remembering J. M. Stuart-Young of Onitsha, Colonial Nigeria: Memoirs, Obituaries and Names," *Africa* 73, no. 4 (2003): 505–30. Thanks are due to the editors and publishers of both journals for their permission to reproduce this material.

Permission to reprint photographic and archival materials came from the following: front cover by permission of Ohio Historical Society; figures 1, 16, 17, and 20 by permission of Manchester Library and Information Services, Manchester Archives and Local Studies; figures 2–8, 10, and 11 by kind permission of the Board of Trinity College Dublin; figure 9 by kind permission of Enyi Onyeomadiko Helen Onochie; figure 12 by permission of the Harry Ransom Humanities Research Center, The University of Texas at Austin; figure 13 by kind permission of Oxford University Press; figure 15 by kind permission of the Ordnance Survey. Every effort has been made to establish the ownership of the photographic material reproduced in this book. Additional information should be sent to the author, care of Ohio University Press.

INTRODUCTION

Buried beneath Imperial History

The Search for "Odeziaku"

> Onitsha had always attracted the exceptional, the colourful and the bizarre. Take the strange Englishman, J. M. Stuart-Young . . . a mystery man who was perhaps a doctor of philosophy and perhaps not.
>
> —Emmanuel Obiechina, *Literature for the Masses*[1]

AT DAYBREAK ON 30 May 1939, approximately 200 senior and influential Igbo women assembled outside a modest wooden house in New Market Road, Onitsha. Quaintly named "The Little House of No Regrets," the property belonged to a British palm oil trader and poet who was known to the educated community as Dr. John Moray Stuart-Young and to the market women as "Odoziaku" (meaning "arranger, manager, or keeper of wealth"), a name he and his elite African friends persistently misspelled as "Odeziaku."[2] He had died two days earlier in Port Harcourt after a long struggle against throat cancer. The women now gathering outside his house controlled the large market in Onitsha and they wished to make certain comments about the life of the deceased.

Inside the house, Solomon Obike grieved for the man with whom he had lived for nearly twenty years, first as a servant, boy-lover, and protégé in the late 1920s; later as a secretary and companion; and finally as a nurse.[3] For many of these years, Obike's wife and children occupied rooms at the back of the house, looking in on the affectionate, shifting relationship between the Manchester trader and the younger Igbo man.

At a signal from the women's leader outside the building, the mourning party started to dance and sing, using the licensed performance space conferred on Igbo women at funerals to construct a forceful commentary on the life of the deceased. A funeral represented a critical chapter in a person's life story in Onitsha at this time: the good name one had built up since birth could be reinforced or shattered by the oral performances of different groups of mourners.[4] Core participants in the ceremonies—especially the different women's groups linked to a lineage—could bring shame on the deceased by boycotting the activities required of them in protest at his or her poor behavior.[5] They could also exploit formal lamentation genres by inserting grammars of disapproval and contempt into the lavish praise songs typically performed on such occasions. Aberrant citizens could thus expect to fall into a web of oral censure at some point in their lives.

The deceased man can be regarded as a perfect candidate for just such critical exposure: judged by the most normative Igbo cultural standards of the day, he had died as an isolated individual with no offspring to continue his patrilineage.[6] Unlike the homes and workplaces of many of his fellow Europeans in the early colonial period, Odeziaku's several houses and stores in Onitsha exhibited no visible signs of a wife, wives, or concubines.[7] Moreover, he had never brought honor to his name by investing in any of the status-conferring titles available for wealthy men in Igboland.[8] Living on the first floor of the Little House of No Regrets, tended by his manservant, Odeziaku remained a "complete bachelor" in all senses of the term. He manifestly refused to embark upon any of the social pathways favored by Igbos to achieve full social adulthood.[9]

The fact that at his funeral the most powerful women in the community did not publicly judge Odeziaku to be a scandalous or anomalous presence reveals a great deal about the reasons for his long residence in Onitsha and provides the starting point for this study of different forms of agency, sexuality, and power in colonial Britain and Nigeria. Given Stuart-Young's perpetual "bachelor" status and his widespread reputation among Nigerians as a "woman-hater," it is surprising that the group of dancing women did not perform satirical or abusive songs, as they might have done for a male lineage member who disrupted community values.[10] Instead, the women praised the way Odeziaku had brought wealth to Onitsha after 1905 and they hailed his long fight for African traders' rights in the face of colonial legislation that favored monopolistic European firms. They also praised his cultural and economic contributions to Onitsha since the 1910s, including his sponsorship of local youths. Finally, they blessed him as an honorary "son of the soil."[11] Declining the opportunity to construct a critical life story around Odeziaku, the senior women showered praises on him instead and, as the local newspapers reported, they "visited all his buildings singing dirges and eulogising his name."[12] Stuart-Young's generosity, justice, and fairness to the community had earned him the honor of dying a "good death" in the public sphere.[13] All the while, the women's economic space, Onitsha's main market—usually one of the largest and busiest markets in West Africa—remained "practically deserted."[14]

Igbo women were the chief, but not the sole, producers of Stuart-Young's name for posterity. In pressrooms throughout Eastern Nigeria in June and July 1939, influential and elite African editors composed front-page tributes, hailing Dr. Stuart-Young's contribution to the intellectual and economic life of the region. Furthermore, at his lavish "second burial" several weeks after the funeral,[15] an estimated 10,000 mourners filled the streets of Onitsha for a celebration that lasted four days.[16] Unprecedented for a white man, this customary celebration involved every sector of African society and publicly confirmed Stuart-Young's good name. Diverse constituencies of Igbos, Nigerians, and West African migrants participated in the ceremonies, including influential political figures such as the chiefs of Onitsha, merchant queens, and elite African newspapermen such as Nnamdi Azikiwe. Market women, clerks, aspiring poets, schoolteachers, untitled youths, and the children of the town also crowded the streets. Special prominence was given to the Odoziaku (or Odeziaku) age-grade of males born between 1909 and 1911, established by one of Stuart-Young's favorite boys, Joseph Etukokwu, who had become a wealthy entrepreneur under the senior man's patronage (see chapter 4). At the command of the *obi* (king), other young men of Onitsha sounded the *ogene* in honor of Odeziaku, and war drums and tom-toms were played "as if for a free Prince of the land."[17] "According to Onitsha customary rights," Etukokwu wrote in his memoirs, "I led my students to the funeral to pay our last respect to a great friend."[18]

Clearly there was widespread local admiration for Stuart-Young between his first arrival in West Africa and his death in 1939. By contrast, colonial officials and members of the Roman Catholic Mission at Onitsha knew him as a peevish trader from the English lower classes who fought against their efforts to introduce "civilization" to African communities on the River Niger (see chapter 6). Other Europeans regarded him a little more affectionately, but also with reservations, as one of the many "queer fellows" to find a home in the British Empire.[19]

Focusing on the period between 1880 and 1940, *The Forger's Tale* asks how it was possible for this unconventional, boy-loving Englishman to earn such a majestic traditional funeral in a society where few Europeans recognized his achievements and where, more importantly, few Europeans achieved such prestige among the local population. Was Stuart-Young's homosexuality irrelevant to the Igbo community, elite and nonelite alike, or were local cultural resources made available at different levels of society to accommodate his sexual difference? In what ways did his record in Manchester as a forger and a liar follow him to Igboland and infiltrate his own and his friends' constructions of his biography? To what extent did his racial and political status as a white man in colonial Africa help protect him from censure by the local community? In attempting to address these questions, *The Forger's Tale* pays close attention to different forms of West African cultural production, including newspaper articles and letters pages, oral naming practices, the symbolic spaces furnished by the spirit realm, and Igbo public debates about sexuality and ethics.

Stuart-Young lived for thirty years in a region that was experiencing rapid alterations to precolonial leadership structures alongside a consolidation of colonial rule. He dwelled in Onitsha during the period of its transformation from a small but strategic missionary and trading post on the River Niger into the regional headquarters of Onitsha Province, complete with colonial cantonments, military barracks, a courthouse, schools, and a European "resident" or district commissioner to oversee the work of a wide network of warrant chiefs and local rulers.[20] Changes in the architectural appearance of the town reflected these political and ideological transformations.

In Stuart-Young's lifetime, Onitsha also experienced the rapid expansion of the international trade in palm oil and kernels, which created fresh opportunities for established and new classes of entrepreneurs—especially Igbo women and lower-class European men, respectively—to make their fortunes (see chapter 2). Indigenous women and lower-class white men thus encountered one another in an arena other than the sexual realm that tends to dominate studies of imperialism and gender. All the while, with increasing fervor and success as the twentieth century progressed, Roman Catholic and Anglican missionaries proselytized from bases at Onitsha, penetrating Igboland along existing trade routes and spreading the Christian word to intrigued, increasingly receptive communities.[21] A politically vocal and influential African-owned press helped to shape and interpret all these processes, while at a popular level the shifts in local power structures were reflected in the wide range of new African titles, names, groups, dances, and relationships that emerged in different Igbo towns.[22] Each of these spheres of activity informs the individual story of Stuart-Young as it appears in *The Forger's Tale*.

As a "palm oil ruffian" on the waterways of Nigeria and as an importer of foreign commodities for barter with Africans, Stuart-Young was inextricable from the economic boom that reverberated up and down the River Niger in the early twentieth century. African communities along the rivers had long-established patterns of consumption for imported commodities; slaves rather than palm products would have been exchanged for them in previous centuries. Economically, the first quarter of the twentieth century differs from earlier decades in West Africa because of the expansion in European trading activity, the arrival of large numbers of men like Stuart-Young to work for the

European firms, and the concomitant rapid expansion of the African consumer economy (see chapter 2). Stuart-Young was different from his fellow traders, however, for he was one of the few independent businessmen in West Africa to survive in trade after the First World War and he was one of the few active poets in the palm oil community.

Local responses to these political and social transformations are frequently missing from cultural histories of imperialism, an omission that is especially problematic in the study of sexualities.[23] For a demonstration of the often subtle ways in which local agency can be erased by historians of empire, one can turn to the opening pages of Robert Aldrich's *Colonialism and Homosexuality*. This encyclopedic book analyzes the lives (and loves) of numerous men of empire, including T. E. Lawrence and Henry Morton Stanley, as well as lesser-known Europeans such as Stuart-Young. *Colonialism and Homosexuality* is not about the "colonised 'other,'" Aldrich emphasizes in his introduction. Rather, the book aims "to provide the context in which local men, *for whatever motivation*, contracted intimate relationships with foreigners."[24] This statement implies that contextual information about colonized cultures can provide few clues about local men's sexual motivations.

Colonialism and Homosexuality exhibits a curious, symptomatic tension between context and agency in the writing of imperial history. Local men's motivations remain unknowable, in Aldrich's view, for the western researcher cannot adopt an "indigenous" point of view and explain the "sexual imperatives and options in non-Western society."[25] While this ethnic humility is understandable in the context of postcolonial debates about "speaking for" the other,[26] Aldrich's lack of curiosity about nonwestern "imperatives and options" is also a form of silencing and disavowal. It serves to push away the very subjects who can provide the most revealing information about the European protagonists of *Colonialism and Homosexuality*, and it marginalizes the people who can reveal how homosexual European men were accommodated in diverse global locations at different moments in the development of imperialism. Such cultural information would help to fragment the monolithic, problematic category of "homosexual" that, as Aldrich himself recognizes, fails to represent accurately the vast majority of nonwestern sexualities that fall outside twentieth-century dichotomies of heterosexual and homosexual.[27]

Aldrich is not alone in his exclusion of ethnographic material from the construction of imperial contexts for European sexual encounters. Among many others, and for different reasons, Ronald Hyam, Joseph Bristow, and Christopher Lane also refuse to speculate about how homosexual Europeans were perceived and remembered by the specific communities in which they fulfilled their desires in the colonial period.[28] In particular, Hyam's survey of "the

British experience" in *Empire and Sexuality* revolves around the idea that colonial lands provided opportunities for "escape" from Victorian sexual prudery in Britain, giving men such as T. E. Lawrence the space to satisfy variegated and otherwise prohibited sexual drives.[29] European imperial expansion coincided with the codification of normative and nonnormative sexualities that made it difficult for homosexual men and women to explore their desires at home, so, in Hyam's view, they traveled to the colonies in search of spaces for freer sexual expression. Political agency is thus reduced to purely sexual desires as Hyam seeks to demonstrate that "the formation of empires can be explained by sex drives."[30]

One of the few exceptions to the trend against ethnography in histories of imperial homosexuality can be found in Rudi C. Bleys's *Geography of Perversion,* which sets out to reread and deconstruct colonial ethnographic documents in the search for examples of "male-to-male sexual behaviour outside the west."[31] In accord with Hyam and Aldrich, however, Bleys also concludes that for homosexual men in the colonial period, "escape from the rhetoric of decadence and marginality itself may have provoked a desire for exile, fed by the hope that the new-found habitat would embrace their sexuality in a natural way."[32]

While the real effects of fear and anxiety on Europeans with proscribed sexualities must not be ignored,[33] what is missing from all of these "great escape" theories of empire is a sense that the different members of the colonized community spent time examining and discussing new arrivals to their societies. Contemporary ethnography has done much to remedy the gaps and silences in the cultural history of postcolonial countries,[34] but the omission of the beloved and the local community from research into precolonial and colonial cultures leaves a vital gap in our understanding of the history of colonial homosexualities. This omission often gives the impression that a singular colonized society encountered a singular European colonizer. Scholars such as Aldrich, Hyam, and Bristow silence the "other" partner in the male homosexual relationship and render him a passive recipient of the white man's desires.[35] Far more than half the story is thereby excluded. None of these studies makes space for a discussion of the complex, nuanced, but difficult-to-retrieve ways in which homosexual white men were treated by women, men, and children positioned on the other side of the imperial divide.

By contrast, the names and titles by which Stuart-Young was known in Onitsha at his death in 1939—including "Odeziaku," "Dr. Stuart-Young," "Eke Young," and "Mami Wata's wife"—offer points of entry into local modes of constructing history in colonial Onitsha. As chapter 5 demonstrates, different classes and constituencies of African conferred names on Stuart-Young, each of which carried its own particular located commentary on his interactions with different sectors of Igbo society. The many local names for Stuart-Young exhibit the agency of local people in their shifting intellectual engagements with European society during the first three decades of the twentieth century.

Recent innovative studies by Ann Laura Stoler, Catherine Hall, Antoinette Burton, Felicity Nussbaum, and other "new imperial historians" have challenged Hyam's and Bristow's assumptions that British colonialism took a similar shape in different geographical locations.[36] These scholars question the notion that whiteness was manifested in the same way around the world and that the metropolis was an uncontested national entity, untouched by colonial cultures and critiques. Imperial cultures, they insist, helped create metropolitan norms and values to the extent that both sets of cultural formations were mutually constitutive.[37] "Metropolitan society," writes Burton, "had been both indissolubly linked to and continuously remade by Britain's colonial possessions since the sixteenth century."[38] "Europe's colonies were never empty spaces to be made over in Europe's image or fashioned in its interests," write Stoler and Cooper in their ground-breaking essay on the importance of indigenous perspectives. "[W]hat Europeans encountered in the colonies," they emphasize, "was not open terrain for economic domination, but people capable of circumventing and undermining the principles and practices on which extraction or capitalist development was based."[39]

Given this starting point and the insistence on a relational model of imperialism, it is surprising that patterns of exclusion toward local communities can be found in parts of the new imperial history. For example, while Hall and Burton carefully highlight the tensions in constructions of identity between metropolitan and settler colonial formations and the unsettling effect of foreign travelers in the metropolis, their lack of ethnographic detail about the places that were colonized serves to push local agency into the background.[40] Meanwhile, Stoler and Nussbaum tend to focus on European colonial settlers, the bourgeoisie, and the tensions between settler identities and metropolitan values. In so doing, these scholars seem to situate concepts of gender, race, class, and sexuality within European post-Enlightenment value systems rather than within local cultural formations.[41]

In spite of the scholarly preoccupation with sexuality, domesticity, and homosocial colonial spaces as "dense transfer points" of power,[42] indigenous homosexualities are rarely considered in this work, which emphasizes miscegenation and the imperial patrolling of male-female relationships.[43] Queer sexualities are excluded and the powerful local response to figures such as Stuart-Young remains inexplicable and lost to history in this framework. Yet, as the new imperial historians insist repeatedly, local perceptions of the colonial encounter are as vital to the study of imperialism as metropolitan and imperial perspectives, most especially when the encounters are of an intimate or a sexual nature.[44] But also, as the story of Stuart-Young will reveal, local perceptions of colonialism are manifested in the literary relationships that developed between authors and readers in colonial settings far away from metropolitan literary culture.

In leaving Britain for West Africa—in becoming Odeziaku—Stuart-Young did not step onto a deserted platform, devoid of cultural colors and perspectives. If the foreign colony provided the freedom for European men to express their variant sexualities, as both Hyam and Aldrich argue in their books, then local communities would have witnessed the economic and emotional negotiations involved in these expressions at a microsocial level. Local people's own kith and kin participated in the sexual and economic possibilities offered by individual white men in their communities. These white men would have been talked about, talked to, observed, and actively interpreted by different classes of "colonized" subjects who would have found places for the newcomers in relation to their own dynamic cultural codes and structures.

One of the reasons for imperial historians' neglect of ethnographic data collected in the colonial period relates to the methodological (and ethical) problems that arise in relation to the reliability, and transparency, of the "information" such studies yield about indigenous values and sexualities. In relation to the history of Igbo women, for example, Ifi Amadiume argues that it is impossible to separate content from tone in colonial anthropological accounts of African gender formations.[45] Whether undertaken by colonial officials such as P. Amaury Talbot and Major Arthur Glyn Leonard, missionaries such as Rev. G. T. Basden, or European women commissioned to study the motivations of African women such as Sylvia Leith-Ross, the anthropological material produced by European researchers in the nineteenth and twentieth centuries is saturated with Eurocentric racist assumptions about the sexuality of Africans.[46] In consequence, Amadiume argues, anthropological texts claiming to describe Igbo intimacies and gender codes can yield no useful or reliable information to the cultural historian and must be discarded in favor of alternative research methods.[47]

Amadiume's forceful rejection of European ethnography and the colonial archive generates an innovative alternative methodology for her research into the history of gender in Igboland, in which local actors and oral historians take center stage.[48] Her best-known book, *Male Daughters, Female Husbands*, reverses the trend against indigenous agency to be found in histories of imperialism and sexuality. Dispensing with English-authored publications, Amadiume turns to Igbo scholarship instead and makes use of indigenous oral and printed histories to construct a precolonial and colonial history of women in the town of Nnobi using local concepts and terminology to describe her material. In the West, she emphasizes, gender is attached to biological sex in a manner that fails to account for the flexibility of gender in Igbo cultural formations, where biological girls can become "sons" and biological women can become "husbands."[49]

Like the new imperial historians, however, and in spite of the provocative title of her book, Amadiume does not address the issue of indigenous homosexualities. Indeed—unlike Stoler, Burton, and Hall and their contemporaries—she is one of several African scholars to suggest that the current western interest in sexuality forms an "obsession" that, in its application to Africa, serves only to perpetuate negative colonialist stereotypes.[50] Other African commentators agree that research into African sexualities endorses racist European myths about the absence of notions of sexual propriety in African cultures.[51]

More problematically, Amadiume also insinuates that there is no indigenous homosexuality in Africa to be researched in the first place when she expresses her opposition to appropriations of her theory by lesbians in the African diaspora: "How advantageous it is for lesbian women to interpret such practices as woman-to-woman marriages as lesbian," she writes, insisting that "such interpretation . . . would be totally inapplicable, shocking and offensive to Nnobi women, since the strong bonds and supports between them do not imply lesbian sexual practices."[52] The "priorities of the West" are, she adds, "totally removed from, and alien to the concerns of the mass of African women."[53]

Amadiume is reacting against western constructions of nonwestern sexualities as exotic or aberrant, but in so doing she sets up homosexuality as an "alien" and recent import to Africa.[54] As Marc Epprecht argues, however, this crudely political labeling of homosexuality gives the impression of prejudice and denial and masks the subtle "cultures of discretion" that existed in many past African societies in order to accommodate diverse sexualities. "Blindness toward indigenous homosexualities . . . appears to have more complex origins and subtle manifestations than critics have allowed," Epprecht suggests, for in many cases indigenous homosexualities were actively and carefully "discoursed into invisibility or 'unsaid' by specific cultural, historical practices" that deliberately placed "a curtain of silence" and toleration over homosexual encounters.[55]

The denial of homosexuality—or the denial of cultural and linguistic discretion—also affects the construction of African social history by more recent scholars. Not once, for example, does Nwando Achebe acknowledge same-sex desire in her impressively detailed study of the spaces created for "extraordinary" women by the "flexibility and fluidity of the Igbo gender system."[56] In a similar manner to Amadiume's, Achebe's history of gender in Nsukka Division deliberately avoids the discussion of sexuality, presenting marital arrangements in terms of economic and social power rather than in terms of desire and pleasure or coercion. Both scholars throw out the baby with the bathwater when they erase sexuality in the process of breaking the European connection between sex and gender. A result of Achebe's refusal to engage with sexual desire, sexual coercion, and African "cultures of discretion" is that her vivid story of the female king Ahebi Ugbabe, who transformed herself into a "man" in the early twentieth century, remains highly narrativized and situated outside theorization or analysis. Achebe's descriptive account of this female king, who surrounded herself with wives, handmaidens, and bathmaids, carefully tiptoes around any encounter with either side of the polarized debate about the existence or nonexistence of African homosexual desires.

For different reasons, more sympathetic historians of sexuality also argue that the word "homosexual" is not adequate to describe the array of sexualities in nonwestern societies.[57] "Even the young man you may have just done everything with sexually will say no if you ask him if he is 'gay,'" writes Nii Ajen of West African men. "And if you should ask that same man if there is homosexuality in Africa, a likely response will be 'No, there is nothing like that in Africa.'"[58] As Bleys suggests, the concept of homosexuality has a distinctly western history and flavor, having emerged out of sexology studies in nineteenth-century Europe.[59] In the late twentieth century it came to connote a permanent identity or at the very least a lifestyle decision rather than a simple description of a physical act or a same-sex encounter that occurs within a range of other identity-defining behaviors that may include heterosexual marriage.[60] The argument that there are no homosexuals in Africa thus stems, at least in part, from the incompatibility between the modern western conception of homosexuality as a "lifestyle," or a constitutive identity, and alternative local constructions of sexuality as one element of human identity among many other more significant elements, including generation, social status, wealth, education, ethnicity, and religious affiliation.[61]

In an attempt to surmount the terminological and ideological hurdles surrounding the historical study of same-sex desire in Africa, I have activated the word "queer" in this book in preference to "homosexual." Of course, both labels are part of modern western discourses about sexuality and desire that are not always helpful in the analysis of historical, or distant, cultural formations. Queer theory is, however, a great deal more flexible and accommodating than theorizations of "homosexuality," for whereas the latter term tends to be oppositional and definitional, caught up in the politics of identity and resistance, "queer" is an adjectival term that admits desire while questioning the very basis of sexual oppositions and identities.⁶² Queer theory "seeks to find the cracks and cleavages between things rather than the things themselves."⁶³ In the words of David Alderson and Linda Anderson, "queer" moves away from a concern with identity in order to privilege those sexualities that "carry the potential to subvert the very grounds on which . . . normative judgments might be made in the first place by refusing or rendering incoherent homo/heterosexual and—often at the same time—masculine/feminine binarisms."⁶⁴

Focusing on discourses that fracture and constitute identity, queer theory accommodates without alarm the gender reclassifications and the delinking of gender from sex that occur in West African societies where women can become "husbands," "sons," and "kings."⁶⁵ Questioning and opening up established western value systems, "queer" is therefore a term that allows space for societies where conceptualizations of sexuality are complex and plural, delinked from the physical body. In spite of its obvious French poststructuralist orientation, then, queer theory can include nonwestern conceptualizations of sexuality and identity.⁶⁶

In breaking away from the dichotomy between heterosexual and homosexual in this book, my aim is to contribute to the "queer history" of Africa. I do not intend to interpret every detail of Stuart-Young's life through the framework of his and others' homosexuality, however, as is the tendency in some cross-cultural studies of sexuality.⁶⁷ Such a move fetishizes and oversexualizes the homosexual male body and, in a colonial context, fails to acknowledge the many and more complex ways in which individuals who are sexually marginalized or discriminated against in their home communities may engage in socially and politically dissident behavior in their host cultures.⁶⁸ As this study of Stuart-Young will reveal, "queer" desire is not necessarily manifested in physical, tactile ways or as a distinctive "gay" lifestyle and identity or even as overt political opposition.

Queer love may be a love that prefers not to name itself rather than the love that dare not speak its name: queer subjects may prefer to remain in a zone of untranslatability, outside names, classifications, and institutions. This is especially the case in places where the culture does not recognize same-sex desire as a permanent characteristic in the individual and in historical periods when mass homophobic prejudice causes secretive and closeted responses among its targets, as in Britain after the Oscar Wilde trials. In the story of Stuart-Young—which takes account of the public shaming of Wilde in 1895— political dissidence and discursive resistance can be identified as much through activities such as his secretive forgery of documents, his self-reinvention, and his chairing of séances as through his political writings and his sexual (and textual) passion for boys.

Ironically, and in spite of their own disavowals of homosexuality in Africa, both Amadiume's and Achebe's accounts of Igbo gender formations help us to set up a "queer" theoretical framework for the analysis of colonial African history. In *Male Daughters, Female Husbands*, for example, Amadiume argues that Igbo gender constructions are far more fluid than the European "sex-gender system" that rigidly insists that biological males must behave in "masculine" ways while biological females must be "feminine."[69] From this starting point, Amadiume's entire study is located in a space of Igbo cultural "contradictions and inconsistencies"[70]—in other words, a "queer" moment of Igbo cultural openness—whereby sexual dichotomies are deconstructed and binary oppositions are permanently destabilized. Her model of precolonial Igboland makes a discovery similar to that of recent queer theory, that classifications of sexuality are social and variable rather than biological, static, and essential.[71] Indeed, she finds that the strict "dual-sex" principle that governed men's and women's separate access to land, wealth, status, and titles in precolonial Igboland was made possible in the first place by the "flexible gender system" that mediated the operation of power until the colonial invasion of the region.[72]

This model has enormous potential when it is applied to the history of homosexuality in Africa, particularly in explaining the reasons why homosexual Europeans were often able to live without harassment in African cultures where gender structures were sufficiently flexible to accommodate their sexual ambiguities. Moreover, the links made by Amadiume and Achebe between individual wealth and the control of others' sexuality[73] greatly assist in our understanding of the manifestations of power in colonial Europeans' relationships with local people, especially in the asymmetrical arrangements that characterize the love of adult men for youths. The connections these scholars highlight between wealth, public status, and domestic power also support the emphasis in histories of homosexuality on the impossibility of regarding personal sexual practice as a private matter, separate from society and political culture.[74] Finally, Amadiume's and Achebe's attention to the wealth and power of "female husbands" helps demonstrate a point made by many historians of homosexuality in nonwestern cultures, as well as by classical scholars, that sexuality may be conceived of in social rather than sexual terms; that is, desire and the sexual act may be structured around power relations in society.[75]

In maintaining a binary opposition between two continents and two sexual cultures,[76] however, Amadiume's model in particular remains rigid and essentialist. It does not fully account for the flexibility of gender in the west or for the links between sexuality and the exercise of power within and between the two communities. If African gender roles were flexible in ways that challenged rigid Victorian sex-gender structures in Europe, not all sexualities in precolonial and colonial Africa were equally accessible and open to the local community. As Amadiume admits, "female husbands" were wealthy women whose "woman marriages" represented public manifestations of power and status.[77] Junior wives in this arrangement could not easily contract their own women-to-woman marriages, take titles, and become "husbands" in their own right. Relatively rigid economic and status hierarchies thus limited these gender-flexible marriages in Igboland.

While Amadiume does not discuss the domestic or sexual encounters between Europeans and Nigerians in the colonial period, the greater flexibility of Igbo gender rules that she describes and the fact that "biological sex does not necessarily correspond to ideological gender"[78] certainly would have facilitated the Nigerian life stories of individuals such as Stuart-Young in ways that were unthinkable in Britain at the time. In the late nineteenth and early twentieth centuries in Britain, the confession of gender irregularities carried enormous physical and legal dangers for the individual. By contrast, Igbo gender flexibility would have eased the intense anxieties of men such as Stuart-Young about their own sexuality (see chapter 5).

The Forger's Tale is an experiment in biography, driven by my wish to contextualize and interpret an area of the imperial past that is neglected in current scholarship. At one level, my intention is to contrast the repression of homosexuality in Europe with a range of more amenable African sexualities. Gilbert Herdt describes this type of framework in *Same Sex, Different Cultures* when he states that "nonwestern societies are typically more tolerant [than western societies] of variations across the spectrum of sexual behavior."[79] While largely endorsing this position, I also aim to show that this popular representation of nonwestern gender flexibility set over and against Europe's sexual rigidity is problematic and overly romanticized. First, it tends to assume that nonwestern cultures place a positive valuation on homoerotic acts and roles;[80] second, it tends to be ahistorical, clumping data into monolithic categories; and third, it tends to essentialize cultural formations in "western" versus "nonwestern" terms. In consequence, the "rigidity versus flexibility" model misses significant moments in the cultural histories of both Europe and Africa.[81]

Many difficulties surround the search for a "queer history" of Africa, however, and this book is marked by several lacunae and methodological problems. Same-sex desire has remained hidden from African history until recently; its multiple forms are barely accessible to the researcher except in ethnographic descriptions of "unnatural vices."[82] There is a near absence of information in the colonial archives, although numerous colonial anthropological accounts of Nigeria refer cryptically to "unbridled license" and "other forms of wickedness" to connote the range of sexualities that fall outside English Christian heterosexual norms.[83] In his extensive studies of southeastern Nigeria, for example, P. A. Talbot comments vaguely on the "licentious character" of several Igbo ceremonies, and notes the "real vulgarity and indecency" of some of the images in Igbo Mbari shrines, without clarifying his descriptions.[84] We cannot simply ascribe a positive valuation to these blurred sexual scenes from the past and expect their logics of perversion and degeneracy to melt away, leaving a clear map of what Bleys calls the "geography of desire" in nonwestern cultures.[85] Rather, this archive of descriptions actively helps to constitute the "ethnography of silences" described by Bill Stanford Pincheon in his forceful critique of ethnographic accounts of homosexuality in Africa.[86]

It is immensely difficult to recover instances of indigenous agency from the colonial archives and almost impossible to retrieve a full range of historical evaluations of sexuality. As Kath Weston writes, the difficulties of "getting data" are considerable when one is looking for evidence of same-sex relationships and gender ambiguity.[87] The problems increase a hundredfold in getting historical data. Contemporary interviewees cannot be expected to produce historically reliable evidence when asked to recall characters and events from the early twentieth century. Nevertheless, it is essential for cultural historians to remain open to the many ways local populations disrupted Eurocentric dichotomies between colonizer and colonized and between heterosexuality and homosexuality in the imperial period. To achieve this goal, life histories and instances of disruptive agency must be reinserted into colonial history.[88]

In response to the difficulties of conducting a purely "oral" historical project for the early twentieth century, *The Forger's Tale* cautiously revisits the colonial anthropological archive, fraught as it is with the dangers of colonialist repetition. In order to construct a biography of Stuart-Young and a cultural history of colonial Onitsha, I make use of the work of British missionaries, anthropologists, and administrators who worked in Onitsha in the early twentieth century and I attempt to disentangle the different colonial elites from one another.[89] When faced with the many ethnocentric truth claims of this material, I try to read European anthropological texts for moments in which their authors appear confused and suspended between cultural categories or when Eurocentric presuppositions are unsettled from within by the sheer force of the African material.

I also analyze the neglected archive of palm oil traders' memoirs and the voluminous writings of Stuart-Young himself with a view to moving beyond "official" documents and exploring the class tensions in colonial locations. I place the palm oil traders' writings alongside material drawn from African newspapers in the early twentieth century as well as material from elite Africans' autobiographies and from recent interviews with residents of Onitsha. In order to appreciate the diversity and magnitude of local responses to Stuart-Young in the 1920s and 1930s, the opinions of his surviving protégés and elderly people in different sectors of Igbo society are also incorporated into the frame of this book in the form of interview material and reminiscences.

Stuart-Young's life story is positioned at a point in history where the tensions and incongruities of imperialism had become particularly pronounced. Members of the British working classes—long regarded by the bourgeoisie through a racialized and highly sexualized language of "savagery"[90]—entered imperial geography as travelers, settlers, and entrepreneurs, actively carving routes for themselves through the imperial map (see chapter 2). When he decided to settle down in Nigeria in 1905, Stuart-Young was not yet known or recognized in Onitsha, then a small riverside market that hosted a handful of missionaries, a skeletal colonial administration, and approximately forty-five white traders working for European firms.[91] Within five years, he had acquired land on lease from local chiefs and constructed his own stores at strategic locations around town.[92] By 1919, he had become the wealthiest independent palm produce trader in Nigeria and a celebrated local personality in Onitsha, especially for his controversial political views, which antagonized the local Catholic mission and the colonial government. With several stores in town and outlying settlements and a staff of African clerks and shop assistants, he conducted a busy trade with local middlemen and merchant queens who brought palm produce to his factories, as the depots were known, along the shores of the River Niger (see chapter 2). He had also become a celebrated local poet, philanthropist, and intellectual who sponsored many young Igbo men through secretarial and clerical training in Onitsha.

What sets Stuart-Young apart from his peers and makes his story exceptional is that at each stage of his own journey he produced copious memoirs, articles, and poems. So great was his textual output by the early 1930s that, in the words of one of his African secretaries, "he wrote very fast like a machine."[93] The two Igbo typists assigned to type up the work of this compulsive writer "hardly coped with the volume of manuscripts he wrote."[94] As we shall see, Stuart-Young's texts played a key role in the production of "Odeziaku."

Given the academic interest in popular literature produced in Britain relating to the British Empire, it is surprising that so little research has been undertaken into this ephemeral literature that was produced by lower-class authors living in the colonies and writing for publication in Europe or America.[95] *The Forger's Tale* seeks to retrieve and historically situate a selection of this neglected but rich archive of material by palm oil traders and lowly clerks in the colonies. Stuart-Young's writings occupy a central place in this canon, revealing a great deal about working-class men's perceptions of class and race in Africa. His life spans almost the entire period of British imperial supremacy in Africa, and whether his topic was London's pederastic poets, the English countryside, or interracial love in the tropics, this author remained firmly located in his various West African homes, participating in the cultural and economic life of his adopted communities. In spite of his enormous literary production and political activity between the 1900s and the 1930s, however, Stuart-Young came from precisely the social class ignored by historians of imperialism in West Africa. Palm oil traders, European middlemen, and clerks lack a place in social histories of the region, and yet they played a vital role in sustaining interracial networks of trade, culture, and communication in the colonial period. Additionally, several of them wrote memoirs and novels in the 1920s and 1930s, few of which have been studied in the intervening decades. Of special interest in this respect is the manner in which Stuart-Young made use of his rural West African locations to forge documents and fabricate friendships with famous British personalities, conferring on himself an entitlement to the very culture and class position from which he was excluded at home.

Alongside this ephemeral European literature, indigenous African newspapers also played a vital role in the literary culture of the colonial period. In Nigeria and the Gold Coast (Ghana), African-owned newspapers were seminal in the "production" of Stuart-Young as a literary personality. Without the active support of his elite editor friends in Port Harcourt, Calabar, Lagos, and Accra, Odeziaku would have been nothing at all. Moreover, without the African newspapers, there would be few textual traces of his extraordinary life. With this in mind, *The Forger's Tale* suggests that African-owned printing presses played an important role in the literary networks that emerged in British West Africa in the early and middle colonial periods. This newspaper history provides a vital context for our study of postcolonial literatures in West Africa.

In his writing, as in his business life, Stuart-Young's primary market was African. He produced copious quantities of memoirs, poems, novels, and newspaper articles on controversial issues ranging from interracial love to the merits of colonialism and the nature of same-sex desire. Stuart-Young was one of the few Europeans to write for the African-owned nationalist press on a regular basis in the 1920s and politically stormy 1930s. Writing always "as an Englishman," he found sites for publication in newspapers that catered to an expanding and increasingly politicized West African readership. For a period of more than thirty years, his work appeared regularly in the Nigerian press. Farther afield in the Gold Coast, in London, and in the United States, his articles and poems appeared often enough to attract a large international mailbag to his Little House of No Regrets (see chapter 2).

British imperialism is a complex and heterogeneous subject area, and one way to comprehend its social history is through detailed, situated studies of specific instances of cultural or textual practice. In clustering sets of topics around the biography of a single individual, my aim in this book is to write against histories that present broad cross-cultural surveys of global imperial circuits. The absence of local perspectives from these broad-sweep histories is especially problematic when scholars discuss the lives of "queer" colonial men whose physical encounters required local bodies and whose lives were enveloped by ambiguous and contradictory relations of power.

One might, however, question the value of "the microscopic study of an eccentric or even an abnormal self" such as Stuart-Young and what it can "tell us about the social world of normal others."[96] In addressing this question, *The Forger's Tale* compiles a cultural and literary study around the figure of Stuart-Young. His biography is used as a magnet for the attitudes, values, aesthetic expectations, and popular tastes of his day. Situated at the center of these diverse currents, Stuart-Young remains pivotal to the progress of the book. Through detailed analysis of his life story—from his childhood and adolescence in working-class Manchester to his maturity in West Africa—I discuss the ways in which this poorly born but ambitious man could reinvent himself in Onitsha and forge his way toward an impressive Igbo funeral while never fully stepping out of the normative gender, class, racial, and imperial standards of his day.

The very smallness of Stuart-Young's contribution to institutional discourses such as imperialism and English letters is precisely the reason why his biography opens up an intriguing and relatively unrestricted space in colonial history. *The Forger's Tale* does not aim to inscribe Stuart-Young's story back into the heart of the colonial project. It aims instead to use his biography and the stories of his African friends to open up an array of topics that have remained on the margins of imperial history, including the criminal and creative uses of forgery in Britain and West Africa, the cultural and literary life of lower-class traders on Nigerian palm oil stations, the complex reciprocity of pederastic relationships in colonial Africa, and the role of African-owned newspapers in producing keen, active, and class-conscious reading publics. In this, *The Forger's Tale* participates in the project started by Antoinette Burton in her study of the life stories of three Indian travelers in Victorian Britain to interrogate precisely "what—and who—has traditionally been considered a legitimate subject of 'British' history."[97] *The Forger's Tale* adds to Burton's agenda by addressing the question of what, and who, are the legitimate subjects of *African* history.

Ann Laura Stoler and Frederic Cooper insist that historians of empire must abandon center-periphery models of analysis in favor of a more integrated "both-and" model in which colony and metropole configure one another in tense, productive, antagonistic, and complicit cultural and economic relationships.[98] This has important implications for the genre of imperial biography, for according to Stoler's and Cooper's model, the biographical subject must not be positioned in a way that replicates the binary oppositions that were generated within colonial discourse itself between colonizer and colonized and between black and white.[99] The search for Odeziaku exemplifies the need to move beyond binary oppositions, for it encompasses material ranging from the British popular response to Oscar Wilde's homosexuality in the 1890s through to the rise of West African newspapers in the colonial period and the local impact of missionary-led debates about monogamous marriage in West Africa in the 1920s and 1930s.

The question of African agency motivates a large part of this book and prevents it from conforming to the rules of mainstream western biography in which the discussion of "other" subjectivities tends to remain secondary to the understanding of an individual's psychological development.[100] *The Forger's Tale* attempts to interpret Stuart-Young's biography in Igbo terms as well as in British cultural terms, for his life story cannot be separated either from the social and cultural contexts that facilitated his choices or from the stories of other people, particularly the inhabitants of the West African town in which he settled and thrived. *The Forger's Tale* thus uses the figure of Stuart-Young to open up a wider study of imperialism, (homo)sexuality, and nonelite culture in Britain and West Africa between the 1880s and the late 1930s, and the resulting life story is not that of an individual in isolation from his context, nor is it a set of cultural histories that can be divorced from this man's particular life.

One factor makes this project especially complicated. Stuart-Young was an individual who was sculpted in important ways by the circumstances of his race, class, sexuality, gender, historical period, and geographical location. But his biography is queerer than allowed for by the relatively stable model of self in relation to setting or subject in relation to context. The problem is this: the chapters that follow trace the life story of a compulsive inventor of identities; a creator of names, titles, and signatures; a liar, a scribophile;[101] and a wearer of multiple masks. Each of these slippery, open, unempirical identities plays havoc with the biographer's method, for Stuart-Young wore each mask in a manner that was equally authentic—or equally inauthentic—as another mask. If we turn, in the search for evidence, to the many memoirs that he produced about his early life in Manchester, we find texts filled with forged documents and fabricated relationships from which it is impossible to disentangle a "true" or "real" subjectivity (see chapter 3). His African memoirs are no more reliable for the intimate friendships they construct with famous men. Indeed, exactly when he took on the names "Moray" and "Stuart" is itself unclear, since he was born plain "John James Young" on 3 March 1881 in Ardwick, a working-class district of Manchester. Thus began a lifelong process of self-production, or masking by naming, through which Stuart-Young effaced young "Johnnie" and forged himself into a better social class.

Colonial Africa was central to this process of self-forging and self-reconstruction. In moving to West Africa in the early twentieth century, this poorly born but ambitious poet could take up one of the few opportunities for economic self-advancement available to lower-class British men. Born to a washerwoman and a manual worker, Stuart-Young made his escape to West Africa, leaving behind the clerical job, cramped housing, and restricted dreams that would have been his lot had he stayed at home in Manchester (see chapter 1).

Stuart-Young's life is bound into complex areas of British and African cultural history, including the history of forgery and pederasty. His decisions and choices, and the ways in which he (mis)represented them textually, offer us singular access to these elusive areas of history. In attempting to account for the hiddenness of the forger's "self," it is therefore necessary to produce a form of biography that respects the careful, secretive ways in which he encoded his desires, but it is also necessary, in tension with this, to respect the performed nature of all his identities, the unrecoverability of his subjectivity, and the impossibility of simply "decoding" his inscriptions. Continually reaching away from his previous selves and constantly recasting himself in response to local expressions of approval or unease, Stuart-Young was the perfect forger in that he was never simply "at one" with himself; rather, he was permanently inspired to produce new, future-oriented selves.

Stuart-Young deliberately manufactured his subjectivity in order to deceive the outside world. Given the creativity of his forgeries, however, the biographical search for Odeziaku should not simply take the form of a quest to unmask a liar or a project to decode his secret language and expose his inner or "perverted" self.[102] While the activity of decoding is vital to the recognition of forgery, the opposition it generates between authenticity and inauthenticity, or truth and lies, does not do justice to the creative agency of this forger. Nor does it recognize the fundamental importance of other people to the process of forgery. Each new incarnation of Stuart-Young depended for its success or failure on his accumulation of deposits of belief and goodwill among the people who witnessed the spectacle of his identity. A degree of mutual complicity was therefore involved in his relationship with his public.

Once again, queer theory can assist in refining our sensitivity toward forgery and the forger, for queer readings highlight "the constructed nature of sexual identities, their contingency and instability."[103] Given that homosexuality is often regarded as "a spoiled identity" in western sexual cultures, and given that forgery involves the spoiling of "identity" as a concept, forgery may be regarded as one of the rituals of queer expression involving the artful fabrication of a true self for public consumption and the equally artful partial concealment of the "spoiled" self in between the lines. As several chapters of this book will reveal, in Stuart-Young's case, forgery, sexuality, subjectivity, and textuality are all woven together into a complicated web that "queers" our search for true biography and identity.

The Forger's Tale adheres to Catherine Hall's request that social historians of colonialism should respect "the imperative of placing colony and metropole in one analytic frame."[104] The inseparability of colony and metropole necessitates a double vision without which it would be impossible to comprehend the sheer scale of Stuart-Young's self-reinvention in Onitsha. The search for Odeziaku therefore begins not in Africa, but in the working-class district of Manchester where Stuart-Young grew up in the last decades of the nineteenth century, tightly confined by the range of imperial and sexual possibilities that were available to working-class men in Britain at the time.

1 ∽ Forging Ahead

The Secret Gentleman of Ardwick Green

ON 4 MAY 1899, a shamefaced eighteen-year-old stood before the City of Manchester Petty Sessional Court. "John Mount Stewart Young," as he then called himself (also "John Mountstewart Young"), pleaded guilty to the charge of theft by forgery and was sentenced to six months with hard labor at Strangeways Prison (see fig. 1). Irrefutable evidence of his theft of a banker's check worth £20 was presented to court, but he confessed to banking a further £180 in recent months by illicitly opening envelopes, forging his employer's signature on the back of checks, and sending receipts to clients in the name of his master, the mantle manufacturer James Hollings.[1] Immediately after the sentence was passed, John Pultney Young, an imposing, red-whiskered railway worker, forced his way to the front of court and rained loud and public insults on his son for bringing the family name into disrepute.[2] Four days later, in a state of abjection, the young invoice clerk with his billycock hat, large amethyst ring, flowing tie, and velvet jacket was taken down to Strangeways with a batch of shabby, unshaven men. There he was stripped of his fashionable clothing and forced to change into prison garments.[3]

Lengthy sentences were passed by the Petty Sessional Court in Manchester for far less serious crimes than those committed by Stuart-Young. For instance, a man named John Rogers was sentenced to two months' imprisonment with hard labor for the theft of twenty-five packets of cigarettes in January 1899; another man, George Harrison, received one month's imprisonment with hard labor in April 1897 for the theft of six currant cakes valued at threepence in total; the theft of thirteen umbrellas by Harry Young in September 1897 carried a sentence of three months' imprisonment with hard labor.[4] In this

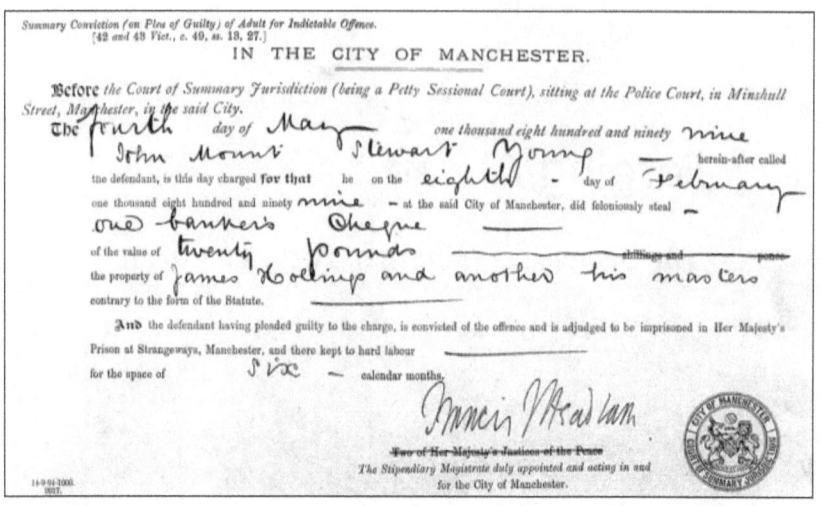

Fig. 1. Conviction of "John Mount Stewart Young" at the City of Manchester Court of Summary Jurisdiction, 8 February 1899. *(By permission of Manchester Library and Information Service: Manchester Archives and Local Studies.)*

context, given the large quantities of money involved, Stuart-Young's prison sentence was relatively lenient. Perhaps the judge showed clemency because this was the youth's first appearance in court and he was obviously contrite once caught, having tried to repay a portion of the stolen money.[5] Perhaps the magistrate—on a salary of several thousand pounds per annum[6]—also felt some sympathy toward this low-paid white-collar worker who earned just a few shillings per week, the bulk of which went to his mother to help maintain their "one-up, one-down" rented home in Ardwick.

The senior policeman who oversaw the investigation into Stuart-Young's forgeries, Chief Detective Inspector George Hargreaves, had, the month before, received a "special report of meritorious conduct" from the Manchester City Police Force to add to an already impressive record of successful investigations.[7] Given the relatively petty nature of Stuart-Young's crime, Hargreaves would have made a special request to undertake this case, probably attracted by its lucrative potential for the cash rewards that were often given for the arrest and successful prosecution of criminals in the financial or white-collar sector.[8] Additionally, the officer may have been curious about the individual involved, for the young invoice clerk was also a dilettante journalist and author who had established a minor local reputation for himself with occasional articles, poems, and reviews for provincial and national journals. Stuart-Young's reputation as an aspiring writer was, however, about to be shattered by the combination of mirth and derision that his case aroused.

Hargreaves's investigation was made easy by the fact that many people came forward to give evidence against the young man. Stuart-Young had few friends, and nobody spoke out in court in favor of his character. Indeed, it soon emerged that "the prisoner had been at several situations in the city and at each place had been dismissed for embezzlement."[9] The case itself proved simple to investigate. When cornered and confronted, Stuart-Young burst into tears and confessed to habitual forgeries and embezzlements in previous months. By the time he was caught, he could forge the boss's signature with such skill that the original name could barely be distinguished from the imitation. Caught red-handed in February 1899, the young man had already paid approximately £200 into his own bank account, using it to fund a secret double life in the center of town.

In the four days between Stuart-Young's first and final appearances in court, Inspector Hargreaves made, in the words of the *Manchester Courier*, "discoveries which point to the fact that Young is, and has been for some time past, a very mysterious youth."[10] It emerged that for several months the young man had been secretly renting a house in Nelson Street, in an affluent part of town, at a cost of £18 per year. Without telling a soul, he paid for this house to be "fitted up luxuriously" with his own choice of furniture.[11] When finished, it looked splendidly middle class, "fitted out like a drawing room" from top to bottom.[12] It is possible that the extra barrels crept into the young man's name at this time, helping transform the social stature and self-image of "John James Young."

One large room in the Nelson Street property was called the "Christian Spiritual Hall." Here Stuart-Young set up a spirit-rapping table at which visitors could commune with their loved ones through his mediumship. This work of spiritual "hosting" meshed perfectly with Stuart-Young's expertise in forging others' letters and signatures. Here was a youth whose body was radically open to the entry of others, whose identity was unfixed in name, in voice, and in social class: he "queerly" lacked a stable identity.[13]

The Christian Spiritual Hall was one of many such venues to spring up throughout Britain in the doctrinally experimental spiritualist 1890s.[14] As with other late-nineteenth-century sects, the Christian Spiritual Hall challenged clerics and Christian hierarchies by its very existence, but it did not necessarily reject, nor seek to compete with, the tenets of mainstream churches, especially the Nonconformist denominations that proliferated around Manchester at the turn of the century. The motto of Stuart-Young's establishment, which was read out in court, was not in the least anti-Christian, for the sign on his door read: "The Fatherhood of God, the living intercession of Christ, the help of the Angel world, the brotherhood of man, and the eternal progress and development of the soul."[15]

Stuart-Young must have possessed enormous reserves of self-confidence and religious energy to set up this establishment without the knowledge of his family or colleagues, especially at the tender age of eighteen. Operating as a young and attractive spirit-medium, he offered positive proof of the afterlife to clients; he followed the paths of angels, creating personalized connections between mortals and the other world, reinforcing clients' faith in the existence of an afterlife. This was to be a lifelong interest.

Beneath his spirit-rapping table Stuart-Young fixed "a small trap and a cord, which was worked by the person who acted as the medium (Laughter [in court], in which the prisoner joined)."[16] To "renewed laughter," the process of cord-pulling in a darkened room was also described in court, although it is likely that by this stage in proceedings the prisoner's laughter had taken on a rather more embarrassed timbre than that of his spectators.[17] Indeed, in spite of his mirth, it is unlikely that the spirit-rapping scheme was simply a ruse designed to defraud gullible bereaved individuals of their money. The pretense was more creative than that, more integral to Stuart-Young's queer sense of self. The youth—a man of independent means now with his regular income of embezzled checks—did not charge people for his spiritual services. Having set himself up as a middle-class gentleman in well-furnished surroundings, the last thing he desired was for clients to "cross his palm with silver" after a séance. Instead, his reward was other people's connection, through himself, with the souls of their loved ones. Relying on Stuart-Young as their medium, visitors to the Hall provided public affirmation of the young man's "special" inner qualities, reinforcing his perception of himself as a child prodigy situated in a separate class from others of his birth.

At the spirit-rapping table, as in other areas of his life, Stuart-Young expressed his creative inspiration through the artful forgery of communications.[18] With or without the material props that were exposed in court, it is necessary to see him as a sincere performer, or a "sincere forger," for throughout his life he believed himself to be in contact with the other world, to be gifted with an intensely passionate soul and a heightened sensitivity to beauty, ugliness, death, and the divine. Even at this tender age, he was open and receptive, acting as a bodily host to the ghostly presence of other selves.

As the mystery of Nelson Street unfolded in court, the public learned about the contents of a second room, located above the spirit-rapping room, where Stuart-Young had installed an organ. In a class-divided world in which one sign of upward social mobility was the acquisition of a piano for the parlor, Stuart-Young's music room furnishes further evidence of his desire to participate in the culture and values of the English middle class. The young man set up this music room—a peaceful, creative space—to compose and perform lyrics, and it is possible that some of his compositions found publication in the many books of verse released after his decision to leave for West Africa. In particular, *Minor Melodies* (1904) and *The After-Life: A Poetic Service of Song* (1905) contain numerous sentimental lyrics offered to the public to be set to music.

The third, perhaps most remarkable, room in Stuart-Young's secret house confirmed this identification with middle-class values, for it contained the young man's large personal library of approximately 600 books, "including the 'Encyclopaedia Britannica' and a large number of novels."[19] From this private library, using notepaper especially printed with an ornate, personalized address, Stuart-Young wrote letters of admiration and friendship to his favorite authors and intellectuals, including Oscar Wilde, Rudyard Kipling, Edward Carpenter, and many other well-known writers. Masquerading as a gentleman proved easy once the youth had obtained good-quality stationery and mastered an appropriate writing style. Such creative, persuasive forgery must have astounded members of the court and confounded his parents. In order to cover his absences from home outside office hours, Stuart-Young told his parents, with whom he lived, that he was working for the Remington Typewriter Company, rapping out letters of a more mundane nature than the communications he received and dispatched from Nelson Street.[20]

In Nelson Street, Stuart-Young's transformation was complete. With the emergence of each detail in court, the levels of shocked laughter increased at the audacity of this social upstart. In between teaching himself French, translating the works of Jules Verne, and reading Baudelaire's poetry, he also studied elocution in an effort to purge himself of his working-class Mancunian accent.[21] The house at Nelson Street exemplified Stuart-Young's desire to flee from his roots and escape from the cultural activities with which his class was associated. Ensconced in his beautiful rooms, composing lyrics and letters, the young autodidact had, through careful and creative forgery, found a way to *become* a middle-class intellectual, surrounded by opportunities and in correspondence with a community of well-educated fellows. By the time he was arrested, the "false" identity was the one he was forced to assume at home in Back Kay Street, his place of birth and the place that, according to the edicts of late-Victorian Britain, determined his education and his income and fixed his opportunities for advancement as a clerk.[22]

Nevertheless, nobody in court, or in the newspapers at the time, could fathom the motivation behind the Nelson Street enterprise.[23] Stuart-Young's use of the stolen money seemed immoral, for he had invested the wealth in neither productive nor ethical ends. While young Johnny Jones, hero of his final two novels many years later, embezzles money to pay for his dying sister's medication and cover the rent on a Manchester missionary station, Stuart-Young could offer no moral justification for his own thefts.[24] He had a clean home to go to each night after work, and his parents were, to all outward appearances, honest, hard-working people, described in court by Inspector Hargreaves as "respectably connected" members of the upper working class.[25] Indeed, John Pultney Young possessed such a strong sense of his family's proletarian respectability and his own good character that he alerted his son's first employer to an embezzlement of funds, leading to the first in Stuart-Young's long chain of dismissals.[26]

Stuart-Young's secret life inverts the late-nineteenth-century pattern whereby wealthy middle-class gentlemen and women such as Charles Booth and Beatrice Webb—alongside numerous less well-to-do missionaries, novelists, and reporters—descended into the "abyss" of the slums to record what they witnessed in "darkest England."[27] Assisted by metaphors from Dante's *Inferno* and Bunyan's *Pilgrim's Progress*, as well as by popular accounts of "primitive" Africa, middle-class sociologists and Christian moralists recorded the horror of England's "darkest" and most "savage" places. Their best-selling publications provided windows through which the educated classes could look out over the region known as slumland, described by William Booth as "the Great Slough of Despond of our time."[28]

Moral tracts such as William Booth's *In Darkest England* (1880) and sociological studies such as Charles Booth's *Life and Labour of the People in London* (1889) and *The Heart of the Empire* by C. F. G. Masterman et al. (1901) captivated British readers at the turn of the century, allowing them to participate in the ongoing "rediscovery of poverty" in their cities.[29] In vivid detail these books revealed layer upon layer of personal stories of unemployment, marital breakup, alcoholism, domestic violence, disease, and desperation, constituting a full human tragedy set in London and the major industrial cities of Britain. They also provided detailed systems of classification whereby degrees of poverty and wealth could be charted. With his small regular wage as a railway worker and assurance of a meager pension, for example, Stuart-Young's father would have been positioned in "Class E" of Charles Booth's eight-point scale of social class, approaching the upper working class but living in a "vile spot" in a two-room dwelling with a wife who was obliged by the family's hardship to take in washing. According to the same scale, Stuart-Young had graduated from his parents' class, having been employed as a clerk in a position that would, ideally, allow the family to evolve out of poverty in coming generations.[30]

A plethora of sensational novels, newspaper articles, and tracts added to the works of these early sociologists, including books such as *The Bitter Cry of*

Outcast London, Ten Years in the Slums, Children of the Jago, and *People of the Abyss.*[31] Written in grippingly realistic prose, this slum writing entered "respectable" households, crossing the threshold that kept poverty and dirt at bay. To readers more familiar with the moral geography of colonial exploration narratives, in which the abject soul was to be found in a far-off country, the moral shock of British slum writing arose from the repeated insistence by authors that the "lowest" ranks of the British working classes lived "the life of savages."[32] With no culture or homes of their own and certainly no sign of soap, it seemed as if these degenerate Europeans bore more in common with the peoples of Africa, where "human beings dwarfed into pygmies and brutalised into cannibals lurk and live and die."[33] Similarly, the white tribe of slum-dwellers owned no possessions and were "living in dirt, fond of drink, alike shiftless, shifty, and shifting."[34]

Comparisons with the racially other African drove this fin-de-siècle writing on British poverty. In an age of popular imperialism—an ideology predicated on the work ethic and the widespread belief that people with "English blood" possessed a superior civilization[35]—many British people were found to be no better than the savage, whose abject condition was also regarded as "hereditary in character."[36] The realization that Caucasians were "toiling like galley slaves" with "appallingly few . . . rescued" fascinated and appalled late-nineteenth-century readers, for whom politicians and liberal historians had served up a very different narrative in which the British were responsible for the emancipation of Africans and the abolition of slavery in favor of "legitimate commerce."[37] Now it emerged that, as with the degraded natives described in the writings of nineteenth-century travelers and traders, many people in British cities "create no wealth [and] . . . degrade whatever they touch, and as individuals are perhaps incapable of improvement."[38]

The general fascination for poverty and slum life in the late nineteenth century must be acknowledged if we are to appreciate Stuart-Young's decision to invest his embezzled money in fine furniture and books, icons of middle-class gentility. The young clerk flowed against the tide of those bourgeois authors and readers whose attentions were focused on "low" society. Enclosed in the opulent surroundings of Nelson Street, cut off from the industrial city, he made the subversive discovery that social class was not a fixed, innate identity. Even as he reinforced class boundaries with his desire to erase his plebeian roots, Stuart-Young's Nelson Street lifestyle demonstrated that any person might become middle class if the occasion arose: through forgery and embezzlement he discovered that social class was an unstable process, a cultural and economic achievement made possible by the availability of opportunities. While newspaper reports on the court case represented him as a charlatan, or a thief of others' original identities, we can regard the eighteen-year-old's speedy transformation into a literary gentleman as a challenge to the dominant social Darwinist model of class (or race). Stuart-Young's self-reinvention demonstrated that class was not a natural condition produced by social evolution spreading through the generations to create distinct types with few immediate prospects of transformation for the better.[39] While his arrest frustrated his project to leave slumland behind, his new lifestyle revealed that a "guttersnipe" could become a "gentleman" through degrees of forgery ranging from counterfeit signatures to more creative types of forgery, including the adoption of gentlemanly manners, names, clothing, accent, environment, and reading matter. Just as the original name could not be differentiated from the forgery on the checks that Stuart-Young stole, so too his class subversion exposed how easy it was to make copies and demonstrated the fluid "nature" of social class.[40]

The bemused spectators in court could not appreciate in 1899 that Stuart-Young was positioned at an important ideological junction, facing both ways at a time of social change, for here was a clerk from a working-class family who spent long hours in a monotonous, poorly paid job but was separated from his father's world by virtue of his minimal secondary education, office work, and ambitions for financial self-betterment. Lower middle rather than upper working class, Stuart-Young was one of many thousands of men from laboring families to benefit from the combined effects of mass education and the growth of clerical jobs in the banking and commercial sectors.[41]

As a clerk in the 1890s, Stuart-Young would have been expected to look as gentlemanly as his meager salary allowed, to dress smartly in a suit, to behave with decorum and display "good character" in all aspects of his life.[42] "Character" was a crucial category in late Victorian moral discourse, signifying a set of stern requirements, including self-discipline, abstinence from (or moderate use of) alcohol, honesty, personal and domestic hygiene, and the ability to save money for the future.[43] "Bad characters," by contrast, were incapable of an honest day's work and were usually to be found in, or en route to, prison.[44] Congenitally programmed by their "drunken and disreputable" parents into lives of crime, the sole hope for this degenerate criminal class was their "destruction" and "demolition."[45]

With the rise of the new consumer in the late nineteenth century, an additional sign of the bad character emerged: failure to own things. "The existing type of what has been termed 'western' civilization," commented Charles Booth in a rare moment of cultural relativism, "requires a great deal of . . . things, and its advance is based on their increase."[46] "Good character" and goods were closely connected in this fin-de-siècle discourse. A person's degree of "western civilization" was reflected in the number, and condition, of objects possessed by a household, and bad characters could be materially distinguished from others by their ownership of "a few miserable sticks" and occupation of a "single room in which they have to sleep, and breed, and die."[47]

Slum writing is characterized by this interest in others' possessions, as authors take stock of the newness, value, and cleanliness of the things in their subjects' households. Studies of poverty in the late nineteenth century refer repeatedly to objects in rooms and their value and to the lack of commodities that characterizes the poorest households: "Their room was almost destitute," writes Charles Booth of two women sharing lodgings in London, for "all it contained would not fetch two shillings—and dirty to the last degree."[48] "The room here was full of rubbish," he comments of another slum; "all in all it would not fetch ten shillings; the dirty walls covered with little pictures never taken down; vermin abounded and the stench was awful."[49] Booth's study of London contributes to the construction of a new consumer mentality in the 1890s, for he assesses people's physical and moral state according to the state and value of their possessions and, in the process, turns them into commodities—textual commodities—for the consumption of readers.

Underpaid clerks from working-class homes, of "good character" but in possession of few material goods, were trapped in a web of contradictions. Expected by their employers and colleagues to distance themselves from rowdy cultural venues such as public houses, music halls, fairs, and the streets, Victorian clerks were, nevertheless, excluded from the "proper" middle class by virtue of their salaries and living quarters.[50] Such men—and clerking was almost exclusively male until the 1920s[51]—were, of necessity, first-class forgers, for they had to simulate the gentleman's behavior and appear to be that which their salaries prohibited. Maintaining appearances required a great deal of the forger's creative ingenuity, especially when it required the simultaneous concealment of poverty and the desperate need for more money.

Recruits to the lower middle classes experienced many anxieties, especially the fear of being thrust "backward" into the working class and losing hold of their fragile new status.[52] In the words of Geoffrey Crossick, "a basic problem of lower middle-class status was that of maintaining it, even progressing beyond it."[53] Clerical workers often lived with their parents in rented accommodation, unable to afford new shirts and suits for work, let alone leave home. They had to maintain their polish against all the odds while their more affluent employers lived comfortable lives in the suburbs.[54] As the young John Holt declared to his father before abandoning his clerical position in the early 1860s and traveling to West Africa, where he made his fortune as a trader, "What am I to do? If I stay where I am I have the prospect of a £60 salary, which to my ambitious nature is beggary. No! It is money I want and money I must have if

I go through fire and water for it."⁵⁵ This future palm oil magnate and Liverpool entrepreneur added, in justification, that his craving was not for "the gold, but the independence it brings and the cares it drives away."⁵⁶ One of Stuart-Young's fictional creations in the 1920s, Johnny Jones, echoes this sentiment in his rather more tearful plea for permission to emigrate to South Africa: "It is not fair that favoured people in society should have so much and that I—we—should want for so little and yet be denied our absolute necessaries!" he tells his father, and begs: "Let me go to wider fields. . . . There I shall be able to earn enough to hold my own in the world. I don't believe I was born to be poor—poor in that grinding hideous sense that I remember so well."⁵⁷

Given the contradictions of their class position and the lack of opportunities for all but the most assertive individuals, it seems inevitable that forgery and embezzlement were endemic crimes among low-paid British clerks in offices and banks. Far from being the passive victims of middle-class exploitation, from the 1870s onward, increasing numbers of clerks engaged in white-collar crime as an expression of their entitlement to a better lifestyle. One of the few ways for a clerk to display the material signs of his own class progression was to become a "skidder" and succumb to the temptation to pilfer money from the workplace.⁵⁸

In Manchester in the late nineteenth century, the ambiguous class position of many local clerks was attested to by the voluminous lists of embezzlers, forgers, and fraudsters who were declared "wanted" by police.⁵⁹ The police obtained photographs of errant clerks from their families and circulated copies around the region. Unlike the lower-class criminals, whose burglaries and muggings led them to be imprisoned as "incorrigible rogues," what is striking about these portraits is the impeccable appearance of the "wanted" men, who pose in their Sunday best in the mock drawing rooms set up in the photographer's studio (see fig. 2).⁶⁰ These were the unlucky individuals, for embezzlement was ubiquitous in the white-collar workplace, far more extensive than the number of names appearing on "wanted" lists. Those who were caught simply signified human "failure at the bottom of an unequal society."⁶¹

Stuart-Young's court case was to be the young man's last appearance in the British limelight before he traveled to tropical West Africa in 1901. His arrest and imprisonment marked the failure of his attempt to supersede social class and to realize, in material form, the lifestyle about which most clerks dared only to dream. While Stuart-Young did not seem to have suffered unduly from moral qualms about his embezzlements, believing himself deserving of a pay raise,⁶² the conviction left him, like other guilty clerks, "without references and with a reputation in ruins."⁶³ It also caused lasting damage to his family's

Fig. 2. Photograph of Stuart-Young taken in the year of his conviction (from *Osrac, the Self-Sufficient and Other Poems with a Memoir of the Late Oscar Wilde* [London: Hermes Press, 1905]). *(By permission of the Board of Trinity College Dublin.)*

reputation as members of the "respectable" working class. Shattered by the publicity the case attracted locally, Stuart-Young's father disowned the boy and drank heavily during 1899. His mother, meanwhile, remained in a state of tearful collapse for the duration of the case.[64]

Upon release from Strangeways, Stuart-Young was taunted as a "jailbird" by his neighbors in Ardwick, some of whom seemed to revel in the fall of this fashion-conscious social upstart.[65] He was more cut off than ever from his roots when he returned home to his crowded working-class neighborhood in November 1899. Hidden away in the downstairs room of Back Kay Street with paper and pens, writing poems on the subject of beauty and journalistic articles about prison life, he waited impatiently for an opportunity to leave the country. In 1900, a clerical position in the tropics arose with Miller Brothers of Manchester, and in 1901 Stuart-Young left "darkest England" behind him for Liberia.

In setting up his well-furnished library and trying to actualize a middle-class ideal, Stuart-Young exposed many of the contradictions and dilemmas inherent in the lifestyles of his fellows, which revolved around the masking of poverty and the denial of material lack. Additionally, his Nelson Street lifestyle made a statement about the difficulties of becoming a "working-class intellectual" in the late nineteenth century and the need some educated lower-class youths felt to avoid the perceived constraints of their class and culture by emulating the intelligentsia. Failing to recognize the intellectual culture of laborers, Stuart-Young used his stolen money to propel himself, like a human cannonball, as far away from his class of birth as funds would allow. Like the hero of his "Johnny Jones" novels discussed in chapter 7, he seemed "determined, willy-nilly, to rise from the class into which he had been born."[66] Like many others of his rank, he was insistent on his entitlement to "rise," and in the wake of his failed bid to achieve gentlemanly status in Manchester, the young man departed for Africa at the first opportunity, exchanging his class inferiority for what he hoped would be a privileged place in the racial hierarchy of the colonies.

2 ～ The Palm Oil Trader's View

> Tensions between bureaucrats and planters, settlers and transients, missionaries and metropolitan policy makers, and petits blancs and monied entrepreneurs have always made European communities more socially fractious and politically fragile than many of their members professed.
>
> —Ann Laura Stoler, *Carnal Knowledge and Imperial Power*[1]

INCREASING NUMBERS OF "POOR WHITES" and lowly clerks such as Stuart-Young traveled to West Africa at the turn of the twentieth century, their interest in the continent aroused by popular novels, exploration narratives, and British newspaper coverage of the Boer War in South Africa. Ambitious young men from the British working classes could seize opportunities unavailable at home and rise to positions of great power and wealth as traders in the colonies. Few men, however, could escape their ranks of birth to bask in an all-inclusive white colonial identity. As Ann Laura Stoler, Antoinette Burton, and other new imperial historians point out, colonial elites were less racially coherent than that.[2] Known as "palm oil ruffians" and "old coasters," men such as Stuart-Young who worked as agents for European companies or set up their own palm oil enterprises formed a distinct socioeconomic group within the European colonial community. Their new imperial identities remained permanently marked by their class of birth; indeed, by the start of the twentieth century, their presence in the oil-rich areas of southern Nigeria caused many Christian missionaries and colonial administrators to label the entire region a "dumping ground for undesirables."[3]

In spite of their educational limitations, several lower-class traders published memoirs and novels between the 1870s and 1930s. Their unusual stories form the focal point of this chapter, for the writing of "poor whites" occupies a distinctive place in the historiography of British West Africa, providing an intensely subjective and intimate glimpse of changing colonial ideologies and gender relations during a century of economic—and physical—contact between Britain and West Africa. This chapter considers the ways in which this hitherto neglected body of writing offers both a commercial and a gender perspective on precolonial and early colonial relations, giving us intimate access to a dynamic set of white working-class accounts of the tastes and consumer habits of West Africans.

Traders' accounts of the past contain a "bias history"[4] of West African consumer relations and tastes in the nineteenth and early twentieth centuries. They draw upon generic and popular narrative forms that include explorers' tales of the "dark continent" and the published memoirs of fellow traders: both genres actively construct heroic masculine identities that contrast with other masculinities in colonial society. The distortions and exclusions in traders' texts are just as significant as the events they relate, revealing the relationships and values of a group of men whose perspectives are largely passed by in economic and social histories of West Africa. Yet in their role as arbiters of African wants and tastes, palm oil ruffians anticipated African demand for particular trade goods, and, as this chapter suggests, in their roles as receivers of African produce and hagglers over prices they became enmeshed in indigenous consumption patterns and forms of power that changed over time and were never wholly determined by the colonial center.

In southern Nigeria, where Stuart-Young worked, British traders established close working relationships with networks of African communities. Often operating without governmental protection, the palm oil ruffians generated new social identities for themselves by forging alliances with local chiefs and employing African middlemen along the trade arteries to the interior. Often skilled linguists, they traveled widely in search of new sources of oil and kernels, forging cultural and economic partnerships along the way. Like the African traders who were their rivals and the African middlemen who were their agents, many Europeans entered traditional elite structures. Some borrowed goods and currencies from chiefs and middlemen, repaying their debts with gifts and interest; others bought titles or special powers for themselves, investing heavily in local cultures and becoming "big men" in African terms, protected by fetishes and surrounded by auras of strength.[5] Many also married one or more well-placed local women traders, consolidating their commercial alliances, obtaining protection, expressing desire, and easing their loneliness in one fell swoop.[6] Such cross-racial marital practices became a major theme in the British popular literature discussed in the final section of this chapter.

Traders' memoirs reveal the degree of ideological and discursive labor that accompanied these interactions with the people on whom their livelihoods depended. As we saw in chapter 1, the parallels between British "slumland" and "primitive" Africa were powerfully evoked in numerous moral tracts and sociological publications in the late nineteenth and early twentieth centuries. Thus,

General William Booth's best-selling book *In Darkest England and the Way Out* (1890) was written as a direct response to Henry Morton Stanley's tale of exploration and missionary endeavor, *In Darkest Africa* (1890).[7] Explicitly connecting the "savage" with the slum-dweller, Booth set up a matrix of shame that implicated the English master race for allowing its own kind to descend to the same depths of "hunger and sin" that justified imperialist intervention in the lives of others overseas.[8] "As there is a darkest Africa is there not also a darkest England?" he asked. "May we not find a parallel at our own doors, and discover within a stone's throw of our cathedrals and palaces similar horrors to those which Stanley has found existing in the great Equatorial forest?"[9]

Writing from the other side of Booth's imperial map, many British missionaries reactivated these descriptions of working-class life when they noted the general moral "dirt" and receptivity to contagion of British palm oil traders in West Africa. A dynamic discourse thus emerged in which racial descriptors fed into the analysis of class in Britain, while class categories in the colonies were fueled by the conjunction of racial and social classifications at home. What emerged among colonial elites was a perception that the colonial environment was "sexually distinct from Britain: sexually loose, sometimes predatory, and frequently excessive," requiring political intervention and management.[10]

In his preface to Samuel Crowther's *Gospel on the Banks of the Niger*, "WK" of Church Missionary House activated these associations and drew attention to "the recklessness and profligacy of our own countrymen in heathen lands."[11] Working-class British merchants lack the "self-control of Christian gentlemen," WK insisted, and a "grave responsibility" rests on their employers to send out a better type of commercial man to West Africa.[12] Class stereotypes such as these increased at the turn of the twentieth century, coinciding strategically with the arrival into West Africa of the ruffian's opposite number, known by the popular stereotype of the public-schooled, stiff-upper-lipped, "clean" and "masculine" colonialist, product of the New Imperialism, trained in his duty to take up the white man's burden. According to popular mythology, in West Africa, this type of man could "develop those inborn qualities which have done so much to make our Empire what it is."[13]

Unlike these "manly" middle-class types, who featured prominently in imperial popular literature and children's books at the end of the nineteenth century, the white palm oil trader was regarded in many missionary and government circles as the product of working-class degeneration in the slum, his "nervous tissue worn out and stamina undermined."[14] British missionaries and colonialists hoped that with the political stability and military presence promised by imperial government after the First World War, a "better class of men" with "improved physique" might be encouraged to enter into trade.[15]

As working-class traders in Africa, "poor whites" were therefore caught in a web of social and discursive tensions. In consequence, in their effort to uphold the vital differences between the categories of race and class, the traders often tried in their memoirs to establish Africa as a fixed negative pole, the moral antithesis of their own whiteness.

One can chart the rise of dirt as a moral category in this writing; traders attempted to appropriate the same Christian hygiene discourse that was applied to the classes from which they had sprung. They tried to displace their own moral dirt sideways, sweeping it away from working-class Britons toward racialized African bodies. Their "half-civilized" African customers thus helped to erase traders' own "unwashed" and "savage" status. Indeed, there was no better figure than the "dirty" African to police the permeable boundary between white and black, especially when traders found themselves wearing "the same old bush-cloth that [the African] wears himself," eating local "chop," and using half rum puncheons for bathtubs, in local style.[16] Traders' feelings of revulsion toward African bodies were a source of constant comment in their narratives. Given their lower-class status in the eyes of imperial elites, it is easy to appreciate the urgency of their project to disavow contagion and substitute African bodies for their own in the moral discourse of cleanliness and hygiene.

In his impressive social history of soap in southern Africa, Timothy Burke explains how Europeans' physical revulsion toward African "dirt" and "ugliness" formed part of their incomprehension of precolonial gender, generation, and status categories: such categories were often expressed visibly in bodily adornment or nakedness, through body-painting (with "dirt") and through body-smearing to protect the skin from dryness (using "dirt").[17] The sense of revulsion Burke describes was not confined to southern Africa. In his Niger journal of 1857–59, the British-trained African missionary Samuel Ajayi Crowther held forth at length on the topic of dirty clothes and washing. "It is a reproach to them all that they go about in [flowing robes . . .] in a most filthy and disgusting state," Crowther wrote of Nupe men on the upper Niger. "They are the receptaicles [sic] for all kinds of vermin, which they are not ashamed to pick out from their garments even when in company."[18] Nupe women did not fare much better in Crowther's account: "Their moderate cloths around their body would have appeared cleaner and more decent still, if they were not stained by being dipped in cam-wood which gave them a dull and dirty reddish appearance."[19] Crowther's physical revulsion at this "dirt" mutated into moral disgust as he continued, "Even their ablutions are an abomination, especially as they are promiscuously performed by both sexes in the sight of each other. . . . [I]t is a violation of the law of decency, sanctity and holiness, which the law of God demands."[20] These comments reveal how

European and Christian-trained commentators observed visible categories of otherness all around them but misread the local bodily practices that were signified by other cultures. Local cleanliness rituals were read in terms of "ugliness" or "filth," processed through European binary markers of acceptability and difference.[21] As a result, even people's washing practices remained dirty, in Crowther's view.[22]

Not all nontraders looked on with disapproval at the moral dirt of palm oil ruffians. In 1897, the explorer Mary Kingsley keenly defended these men and placed them on the side of "civilization" when she insisted that "the greatest recantation I had to make I made humbly before I had been three months on the Coast in 1893. It was my idea of the traders."[23] Praising these rough men's "kindness to me," Kingsley emphasized her dependence on them during her travels, describing how "when I have arrived off his factory in a steamer or canoe, unexpected, unintroduced . . . he has always received me with that gracious hospitality which must have given him, under Coast conditions, very real trouble and inconvenience."[24]

In presenting the traders' hospitality and chivalry toward women, Kingsley carefully highlighted her own political desire for the civilizing mission to occur peacefully and consensually through trade rather than forcibly through the imposition of colonial state structures on African communities. To drive this argument home, the civility of traders is situated in close proximity to her own civility, above the more obvious differences of social class and gender, for "although he holds the meanest opinion of my intellect for going to such a place as West Africa for beetles, fishes and fetish, he has given me the greatest assistance in my work."[25] Kingsley's bestselling *Travels in West Africa* thus went a long way toward correcting the poor reputation of the palm oil ruffian at home.[26]

In their autobiographical writings between the 1870s and 1930s, working-class traders attempted to revise the popular stereotypes about them and rewrite their activities in a more heroic or procolonial light. Some autobiographical narratives, such as Harry Cottrell's, represented the trader as preparing the way for colonial rule, while others, such as James Deemin's and John Whitford's, represented the trader as a neutral, nonideological presence with no political or moral impact, for better or for worse, on local communities. In the words of Stuart-Young, himself an old coaster by 1916, "We are not Colonists,—we are simply cogs in a huge machine! Every Coaster knows in his heart that he is here to make what he can, and then clear out again!"[27]

Stuart-Young's morally and politically neutral posture was taken at face value in many missionary circles, inspiring a predictable response. For example, the famous African missionary Rev. Samuel Ajayi Crowther commented in disappointment on his way up the River Niger in the late 1850s that "though the palm oil trade has been carried on with this people for years, yet it makes no impression or change in their social or moral condition."[28] Whereas missionaries such as Crowther traveled the waterways and trade routes of Nigeria in order to intervene in local people's lives and "improve" their "social and moral condition" by encouraging them to cover their nakedness and hear the Word of God, palm oil traders occupied a morally ambivalent position on the rivers. They inhabited an interface between races and cultures, profiting from their control of supplies of credit and trade goods and asserting their racial superiority over Africans on many occasions but refusing to be physically segregated from the "pagan" African communities with whom they exchanged gifts, favors, and goods. As we have seen, to many a white bourgeois onlooker, such a lack of boundaries illustrated the consequences of allowing the products of slumland to enter the tropics, for slum-dwellers and "savages" were seen to be similarly contagious, similarly dirty, requiring the same soapy intervention from above.

The tropics provided a space for "poor white" men to distinguish and define themselves, especially in relation to Africans and women. Eager to memorialize their long careers as pioneer businessmen and adventurers in exotic, unmapped locations, many traders put pen to paper in the late nineteenth and early twentieth centuries, producing self-consciously "masculine" narratives ranging from memoirs and adventure novels to sensational testimonies that confessed to kidnappings, punishment beatings, and massacres of Africans hostile to trade.[29] In their writings, many of these palm oil ruffians looked back to the old days of precolonial trade from a colonial vantage point and from a position of personal opulence, proud of their achievements in the post–slave trade era but conscious that the new imperial standards and bourgeois morality of twentieth-century colonialism might call their actions into question.

I. WEST AFRICAN TASTES

What is particularly striking about the texts this chapter explores is their disclosure of a set of stories about production and consumption in West Africa in which it becomes clear that imported commodities and the global economy predated the presence of European traders in West Africa.[30] In order to succeed as businessmen in the tropics and secure supplies of palm products from the interior, European traders had to adapt their practices and perceptions to suit existing West African systems of exchange: they had to occupy and expand existing African networks of trade routes, which were often monopolized by women, and take seriously local tastes and consumption patterns, which frequently baffled or revolted their senses.[31] Only in this way could they harness African labor to the global economy and secure sufficient quantities of palm oil and kernels to satisfy the voracious demand from Europe. Theirs was a commercial type of "indirect rule" in which existing precolonial structures were exploited while, simultaneously, great efforts were made to restructure local economies to meet the needs of global trade.

The primary reason for traders' efforts to comprehend African tastes and consumption patterns was the palm nut, which grew abundantly in the wild, especially in eastern Nigeria in the densely populated regions from Warri to the south and east.[32] Although palm nuts called for little formal cultivation, they required a great deal of human labor to be transformed into oil and kernels, essential products that helped fuel the European and American industrial revolutions. Palm oil was widely used as a lubricant for industrial machinery, in the manufacture of soap and candles, and, in the tinplate processing industry, as a source of glycerin until mineral oils displaced palm oil after the 1850s.[33] Meanwhile, palm kernel oil was found in the 1880s to be ideal for the mass production of soap, an industry dominated by Lever Brothers after the Great War.[34]

At the peak period of the trade in the mid-nineteenth century, the white palm oil ruffian made a double windfall: he imported cheap trade goods from Europe and India and made them available to African producers and middlemen in exchange for valuable raw materials, which would be shipped home and sold at a profit to British industrialists. In the brutally honest words of the trader and famous ruffian Aloysius Horn (aka "Trader Horn"), "the art of trading was to get the natives to exchange cheap articles for dear ones."[35] Although profit was distributed unevenly along the chain of command, their control of the interior routes enabled some African chiefs and suppliers of oil to become immensely rich in the nineteenth century.[36]

Large fortunes were lost as well as made by traders in palm products, especially in the 1880s and 1890s, when oil prices plummeted and the value of trade decreased by up to 40 percent.[37] This period also witnessed the end of the era of African "merchant princes." These independent African and "mulatto" traders, many of whom were liberated slaves, had accumulated enormous wealth from commerce in the early nineteenth century and had built palatial residences along the coast with "coloured glass panes in their gothic-shaped windows."[38] But by the late 1920s, many independent African traders had been squeezed out, as had the majority of European small traders, and the field was dominated by a small number of European "combines" who met the demand for palm oil and kernels.

Palm products became so integral to late Victorian manufacturing that commodities making use of oil or kernels, such as domestic soap, came to be identified with Rev. Livingston's three "C's"—Civilization, Christianity, and Commerce—which justified British imperial expansion.[39] A fourth "C," Cleanliness, should be added to this list as the bonding agent, for as Anne McClintock convincingly argues, a large part of the rationale for British imperial supremacy in Africa was expressed through the "fetish" of soap. Made from African raw materials and promoted in Britain as the epitome of "civilized" hygiene, the bar of soap provided material and moral inspiration for colonial expansion.[40] One Pears soap advertisement neatly reflected these two sides of soap: "The consumption of soap is a measure of the wealth, civilisation, Health, and Purity of the People."[41] Stimulated by the Victorian preoccupation with hygiene and the popular fascination for "darkest Africa," soap manufacturers released numerous advertisements that reaffirmed the connections between cleanliness, commodity culture, white skin, imperial expansion, and the advance of humanity. Unilever's company slogan expressed this succinctly: "soap is civilisation."[42]

In the metropolis, as McClintock and others have shown, soap represented, in a single compact commodity, the coming together of an array of Victorian cults, ideologies, and scientific concepts that included sexual hygiene, industrial precision, Christian ideas of purity, Victorian femininity, and the physical and moral "cleaning up" of European slums and African savages.[43] For traders in West Africa, however, operating in terrain outside the Victorian commodity culture, it was the provision of soap components and their exchange for goods rather than the use of soap itself, that came to be associated with the qualities of wealth, health, and purity.

Benefiting from the fetishization of soap in Britain, traders developed their own moral discourse to justify their efforts to transform West African consumption and production patterns. The prevailing belief among merchants was that the palm oil trade would help turn locals away from consuming one another in "cannibal feasts" and transform them into "model Victorians keen to encourage commerce and to buy British goods."[44] Civilization came to be connected with the hard-work ethic of Victorian Britain. As trader John Whitford commented with pleasure, "There is a common interest developed by the creation of new wants amongst the heathens, and habits of industry are thereby so engendered that they eagerly seek out whatever we require to enable them to get what they want."[45] Representing their own actions through the vector of Victorian bourgeois ideals, many traders' memoirs convey an almost religious belief in consumerism as a force for good in Africa, inciting people to labor to produce palm oil and kernels. Thus, the cure for Africa's moral "dirt" was the production of the components of soap.[46]

In the process of creating wants and needs among palm oil producers, traders had to study the economies and social systems from which new needs might emerge. On their numerous tours to ascertain local demand and gather information about their competitors, they generated an early form of market research that reveals much about local responses to globalization. Traders' memoirs reveal that African tastes for imported commodities changed rapidly in response to internal and external stimuli, and within each community tastes clearly differed depending on the individual's gender, status, and generation. In addition, "each district had a fancy for distinct sorts of goods."[47] British traders might have had privileged access to suppliers of commodities in Liverpool and Manchester, but unless Africans actively desired their goods, the flow of palm products would dry up. As Allan McPhee commented in frustration, "the natives preferred to produce nothing, when they could not get what they wanted."[48]

The European palm oil and kernel trade thus revolved around the tastes and values of each particular African market and its hinterland. This fact created numerous headaches for European traders, for many Africans simply would not become peaceful producers and consumers. "It was found utterly impossible to get them to take any interest in [trade]," recalled James Deemin of his period as a trader in the 1880s, "without first giving them credit and afterwards harassing them in every possible way for its settlement."[49]

Late-nineteenth-century traders spent a great deal of time attempting to initiate people into the rites and manners of British consumer culture. In the months before the development of such a culture, palm oil traders faced many hazards, including "mobs of noisy, dangerous, thieving savages all over his place all day" instead of orderly queues of customers.[50] In Deemin's case, when the lure of rum failed to excite agricultural productivity, he adopted modes of harassment that included kidnappings with ransom demands and punitive raids on villages by his private army.[51]

What many traders failed to appreciate was the existence of established complex consumer desires and trade economies in West Africa that preceded the expansion of global trade by many decades. In consequence, even when the "savages" had been tamed and rendered "customers," their shopping habits, carried over from previous decades, would test the nerves of the most patient trader. "As soon as we thought we had got one gentleman's mind settled as to what goods he would take his pay in and were proceeding to investigate another gentleman's little fancies," Mary Kingsley explained in frustration, "gentleman number one's mind came all to pieces again, and he wanted 'to room his bundle,' i.e., change articles in it for other articles of an equivalent value, if it must be, but of a higher value if possible."[52] Kingsley's account of the negotiation process serves as a template for the problems many traders experienced with African customers, who had their own tastes and modes of discrimination: "Oh ye shopkeepers in England who grumble at your lady customers," Kingsley concludes, "just you come out here and try to serve, and satisfy a set of Fan [customers]!"[53]

Traders were well aware that "constant trials of new lines" were necessary from the outset if they were to fathom local consumer cultures that shifted rapidly and without apparent logic.[54] The key problem was how to maintain the flow of oil and kernels to international markets when the native seemed, in the merchant capitalist's terms, to be fickle as a consumer, "lazy" as a worker, and resistant to developing the "wants" upon which the entire export economy depended. These problems surface repeatedly in the autobiographies of nineteenth- and early-twentieth-century traders. Writing in 1840 in distinctive English prose, Captain Harrington, master of an American trading vessel, voiced a set of conclusions that persisted for a hundred years:

> The Blacks cannot perceived [sic] any comprehensible motive to impel them to sustain and practice a purity of Caracter [sic], being naturally Depraved and indolent and imbued with their disgusting customs and savage supersititions [sic] and leaving [sic] in a filthy mud hovels [sic] as long as they obtain enough to gratify their personal wants and as long as such last nothing can move them to exertion.[55]

Harrington's strong response to the "Black"—that is, the non-"Mulatto"—African reveals a complex set of associations and assumptions relating to the emergent African consumer of imported commodities. "Naturally" lazy, inhabiting "filthy mud hovels," and incapable of frugality or saving for the future, the undomesticated African body is stranded outside the hard-work ethic and soapy bathtubs that defined cleanliness and "purity of character" in industrial bourgeois Europe. In the words of another frustrated palm oil trader when he saw rows of empty palm oil canoes, Africans "have got no idea of industry beyond supplying present wants, nor any notion of the value of time."[56]

The central problem facing Harrington and his successors was the apparent self-sufficiency of African nature, which seemed, to many European eyes, to provide ample foodstuffs and materials for people's needs without requiring any labor or processing on the part of farmers.[57] In this, of course, the Europeans failed to recognize African modes of labor and agricultural cultivation. The conclusions they drew reflected their assumption that European trade goods introduced the concepts of labor, cleanliness, and consumption to West Africa. As John Whitford wrote of the 1860s and 1870s, "but for the inducement to purchase gorgeous apparel and truly ardent spirits very few negroes would work at all."[58]

Whitford's memoir, *Trading Life in Western and Central Africa*, is typical of nineteenth-century "ruffian writing"; it is written in a kind of utopian mode, conveying a constant sense of wonder at the bounty of African nature. The landscape is celebrated and described solely in terms of its usefulness to Europe. This trader saw not earth and rivers but "mineral deposits" of gold and iron ore, not trees and forests but "excellent hard timber."[59] Most revealingly, human beings are described not as "people" but, in a manner reminiscent of slave-trade discourse, as "raw material."[60] Thus Whitford asked of the West African, "What kind of raw material does he make for civilisation to operate upon?"[61] He sees supplies of these multifarious African raw materials as infinite and untapped, simply awaiting European exploitation. "Nature has been kind in abundantly furnishing this land with valuable but uselessly-excessive produce," he wrote, insisting on the need for "commerce [to] step in to take the surplus away, and, in return, supply the people with goods, which they ardently covet when they see them."[62]

Trading Life in Western and Central Africa communicates great optimism and awe about the limitless quantities of "valuable produce" stored in Africa's tropical forests, awaiting export under the power of "King Steam": "We know about palm oil," Whitford mused, "but we know absolutely nothing of other valuable products lining the banks of the river, and abounding in the country on either side of us far inland, which it will take at least a hundred years of extending commerce to appreciate, and, to the eye of a trader, properly ferret out and take home to pay."[63]

In comments such as this, Whitford offers the merchant's-eye view of Africa. It is a view that flattens and de-exoticizes the sinister animated African landscapes described by later authors such as H. Rider Haggard and Joseph Conrad in their popular novels of the 1890s and 1900s. So thorough is Whitford's de-exoticization of Africa that on occasion he actually represents West Africa in terms of northern English landscapes, likening the River Niger to the River Mersey and describing its ascent "upwards into wolds like those of happy Lincolnshire."[64] As we will see in Stuart-Young's African pastoral poetry, discussed in chapter 8, the trader's text is anything but Orientalist. It corrects and contrasts the canon of imperialist fictions about Africa, for the rationale of commerce is not to dwell on an exotic "otherness" but to constantly seek similarities and "ways in" to local economies and, in so doing, to reject, or ignore, major cultural differences.[65]

Whitford's typical view of an abundant African nature persisted well into the twentieth century, although few of his successors held such a comfortable, domesticated vision of the landscape. With the arrival of the colonial state, "the bounty of Nature" came to be regarded as more of a problem than a promise, responsible for making "the Coast native, to a great extent, an indolent, improvident animal."[66] Rendered effeminate and degenerate by an all-providing nature, the African man was, in this persistent view, unlikely to produce a steady flow of raw materials for export to the industrialized nations. Such people thus remained unfathomable to the merchant capitalist, impossible to absorb into his frame of reference.

A rich array of trade goods arrived in tropical Africa from British ports. Recreating his youthful vision of trading vessels setting out from Liverpool in 1916, Raymond Gore Clough named the range of exports to be sent off to the West Coast:

> To the swampy delta of the Niger they carried Cheshire salt, Burma rice, herrings in brine and dried stockfish; rum in puncheons, whisky from Scotland and "trade gin" from Holland. There were coloured printed cottons from Manchester, and natural Madras cloth; long flintlocked guns, kegs of gunpowder and lead shot; rods of copper and brass; beads and clay pipes; iron pots, matchets, tools and fishing hooks. All this to win in a cargo of dark red palm oil.[67]

A short history of British–West African trade relations is contained in this compact list of commodities: on the outward journey, vessels carried copper and brass trade currencies alongside goods designed to supplement, if not to displace, indigenous products, including salt, dried fish, cooking pots, farming implements, and cloth from the furthest reaches of the British empire.[68] Wherever he traveled on the "oil rivers" of Nigeria, Clough encountered deposits of this merchandise, in warehouses, in stores of European merchants, or in the bundles of African market women. He was unable to tear his eyes away from the spectacle of "Bombay bowlers and even top hats . . . evening dress suits, faded a little green, old fashioned striped blazers and a fine but faded cutaway coat in hunting scarlet, probably a long-time favourite of some m'lord in Leicestershire."[69] Clough's lists and inventories recur throughout his memoir, stretching for pages at a time, rendering the British products exotic and alien, imbued with a fetishistic power of their own.

Again and again in their memoirs, British traders produce extensive lists of their goods. If African customers were bedazzled by the spectacular array of things in the European stores, the traders responsible for converting trade goods into palm oil were equally mesmerized by the plenitude of European commodities. From Whitford in the 1870s to Stuart-Young and Clough in the

1920s and 1930s, these men did not stop commenting on the spectacle of "shelf upon shelf of every kind of merchandise" in their stores, cataloguing the "infinite variety" of stocks.[70] In so doing, they reaffirmed the supremacy of British mass production over an African subsistence economy. At the same time, however, they also conveyed anxieties about the success of the British consumer project. Taken together, their numerous lists betray a lapse in the cultural confidence of the imperial race, for the commodity rather than the trader is invested with the magical power to civilize and transform the "savage," yet the sheer tonnage of commodities devalues each item, depriving it of cultural power.[71]

On a practical level, a careful balance had to be maintained between supply and demand, and several traders encountered severe difficulties in persuading African customers that the supply of imports was not endless. "They were lost in astonishment at the enormous quantity of goods coming from the ship," Whitford wrote of his African onlookers at the wharf, and "when it came to trading they were too anxious to get more beautiful things than we could afford for the produce that we wanted."[72] As a consequence, the white traders learned to hide their stocks away, displaying only limited samples of goods "so as to keep down their energy."[73] The sheer plenitude of commodities arriving from Britain gave the same impression to Africans as the apparently limitless supplies of African raw materials and the plentiful nature noticed by white traders such as Whitford. Whether it was cloth from Manchester or palm oil from African villages, both sides of the trade relationship seemed convinced that the other's products appeared by magic, in great quantities, requiring little or no human labor to transform them into commodities.

II. AFRICAN RESPONSES TO THE EUROPEAN TRADERS

Traders experienced high levels of "reverse anthropology" from the African producers who delivered raw materials to their factories and purchased goods from their stores, observing European behavior in the process and reaching definite conclusions about the other culture. The white men commented repeatedly on being watched and interpreted. Thus, John Whitford described how people on the upper Niger "got it into their heads that we wanted the large tusks to make ivory anklets for our wives and daughters, like the heathens lower down the river."[74] Even though the interpreter "violently gesticulated and endeavoured to prove that English ladies would never dream of wearing ten or a dozen pounds' weight of ivory over their delicate ankles, yet they would not believe him."[75] Clearly, European cultural difference was regarded locally as no greater than the differences separating neighboring African communities from one another. Finally, when the interpreter "assured them that we made knife handles and numerous other articles in common use out of ivory, they simply said 'pooh' in their own language, and laughed him to scorn."[76]

Examples such as this reveal that it is possible to extract a set of intriguing but heavily mediated African responses to the colonial economy from the biased archive of traders' memoirs. When Whitford and his fellow traders report the scorn and laughter of their customers, they make space for fragments of a social history of West Africa that is situated outside colonial and European ways of knowing Africa. These moments of European bafflement and African interpretive agency help in our effort to piece together a century of changing African reactions to the new goods and traders in their midst. The global economy had become increasingly homogenized by the 1860s and 1870s, when Whitford entered trade, but the cultural untranslatability of the British uses for ivory signals a failure in the transmission of those western consumer (and gender) ideologies that were supposed to accompany imperialism and globalization. African perspectives can be located within these gaps and failures of comprehension.

From the earliest days of commerce along the West Coast, a major component of traders' narratives was the expression of bafflement about African culture. Traders' autobiographies display many lapses in their comprehension of the Africans with whom they worked. It was not only the supposedly untouched Africans who confounded traders' senses, but the confusing spectacle of commodities "wrongly" deployed by consumers who had discovered unimagined cultural potential in foreign goods: confused, or amused, traders repeatedly described such wrongful deployments.[77] The traders showed great ambivalence toward the figure of the African consumer, especially regarding his or her manner of appropriating European items of clothing. When confronted with the sight of African men wearing admirals' cocked hats, flamboyant trousers, or top hats, many Europeans failed to recognize that statements about status and power were being conveyed through this clothing.[78] Yet traders had to sustain precisely these "alien" consumer habits in order to procure palm products for export. In spite of their criticisms of West African elites for "imitating the Unsuitable fashions of Europe" and despite their open hostility toward "half-educated young male negroes" who spent all their money on "fine clothes and jewellery [and] are most offensive and insolent," white traders were heavily invested in supplying such "mimics" with their pince-nez and parasols.[79]

African hands—particularly those of women, children, and domestic slaves—had to be inspired into action to keep the industrial revolution supplied with its precious oils. Traders constantly sought new ways to wean the controllers of this labor from consumption of their own locally made commodities. The controllers of labor—often powerful broker-chiefs who controlled the means of transportation and access to credit as well as labor[80]—had to be tempted into the world market. An absence of new lines of "attractive articles" would cause the flow of oil to dry up, and traders therefore constantly "taxed their ingenuity to think of new goods to attract the golden red oil."[81] Consumption and production were intimately bound up with one another. In the words of Clough, "the only way to induce the Africans to bring their oil in was by . . . creating a desire on the part of not only the canoeman himself, but of his wives and children in their bush villages, for all the attractive articles displaced in the factory store."[82] Of primary importance to traders was the transformation of oil production from an "incidental activity" that enabled the purchase of luxuries into a primary activity to acquire necessities.[83] Traders' attempts to convert former luxuries into essentials seem to have succeeded in many parts of West Africa by the 1890s, for during her travels in villages along the most far-flung trade routes, Mary Kingsley found palm oil and kernels waiting by the riverside ready for export, accompanied by "gentlemen half wild for want of tobacco" and "ladies . . . impatient for their new clothes."[84]

III. AFRICAN WOMEN AT THE PALM OIL STATION

Palm oil ruffians were members of a gender-exclusive profession, and they often represented themselves as bonded together by a shared masculine working-class culture.[85] That culture was sustained by the fact that European wives did not join their trader husbands in significant numbers until the 1920s, when shifts in the colonial management of sexuality and fears over racial miscegenation made their presence more desirable.[86] Until then, as Ann Laura Stoler points out for colonial culture generally, "European manhood in the colonies, whether measured by 'character' and civility or by position and class, was largely independent of the presence of European women."[87] Some wives tried to break into this racially marked homosocial sphere of power and "pluckily followed their men-folk" to the tropics; but men often resented "the keeping up of appearances which the presence of ladies demands."[88]

One old coaster in the 1920s explained his opposition thus: white women "would see us as we are, not as we would like our wives to see us."[89] Such a comment indicates that the construction of "masculine" cultures in the colonies depended on the absence of the British female gaze and the keeping of secrets from European women: colonial masculinity emerged without women's surveillance of men's conversations, clothing, humor, eating and drinking habits, and recreational activities.[90] Viewed in this light, Mary Kingsley's description of the traders' kindness and chivalry toward her represents precisely the behavioral modifications that traders feared would arise from European women's presence in the colonies.

No European women seem to have worked as full-time traders in West Africa, although Kingsley carried commodities on her travels, which she used to "talk trade" with locals and distribute as "dashes" to her acquaintances.[91] Some female missionaries would also have been involved in the running of stores, for until systematic government efforts to enforce the cash economy in the decade after 1918, each mission's staff of teachers, catechists, and servants were paid in trade goods rather than coins. Thus, several of the missionaries Kingsley encountered in West Africa were also involved in the "hard, tiring and exasperating work" of paying native teachers and laborers in goods from the mission store.[92]

If European women traders were a rare breed, there was no shortage of African women entrepreneurs and brokers in West Africa, trading directly with the European firms and controlling major trade routes to the interior. Gifted women traders could establish, and exploit, relationships within the extended family to secure lucrative long-distance trade routes.[93] Madame Tinubu of Lagos and Omu Okwei of Ossomari are perhaps the most famous examples of female entrepreneurs, attracting the attention of feminist historians for their distinction as "merchant queens" who transformed their wealth into social and political power.[94] While Madame Tinubu operated around Lagos, Omu Okwei operated in and around Onitsha between the 1890s and 1940s as an independent palm oil trader and a "buying agent" for hinterland chiefs. To the chagrin of European traders, including Stuart-Young, the chiefs "depended solely on her tastes for the selection of manufactured goods."[95] By the 1920s, Omu Okwei was receiving shipments on her own account from firms in Manchester and Liverpool, which she transported using her own fleet of vehicles.[96] Stuart-Young had many dealings with this powerful woman, which led him to grumble in 1918 that "she drives a hard bargain and [is . . .] able to make her own market and at her own price without competition."[97]

"It seemed as if all Ibo women were traders seeking to make a profit in their own villages from goods they could acquire on their travels," commented Raymond Gore Clough of his time in the Niger Delta between 1919 and the 1930s.[98] The ubiquitous presence and leadership of West African women traders is recorded in many other white traders' accounts of eastern Nigeria. In particular, these memoirs testify to the role of Igbo women as go-betweens and taste-setters and as agents who responded to and regulated the demand for particular products. As their descendents confirm, Igbo women controlled many of the European men's preferred trade routes, governed the distribution of raw materials and commodities, and exercised political authority and leadership.[99] This important zone of cross-cultural, cross-gender contact between African women and European men was not necessarily sexual, nor can it be reduced to the "torrid zones" and "genealogies of the intimate" that tend to preoccupy historians of imperial cross-racial relationships.[100]

Women traders' autonomous political power was utilized on at least one occasion by terrified white male traders in the Niger Delta, when leading women merchants were asked to mediate between the European commercial community and African women farmers. At Olomo during the "Women's War" of 1929, three powerful "merchant queens," Mesdames Unuka, Osika, and Omvaro, were asked to intervene on behalf of Raymond Gore Clough and other palm oil traders to explain to women protestors the differences between government administrators and white traders in the area. Insisting that stark differences separated groups of colonial elites from one another, Clough and his fellows asked the merchant queens to explain that they were not responsible for local taxation regimes; additionally, they asked them to explain "circumstances in the outer world" whereby the global price for palm kernels—the source of women's profits—had slumped along with palm oil to such critically low levels that European traders refused to buy further palm products from local women, even though imported merchandise continued to fill up their stores.[101] Traders hoped that "the presence of the calmer English-speaking [Igbo] women," dressed in their smartest outfits, would "have a sobering effect on the hysterical mob" with their blue-dyed bodies and militant, confrontational clothing.[102] While the three female intermediaries failed to stop the advance of the "singing and dancing mass of several thousand women" on Olomo and the carnage that followed the district officer's order to open fire, their central role in the crisis reveals a great deal about elite Igbo and Ibibio women's position at the intersection of the local and global economies as political and cultural arbiters between white traders and ordinary women.[103]

These examples reveal that European male traders in West Africa were not cut off from the presence of women, nor were their interactions with local women solely sexual and domestic. Even the most "woman-hating" and boy-loving man, such as Stuart-Young, was surrounded on all sides by Igbo merchant queens, titled women, women farmers, and market women. Stuart-Young could not avoid dealing with these spirited female entrepreneurs whom it was necessary to attract to his stores with new ranges of imported commodities.

Sexual liaisons formed one dimension of this complex bundle of cross-cultural interactions between European men and African women. From the earliest days of trade in West Africa, African women embarked on formal and informal liaisons with European men. At Mr. Swanzy's fort in Dixcove in 1840, for example, Captain Harrington noticed "Mr. Swanzys [sic] Lady 'pro tempore' or for a time a young molatto Girl of considerable attraction."[104] Taken aback by their intimacy, Harrington remarked, "Such a distinction and indulgence to a Lady by their Lords I have never witnessed on the coast. Probably Mr. Swanzys [sic] greater liberality of sentiment and his lonely situation prompted him to admit his Lady to his board as to his b-d."[105] Such liaisons produced lines of "mulatto" descendents along the coast and furrowed the brows of many missionary educators and colonial officials, for, as several historians of empire have observed, by the first decades of the twentieth century such offspring were believed to be both the symbol and the symptom of European men's moral laxity in the colonies.[106]

The intimate company of African women eased the "lonely and forlorn" situation of white traders and is remarked on repeatedly by all except Stuart-Young in their autobiographical writings.[107] Alongside "sentiment" and "loneliness," however, several other reasons help explain traders' relationships. "The Girls are very useful to the men in Business," Captain Harrington commented in the mid-nineteenth century, not least because "their knowledge of the native tongue renders them almost indispensable with every trading establishment."[108] This linguistic expertise earned the women the euphemistic name "sleeping dictionaries." For both sides in these mutually beneficial relationships, the partnership played an essential role in the maintenance of trade networks, keeping alive contacts and bonds of loyalty in the interior.[109]

As late as the moralistic 1920s and 1930s, when such liaisons were regularly condemned in the British popular media, African women entrepreneurs continued to offer their daughters, female trainees, and servants in marriage to white traders to consolidate trading rights on both sides. Thus, the merchant queen Omu Okwei of Ossomari and Onitsha "acquired beautiful girls" in the 1910s and "brought them up and gave them out as mistresses or wives to influential businessmen and others."[110] As the wealthiest palm oil trader in Nigeria by 1919, undoubtedly Stuart-Young would have been offered one of Omu Okwei's girls, and his refusal would have contributed to the market women's perception of him as a "woman-hater" whose interests lay elsewhere.

With the formalization of colonial power in West Africa, metropolitan writers became increasingly sensational and moralistic in their representations of these relationships. White palm oil traders' lifestyles represented a continual challenge to the new imperialist ideology with its bourgeois ideals of sexual self-restraint and racial segregation. As Robert Young points out, one of the props on which the ideology of British imperialism rested was the concept of racial purity, sustained by late-nineteenth-century theories that racial degeneration occurred through miscegenation.[111] The relatively relaxed attitudes that characterized the eighteenth and early nineteenth centuries gave way to this fierce sense of racial hygiene, and "poor whites" from the working classes represented the most potent transmission route for racial contagion.

The most dramatic representation of the trader's moral slide—and with it, the British empire's slide—into sexual and racial degeneracy was the stage play *White Cargo: A Play of the Primitive*, written by Leon Gordon in 1923 and based on the bestselling novel of 1912, *Hell's Playground*, by Ida Vera Simonton. Immensely popular throughout the first half of the twentieth century, *Hell's Playground* and *White Cargo* traced the fall of a young English trader, Allen Langford, into the moral abyss in West Africa. His fall is manifested through his decision not just to have a relationship with but to marry a local "half-caste" woman named Tondelayo.[112] In this, Langford exemplifies a point made by Stoler in her study of the Dutch East Indies, that by the 1920s and 1930s "it was not interracial sexual contact that was seen as dangerous but its public legitimation in marriage."[113]

The Hollywood movie version of *White Cargo*, released in 1942, starred Hedy Lamarr as the "sensual half-caste." Curiously, given the class dimension of the discourses of dirt, savagery, and degeneration, the white trader in *Hell's Playground* and *White Cargo* is no working-class ruffian but a cultured, sensitive middle-class youth who dresses impeccably in a pith helmet and flannels. He thus represents the very epitome of English colonial masculinity: the fall of this figure from a position of moral and masculine power presents a forceful warning to all classes of the dangers to imperialism posed by sexual liaisons with locals.[114] The moral tableau is sharply focused through the vector of class in both narratives: Langford is reduced at the end of each version of the story to an effete, sickly, unwashed, and unshaven figure, entirely lacking in physical and moral stamina. In this way, the bourgeois British trader's sexual relationship with an African woman is shown to lower the rank of the imperial male and weaken the empire itself.

How did working-class traders address these increasingly racist readings of white men's African wives and lovers? Escalating moral panic in the metropolis in the 1920s and 1930s influenced the themes of many trader-authors, who often turned away from the memoir toward fiction in order to present their arguments. Published nearly thirty years apart, *Merely a Negress: A West African Story* (1904) by Stuart-Young and *Fantee Carter* (1931) by the trader Warren Henry both engage directly with the popular debate about interracial sex in the colonies—what Stuart-Young termed "the demoralising effect of West Africa"[115]—and their conclusions reflect the gradual hardening of sexual attitudes that occurred alongside the expansion of colonial government between the 1900s and the 1930s.

Stuart-Young's first novel, *Merely a Negress* (1904), produced when the author was only twenty-three and working as a trader in Grand Bassa, Liberia, is a deliberately controversial intervention in the debate about interracial relationships. Published by John Long as part of a six-shilling "popular novels" series, *Merely a Negress* is hailed in the promotional blurb as a "new experiment in fiction" deserving of "careful attention."[116] Preceding *Hell's Playground* by eight years and *White Cargo* by twenty, this is one of the earliest popular novels to introduce the theme of interracial marriage between a white man and a mixed-race woman. In the words of the publisher, Stuart-Young's novel is a "new and original contribution insomuch that it deals with the problem of the marriage of an Englishman and a Negress."[117] Such marriages, these remarks indicate, were already regarded as a "problem" in Britain by 1904.

Stuart-Young's hero, Frank Benson, is represented as a solidly bourgeois character rather than a trader. With "indulgent parents" and "few wants," he is of a different social class than the typical traders and clerks who went to work in West Africa in the early twentieth century.[118] Like the protagonist of *Hell's Playground,* this reserved 23-year-old leaves the city behind him and sets off for Liberia in search of freedom, solitude, nature, and beauty.[119] Despite being a renowned "woman-hater," Benson, while working in Liberia as a palm oil trader, falls in love with Lily Summerton, who has "negro blood in her veins" but a "face that was almost thoroughly Caucasian."[120]

Merely a Negress addresses the popular theme of racial "degeneration" through miscegenation, tracing the weakening of character and physique across three generations of Liberians, from the half-African Mr. Summerton to his quarter-African daughter Lily and her sickly nearly white son, who dies in the sequel to this novel, *Passion's Peril* (1906). After a valiant effort to stay alive in the metropolis, Lily is also killed off in the sequel, punished for the "degenerate" blood that renders her sexually and emotionally unstable and easily led astray when she settles in London. "White blood" and "African blood" are shown to curdle when mixed, causing "retrogression" in the "descendents of barbarians and cannibals."[121] Such themes clearly reveal the influence of Victorian racial science on Stuart-Young, who seemed incapable of thinking about interracial marriage outside the terms of degeneracy discourses.

Unlike the protagonists of *Hell's Playground* and *White Cargo,* however, Benson does not symbolize the collapse of a virile imperial masculinity when it comes into sexual contact with an African or half-African woman. Stuart-

Young seems to resist the easy ideological conflation of interracial sex with the downfall of empire, and the reason relates to his own class position, for he mounts a moral critique of the white bourgeois male, locating one source of moral degeneration and irresponsibility in English middle-class manhood. It is vital to note that Benson has been "spoilt" already by the time he arrives in Liberia. He has been "bred in the atmosphere of uprightness, fed with good sound moral law, and fully catechised from the cradle onwards in the paths of virtue."[122] This combination of protective middle-class values—the very codes promoted for the ideal imperialist—is shown to leave Benson with few inner resources, unable to take responsibility for his sexual desires and decisions. Stuart-Young thus presents a double reading of interracial relationships, upholding the views of racial science but also redeeming his own trader class by holding the metropolis to account for producing middle-class failures such as Benson.

In a three-page postscript to the novel that reiterates his publisher's promotional material, Stuart-Young suggests that "the problem of my story is, I believe, new."[123] In the remainder of the postscript he develops a theory of the function of fiction in imperial settings. Through the portrayal of "true types" such as Lily and Frank, he writes, the "white man who has traveled among the darker races of the earth" can help people in Britain to "understand" the native.[124] Stuart-Young envisages a momentous role for authors and small traders in West Africa; their literary evidence and well-observed narrative scenarios are pivotal, he believes, to the functioning of colonial government. Working alongside scientists and ethnologists, white traders in the colonies can offer "unbiased" assistance to Britain, helping the homeland to achieve "her great responsibilities."[125]

While Warren Henry has far less to say about the role and bias of trader-novelists, this old coaster also addresses the topic of interracial relationships. The theme was no longer new by 1931, when Henry's African novel *Fantee Carter* was published; by then, generations of popular authors had played out the colonial fantasy of interracial desire under titles such as *The Sheik* (1919) and *Gone Native* (1924), reviving it in theaters, newspapers, cinemas, and novels throughout the 1920s. Bored with the entire debate in the 1920s, Henry writes in his autobiography that men such as Allan Langford would never survive in the tropics.[126] Additionally, he insists that such narratives "travesty" the tender "pseudo-connubial" relationships that develop between white traders and "ordinary, simple and often virtuous" African women.[127]

When Henry turns from autobiography to popular fiction, however, he seems pressed by the sheer weight of the popular canon to engage with the issue of miscegenation. Writing nearly a decade after the staging of *White*

Cargo, he responds to the popular theme by removing the decadent, effeminate bourgeois male from representations of West African trading life and inserting a ruggedly "masculine" working-class trader into the popular template. Henry's hero, Gordon Carter, rejects the "spit and polish and veneer" of an academic education that renders a man bourgeois and effeminate, like Stuart-Young's hero.[128] Handsome, healthy, "well-built," and "straight" in character, Carter is the manly replacement for empire boys such as Benson and Langford.[129] Indeed, Carter spends many lonely hours in his remote West African trading station struggling against Benson's and Langford's type of passion. Like them, however, he slowly "goes native" in the absence of European company, and the sign of his mutation from white to black is his desire for "a beautiful dusky fawn."[130] His dreams about her express attraction and repulsion to her race in equal measure. The crucial marker of Carter's virile masculinity, however, in contrast to Stuart-Young's bourgeois hero, is his ability to resist the temptation posed by the nubile African woman. *Fantee Carter* holds a firm position in the miscegenation debate. In the end, the hero would rather marry an English "tomboy" named Rhoda K. Marlowe—a trouser-wearing explorer shown to be dangerously out of touch with her "feminine" side—than give way to his desire for an African woman.

Both Stuart-Young's and Henry's novels expunge the figure of the African or "mulatto" wife, writing out the woman who was normative in palm oil traders' lives in the nineteenth and early twentieth centuries. Either such women are killed off after marriage, as in Stuart-Young's work, or the white man's sexual desire for her is resisted from the outset, as in Henry's novel. However, while both of these novels contain essentialist racial and gender stereotypes, in which English imperial masculinity is set against the degeneracy of interracial relationships, they complicate the equation in important ways. Stuart-Young critiques imperial middle-class masculinity, locating in it the seeds of (white) decadence; meanwhile, Henry rejects bourgeois masculinity altogether, declaring it unfit for a career in West African trade.

∽

The memoirs and novels discussed in this chapter read like a subgenre of the more famous travel and exploration narratives of the nineteenth century, benefiting from what Timothy Burke perceptively terms the "quasi-plagiarism endemic to much colonial writing."[131] Many palm oil ruffians read the work of Mary Kingsley and Mungo Park, soaking up the exploration genre and quoting favorite descriptive passages in their own narratives. Theirs, however, is a vastly different symbolic landscape than that traversed by bourgeois British explorers, missionaries, and colonialists. Over and above anthropological description and moral commentary, traders' writings prioritize consumers and consumables in Africa: indeed, so urgent was John Whitford's desire to collect African "valuable produce" that he decided not to make a pilgrimage to the place on the Niger where his lifelong hero, Mungo Park, died in 1805. The lack of trade in the vicinity made this journey seem a waste of effort.[132]

The export of palm oil in the nineteenth and twentieth centuries brought dramatic transformations to local West African economies, tying African communities into world markets and world prices in new ways.[133] The ruffian-writing examined in this chapter is captivating for the set of perspectives it offers on these changing social, political, and commercial conditions in West Africa. White traders bear witness to the customs of Africans, the arrival and consolidation of the colonial state, and the social effects of fluctuations in world prices for West African produce. Above all, they demonstrate the centrality of gender to the construction of white men's identities in the tropics. Filled with advice from old coasters to young newcomers alongside anecdotes about African economic and domestic life, these texts contain much masculine posturing through which "poor white" traders grasp a place for themselves as rightful members of the imperial race. Alongside this manifest prejudice and posturing, however, I hope to have shown that—often in spite of itself—"ruffian-writing" also shows sensitivity toward the tastes and consumer preferences of the African communities in which individual traders worked. These pragmatic entrepreneurs participated at a more intimate level in local communities than many other classes of European residents in West Africa, and, as the remaining chapters of this book will show, as one of the region's wealthiest and most locally celebrated traders, Stuart-Young participated the most intimately and vocally of them all.

3 ∽ Fragments of Oscar Wilde in Colonial Nigeria

IN 1905, STUART-YOUNG stepped off the steam launch that had brought him up the River Niger on the last leg of his journey from Britain and, wielding an umbrella, walked into Onitsha town. In his luggage was an extensive collection of signed photographs and handwritten missives sent to him by British and French actors, music hall stars, novelists, personalities, and poets that he had assiduously acquired over the previous ten years.[1] He also carried copies of his own publications, including a novel, a recent memoir, and the notes for a further novel, as well as albums containing his articles, poems, and reviews, published in a variety of British periodicals.[2] Additionally, he carried quantities of photographic portraits of himself, which he would later sign "John Moray Stuart-Young" and hand out to African visitors and admirers. To all appearances, this new arrival was a well-connected "literary gent" of some social standing, and he certainly intended to keep it that way.

Since 1901, Stuart-Young had been stationed at Grand Bassa in Liberia and Conakry in French Guinea, working as a clerk and accountant for Miller Brothers of Manchester on an annual salary that rose from £60 to £100.[3] In the three-year period of this first sojourn, he gained a great deal of experience in the produce trade, learning about collecting African raw materials—including timber, palm oil, ivory, rubber, animal skins, and other products—and exchanging them for imported European goods. Responsible for helping maintain the flow of products in an increasingly competitive trade environment, he also learned how to "dash" goods, negotiate for produce, and give credit to African women traders and middlemen.[4] Meanwhile, in his private time, Stuart-Young avoided the traditional coaster's fare of alcohol, card games, and formal or informal liaisons with local women. After a hard day's work in remote African trading posts, while his houseboy prepared food, he wrote poems, memoirs, articles, and novels, which he delivered to publishers and newspapers in Britain and West Africa.

One name stands out in this writing from West Africa. Stuart-Young forged a friendship with the most sexually (in)famous writer of his time. Within a year of arriving in Conakry, French Guinea, he completed his first "memoir," entitled *Osrac, the Self-Sufficient and Other Poems with a Memoir of the Late Oscar Wilde*. Printed privately by Thomas Olman Todd in Sunderland and then reprinted in London by the Hermes Press, which specialized in homosexual publications, this eclectic book includes reminiscences and a lengthy poem diagnosing Oscar Wilde's "disease."[5] The first-person narrator claims to have had an intimate friendship with Wilde between 1894 and 1900 that involved regular visits to London and Paris and an exchange of letters. "Unfortunately," however, as Stuart-Young confesses, "I have retained [only] a few of his epistles."[6]

The narrator of the memoir reveals how he met Wilde regularly in London during the ten-month period before the Wilde trials commenced in April 1895. "When do you come to London my pride?" Wilde urges in his letters. "Nobody need know."[7] As evidence of their relationship, Stuart-Young offers two facsimile letters from Wilde alongside a carefully censored selection of excerpts from the other letters containing "a few sentences of special interest," which he has chosen for their "purely literary" qualities.[8] They last met in Paris after Wilde's release from prison, he claims, and in support of the Parisian connection, one of Stuart-Young's poems in *Osrac* is inscribed "Paris, 1st December 1900," clearly indicating the poet's presence in the vicinity of Wilde's deathbed, for Wilde died on 30 November 1900.

The narrator inserts a prim, sexually abstinent "I" into each and every exposure of Wilde's sexuality and claims to be present during key episodes in Wilde's life. Thus, the young man is seated at dinner with his illustrious mentor during Wilde's outburst against a scandalous book by Robert Smythe Hitchens, *The Green Carnation* (1894), which contained a series of damaging revelations against Wilde. "He forbade me to read the book at any cost," Stuart-Young comments of this scene.[9] Again, Wilde supposedly takes the boy to visit Alfred Taylor's rooms in Little College Street; this was the scene of salacious newspaper revelations concerning blackmailers and working-class boys of Stuart-Young's age.[10] Finally, he is present in Paris to see the completion of *De Profundis* and to read it in manuscript.[11] Here is a youth at the very center of literary history in the making.

Stuart-Young's truth claims in *Osrac, the Self-Sufficient* begin with a photograph of the author holding a volume of Wilde's poetry, signed "Yours sincerely

Fig. 3. Photograph of Stuart-Young taken in 1904 or 1905 (from *Osrac, the Self-Sufficient and Other Poems with a Memoir of the Late Oscar Wilde* [London: Hermes Press, 1905]). *(By permission of the Board of Trinity College Dublin.)*

J. M. Stuart-Young" (see fig. 3). The book of poetry has been etched into the photograph in such an amateurish two-dimensional fashion that its title, spine, and pages have the quality of a cartoon. Its proportions are all wrong: the book draws attention to itself, marking its difference and distance from the more realistic—but also heavily touched up—photographic image of the handsome young man with downcast eyes. The result is that from the outset

Fig. 4. Photograph of Stuart-Young taken in 1895 (from *Osrac, the Self-Sufficient and Other Poems with a Memoir of the Late Oscar Wilde* [London: Hermes Press, 1905]). (*By permission of the Board of Trinity College Dublin.*)

of *Osrac*, Wilde becomes the least real, the most forged and inscribed presence in the book. Within a page or two, there is a photograph of Wilde dedicated "To Johnnie," dated September 1894. This may well be an authentic image, sent to the author in response to one of his "boyish expressions of admiration" from Manchester that included enclosures such as the photograph featured in fig. 4.[12]

There can be little doubt about the veracity of Wilde's handwritten letters to "My own Jack," facsimiles of which appear a little farther on in the memoir. Stuart-Young seems to be barely trying to make the handwriting look like Wilde's in these documents, and he makes no effort to forge the variety of headed notepapers that Wilde used. Curiously, however, forensic evidence suggests that the writing in these letters is neither Wilde's nor Stuart-Young's, but that of a third person (see figs. 5–7).[13]

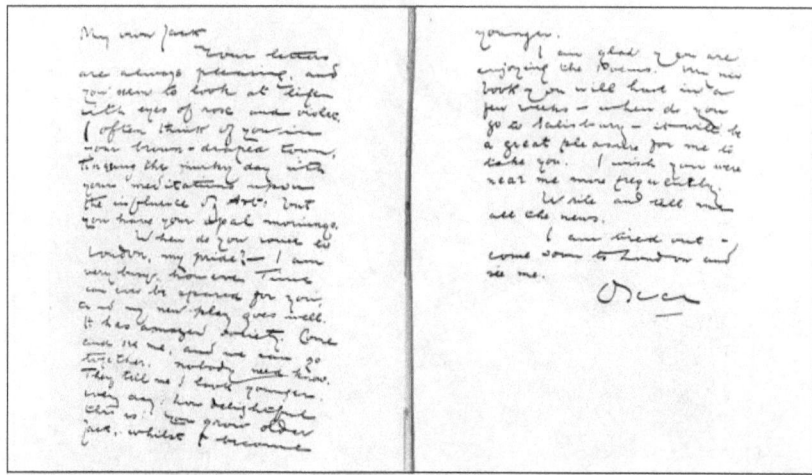

Fig. 5. (above) "My Own Jack": letter purportedly from Oscar Wilde to Stuart-Young (from *Osrac, the Self-Sufficient and Other Poems with a Memoir of the Late Oscar Wilde* [London: Hermes Press, 1905]). (*By permission of the Board of Trinity College Dublin*.); fig. 6. (below) "My Dear Jack": letter purportedly from Oscar Wilde to Stuart-Young, with Stuart-Young's caption about Wilde's habitual misquotations (from *Osrac, the Self-Sufficient and Other Poems with a Memoir of the Late Oscar Wilde* [London: Hermes Press, 1905]). (*By permission of the Board of Trinity College Dublin*.)

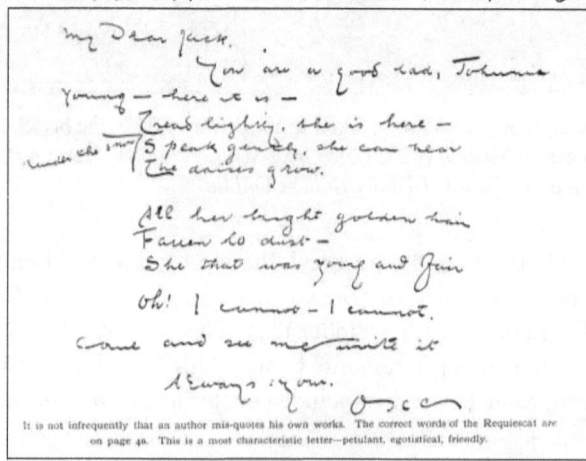

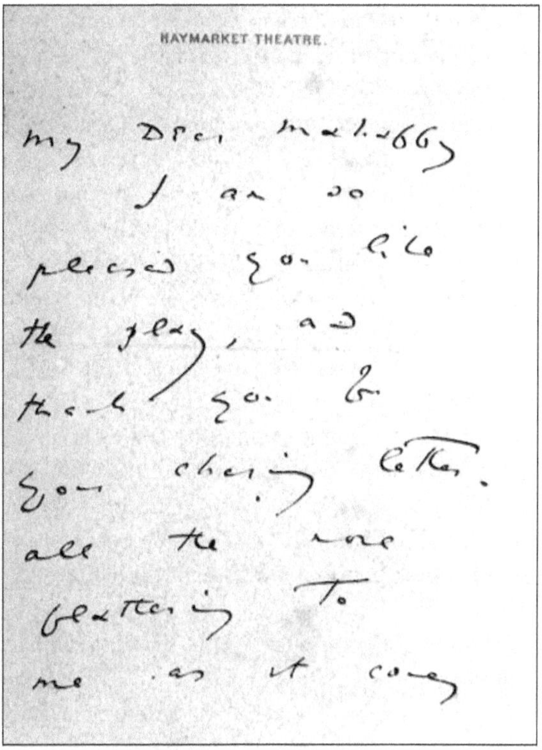

Fig. 7. "My Dear Mahaffy": authentic letter in Wilde's handwriting. *(By permission of the Board of Trinity College Dublin.)*

HAYMARKET THEATRE.

My Dear Mahaffy,

I am so pleased you like the play, and think you so kind — your charming letter, all the more flattering to me as it comes not merely from a man of high and distinguished culture, but from one to whom I owe so much personally, from my first, and my last teacher, from the scholar who showed me how to love Greek things. Believe me, myself, in affection as admiration,

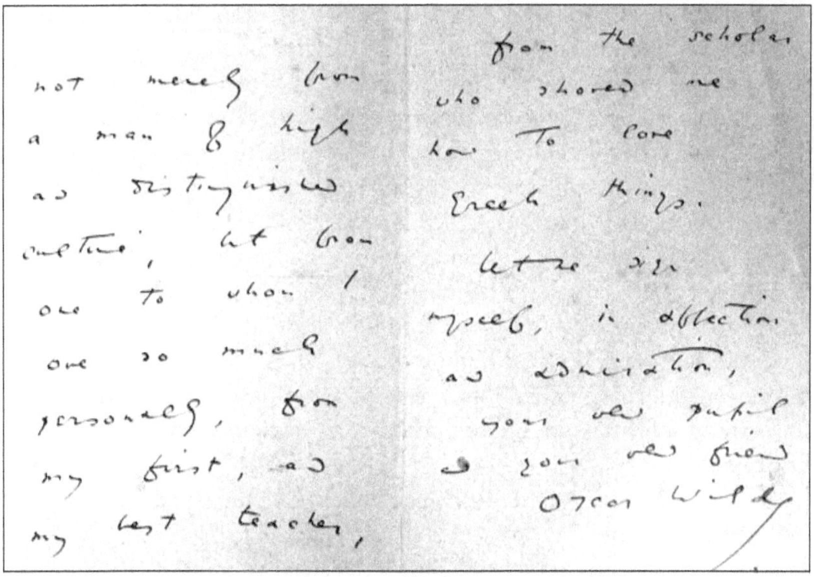

your old pupil
and your old friend
Oscar Wilde

From his writing desk in West Africa, Stuart-Young generates an entire relationship, forging a famous friend for his adolescent self, complete with photographs and counterfeit correspondence. So central does the writing body of the youth become in the memoir itself that Wilde's voice is repeatedly submerged by the fan's, even in the older man's letters: "You have quoted from one of my letters (an unpardonable offence) and say (maliciously) that no woman could receive such tender nothings without a qualm of misgiving," Wilde writes, comically committing the very "unpardonable offence" for which he reprimands the young man.[14] In this letter, Stuart-Young self-consciously mimics Wilde's witty speech style while also inserting his own voice into the moral core of the relationship. Thus, Wilde's letter revolves around the quotation of the young man, who expresses "misgivings" about the flirtatious nature of Wilde's communications. When finally allowed its own expressive space in this letter, Wilde's voice is filled with risky innuendo as he addresses the youth's concerns: "Deliciously impressible and convincing as you deem them, I can only tell you that no true poet would pluck a flower half-blown. Should it not grow to maturity first? Little flowers bleed so piteously! Poor passionate little blossoms . . . !"[15]

In spite of the narrator's claim that "I saw him frequently,"[16] it is unlikely that this particular "little blossom" ever had an actual friendship with Wilde. Stuart-Young probably received a letter and a signed photograph from Wilde in response to a fan letter, although it is unlikely that the letter is either of the two contained in *Osrac*. It is also conceivable, but unlikely, that the thirteen-year-old boy traveled to London in 1894 to meet Wilde for dinner at the Savoy, as he claims in the memoir. "I had the privilege of listening to his conversation over dinner," he recalls.[17] His description of this meeting conveys the impression that if Stuart-Young was present at the Savoy, he sat quietly, wide-eyed, at the far end of a table while his mentor held forth to a large group of admirers.

These threads of truth are twisted and spun into the narrative that is the "Memoir of Oscar Wilde." Just as Wilde had a fascination for forgeries, which he explored in the story of a homosexual relationship between Shakespeare and Willie Hughes in "A Portrait of Mr. WH" (1889), so too Stuart-Young attends to the minutiae of his own relationship with Wilde. *Osrac* is a thoroughly "self-sufficient" text. With the transposition of "Oscar" to "Osrac," real historical personalities are inserted into a new story. In this way, the author creates an alternative life story for himself, summed up affectionately as "the years of our friendship."[18]

Stuart-Young's account did convince at least one respected biographer of Wilde, although the Oscar presented in *Osrac* is seen to be behaving in an extremely uncharacteristic manner. Hesketh Pearson comments of Wilde, "So innocent or obtuse was he that it never occurred to him that he was doing anything out of the ordinary when he invited a schoolboy admirer of his own class named Stuart Young, aged 15 [sic], to dine with him and one of Alfred Taylor's young men at the Savoy."[19] Persuaded by the grammar and vocabulary of *Osrac* that its author is a well-educated middle-class youth, who stood in contrast to Taylor's working-class boys, Pearson interprets the relationship Stuart-Young described as a unique instance of indiscretion on the part of Wilde. "So far, so bad," he comments in response to Stuart-Young's revelations. "But worse was to follow, for when next they met Wilde took the lad with him to Taylor's rooms, solely for the purpose—of this there is no shadow of doubt—of letting him enjoy an hour or two's talk on art and literature in congenial surroundings."[20] For the folly of introducing the wrong caliber of boy to Alfred Taylor's rooms in Little College Street, Pearson concludes, Wilde "must be regarded as . . . one whose innocence approaches imbecility."[21] His endorsement of *Osrac* is therefore shot through with doubts about Wilde's "imbecilic" behavior.

Evidence against Stuart-Young's experiences with Wilde outweighs Pearson's careful accommodation of the story. Letters survive that indicate that there was no ongoing connection between the two men. For example, despite Stuart-Young's statement in *Osrac* that "I have several times seen the young Lord, whose egregious folly hastened the death of my friend,"[22] a furious letter from Lord Alfred Douglas puts a halt to such truth claims. Supremely self-confident, Stuart-Young wrote to Douglas on two occasions and alerted him to the existence of the third edition of *Osrac*, in which a photograph of "Bosie" had been added to the existing illustrations and facsimile letters. On July 29th 1907, the irate Lord responded from Lincoln's Inn Fields:

> Sir,
> Please understand that I object most strongly to the impertinence which you have shown in writing to me a second time. I do not know you and have no desire to know you. As for the disgusting publication to which you refer, I have not seen it and had I known at the time that you had ventured to publish one of my photographs in it, I should have put the matter in the hands of the police.[23]

Lord Alfred found Stuart-Young's book offensive and tasteless and denied ever having met the "impertinent" youth. It is interesting to note that—perhaps under threat of prosecution—the photograph of Bosie and the facsimile letters were withdrawn from subsequent editions of the book and the "memoir" preceding the poem "Osrac, the Self-Sufficient" was also withdrawn from the final edition.

Other documents survive that testify to Stuart-Young's exclusion from Wilde's social circle. In a letter to Wilde's trusted ally Robert Ross, written from Manchester and dated 30 September 1905, Stuart-Young requests a photograph of "Oscar's dearest friend." He probably means Ross himself, although it is possible that his request is for the very photograph that infuriated Bosie.[24]

> My Dear Mr Ross,
> You do not know me, and I feel myself something like an interloper—but the sincere friendship which Oscar extended to me was not diminished by the fact that I am "of the ranks"—one of the "workers" of this great Empire of ours. I thrill to the centre of my being, at the memory of the glorious days of my early teens, developing under his guiding hand. . . . [I] would like the photograph of Oscar's dearest friend to add to my collection of souvenirs.

While insisting on "the sincere friendship which Oscar extended to me," this letter reveals no intimacy with Wilde or any connection with Douglas, and clearly there is no previous acquaintance with Ross. This situation would be strange for such a close friend of Wilde's.

Stuart-Young's many hostile critics saw *Osrac, the Self-Sufficient* as the reckless bid of a literary nobody to promote his own name and to try, through forgery, to insert himself in the life story of a famous man. One critic, Rupert Croft-Cooke, railed against the "effrontery and imposture" of this upstart. "Who was this Stuart-Young," he asked aggressively, "and what induced him to publish a memoir imagining himself to have been a friend of Wilde's, addressed by him as 'Johnny'?"[25] The answer, for Croft-Cooke, "takes us into a madhouse of fraud and sheer silliness, books of agonizing verse printed to exhibit photographs of the author . . . excessively bad autobiographical novels . . . and snapshots of an insane-looking strabismic Stuart-Young sitting with a ten-year-old African in a knickerbocker suit known as 'Ibrahim the Unkissed.'"[26]

Many questions are suppressed, however, by Croft-Cook's appraisal of Stuart-Young. Why, for instance, did the young man insert himself as a full-blown "I" into the center of the life of such a scandalous personality as Oscar Wilde? Why should somebody deliberately step into the orbit of a man marked out by the media as a danger to society and have documents forged in order to reinforce that connection? Did Stuart-Young's location in West Africa somehow facilitate this "relationship" with Wilde?

What *Osrac, the Self-Sufficient* reveals in great detail is the manner in which one adolescent reader processed the newspaper reports and public debates generated by the Wilde trials of 1895. It also shows, in Regina Gagnier's words, "the extent to which Wilde's fiction affected the lives of real boys for a half-century."[27] Composed five years after Wilde's death and ten years after his sensational trials, *Osrac* shows one young reader's struggle to rehabilitate and understand Wilde's sexuality from the geographical and cultural distance of the tropics. His responses are then plotted onto Wilde's life in the form of a memoir. What stands out above all else in Stuart-Young's text is the account of this young man's private reading experience as he absorbed Wilde's published material. "I had for many months felt strangely impressed by his work," he reports in the opening pages, "and certain of his poems haunted me."[28] The effect of Wilde's writing on the young reader is dynamic and "strange," "haunting" him, reaching up from the page to "impress" its presence upon him without naming itself. Through the medium of the printed text, Wilde is manifested to the boy in the form of an emotional specter who flickers in and out of view like a forbidden desire. The poet's "wild fancies had filled my years of adolescence with dreams," he writes.[29] Fulfilling the criteria of the modern queer teenager described by Eve Kosofsky Sedgwick in *Tendencies* (1994), Stuart-Young latches onto Wilde because of his "mysterious, excessive, or oblique" connection with dominant social and sexual codes.[30] Stuart-Young becomes the archetypal queer reader, surviving his own sexual difference from the norm through his adoption of, and overidentification with, Wilde's texts as cultural objects.[31]

Stuart-Young's momentous private reading experience would have coincided with the public transformation of Wilde in the press from hero to beast, from a master of epigram to a man who sparkled wittily but "indecently" in court. What is crucial for Stuart-Young is that the Wilde trials occurred during the period of the young man's entry into adolescence and awareness of his sexuality. As the sexologist Havelock Ellis commented at the turn of the twentieth century, in a diagnosis that is loaded with the negative language of perversion but full of cultural awareness, "the celebrity of Oscar Wilde and the universal publicity given to the facts of the case by the newspapers may have brought the conviction of their perversion to many inverts who were before only vaguely conscious of their abnormality."[32] To put the same point more sympathetically, as Joseph Bristow does, Wilde "became the most influential figure of a specific homosexual style that would prove to be the most significant point of definition for practically every man-loving male writer whose work went into print after his death."[33]

With or without its amorous plot, *Osrac* therefore contains a powerful memoir, not of Oscar Wilde but of Stuart-Young as he reflected from West Africa on the relatively recent public exposure of Wilde. "In murky Manchester," the narrator confesses, momentarily adopting the position of an "ordinary" reader who keeps abreast of the story in the newspapers, "I had followed the case with intense interest, vaguely frightened, vaguely ashamed.... The days that followed were days of anguish to me."[34] Such comments reveal the necessity of the forged documents, for the counterfeits provide a way for Stuart-Young to externalize his own sense of "abnormality." He needs the story of actual physical meetings with Wilde in order to carry the weight of the very real but unnameable and "vague" feelings of sexual shame he experienced in "murky Manchester" during the public humiliation of his favorite author.

The memoir carefully negotiates between these competing strands of desire, shame, and anguish. In the first place, Stuart-Young emphasizes his proximity to the desiring homosexual body of Wilde while insisting repeatedly on his own untouched, physically intact status in the relationship: "Our conversation was always free, but never by any chance tinged with obscenity," he repeats, even though Wilde "had shown unmistakeable signs of armour [sic] in my company."[35] In this representation, Wilde occupies the status of aesthetics teacher, discussing "art and literature" with the youth and conveying his queer poetics without interfering with the young man's body. A second, related strand of sexuality involves an insistence on the nonactive nature of Stuart-Young's own desire, which is contrasted with Wilde's unrestrained sexuality. In *Osrac*, Stuart-Young presents himself as "homo-celibate" rather than as homosexual. Desiring without pursuing, he expresses impulses in writing that he feels incapable of acting upon. From this standpoint, he suggests that Wilde attempted, persistently but unsuccessfully, to seduce him each time they met and that the great man's failure was due to the boy's moral restraint over his own erotic urges. "If only I had a boy of your calibre near me oftener," confesses Wilde, "I might be a better man."[36] A third strand of sexual discourse in the memoir, explored in more detail below, asserts the "diseased," "morbid," and "morally debauched" nature of Wilde's desires and offers a diagnosis that the man's "aberration" and "neurosis" were caused by unrestrained masturbation in childhood.[37] A fourth and final strand involves a defense of Wilde against the newspaper images of him as a predatory and lustful pederast. With himself at the center of a potentially homosexual scenario, Stuart-Young insists, "Had he been as bad as the public have been led to conceive him, that night would have been the initial step towards my destruction, for I offered no protest to his influence."[38] Wilde's decency and moral integrity are here asserted, and the safety of the young male body is guaranteed.

Juggling sexual desire with popular taboos in this way, Stuart-Young simultaneously reinforces and denies Wilde's homosexual agency and his own. His defense of Wilde's sexual inclinations turns into a defensive denial of his own homosexuality. Multiple modes of male bonding are combined in the narrative, and caught up in this lattice are the two central bodies of Wilde and the boy, which Stuart-Young defends against the singular dominant image of homosexuality that took hold of the British popular imagination after 1895.[39]

It is from texts freely circulating in the public sphere rather than from any personal missives that Stuart-Young draws his descriptions of Wilde. Ironically, this close comrade of Oscar's seems to have gleaned most of his material for *Osrac* from the same sources as the general public. The British newspapers are omnipresent in the memoir, setting the vocabulary and framework for the account of Wilde. Where readers of *Osrac* have been primed to expect details of intimate discussions of art and literature, in fact one finds Wilde's most famous statements from the witness box, strung together in loose epigrammatic chains. "There can be neither morality nor immorality in Art," the narrator quotes. "Either a thing is done well or it is done ill. A man can never be judged by an accepted code of ethics. Each soul has its own laws."[40] Fragmentary quotations such as these indicate that Stuart-Young carried back issues, or perhaps scrapbooks, of newspaper reports to West Africa, where he composed *Osrac*. Wilde's speeches in the memoir are all traceable to his public utterances through published accounts.

Wilde's famous aphorisms also circulate in *Osrac*, and it is revealing that despite his self-confidence in the art of generating forged letters, Stuart-Young rarely attempts to imitate the voice of the "inimitable" Wilde. Rather, what he presents are descriptions of Wilde's style: without filling in the image with specific quotations, he prefers to evoke the "sparkling stream of epigram and satirical wit to which I was privileged to listen."[41] Wilde's "conversation was brilliant and epigrammatic in the extreme," he remembers again, recalling how the great man poured forth "a torrent of paradox."[42] Empty of content, however, the actual figure of Wilde remains rather spectral. "A few of his bonmots" are provided at the end, as Stuart-Young recounts his visit to Paris in 1900, shortly before Wilde's death, and fills out his hero with some clever verbal barbs against Émile Zola, Arthur Symons, George Moore, and others.[43] However, this short scene ends with the unlikely phrase from Wilde, "Goodbye Jackie. Luck to you."[44] With the stereotypically Irish phrase "luck to you," the poet bids farewell to his protégé.

Alongside Stuart-Young, a national mass readership followed the Wilde trials in detail, and the trials marked a turning point in the history of the British popular press. Images of Wilde were made available to readers throughout the British Isles, reaching regions far beyond the city in which the so-called crimes took place.[45] These newspaper representations of Wilde overshadow Stuart-Young's writing like a warning against ever "coming out" in late-Victorian or Edwardian society.

A full year after the publication of *Osrac*, Stuart-Young remained preoccupied with the effects of the newspaper coverage of the trials and conviction. He seems perfectly aware of the way this media involvement "altered the shape of the Victorian sexual imagination."[46] For example, a short scene in his early novel, *Passion's Peril* (1906), shows a group of working-class men standing in a circle around a shared newspaper on a London street, where they follow recent developments in the trial of Wilde. The heroine of *Passion's Peril*, Lily, observes how "they scanned the column of matter which referred to the fallen giant of epigram, and only contempt, derision and laughter, foul jests and filthy innuendoes reached her ears."[47] Londoners on Lily's omnibus also discuss the case, echoing the sentiments of the popular press: "Served 'im right. 'E's a bad lot any 'ow," they say, "Them young toffs wouldn't be so careless about their good name if they had no money."[48] Here, perhaps, is a further reason to explain why Stuart-Young decided to leave England for Africa: if a well-connected "toff" could not escape condemnation by the rough-spoken newspaper-reading masses in Great Britain, what hope was there for a young working-class "nobody" whose natural place should be *within* the circle of newspaper-reading men?

Given the "contempt" and "derision" presented in this scene, it is not acceptable simply to regard Stuart-Young with contempt and derision as a self-promoting literary pest who set out to exploit Wilde's conviction and death. His writings on Wilde are saturated with social commentary on the power of the press to form public opinion at the turn of the twentieth century and on the ways in which sexual identities are formed through writing and reading. Croft-Cooke is particularly keen to deride the charlatans, fantasists, and eccentrics "who have chosen Oscar Wilde as their theme."[49] A more flexible framework is required, however, in order to understand the cultural and psychological forces that were at play in these fantastic imaginings of Wilde.

According to Stuart-Young, the great writer's personality boils down to a secret "aberration which brought his splendid life to ruins, which had ruled him since childhood," and is "known only to the favoured few."[50] Speaking as one of the "favoured few," he only hints at the nature of Wilde's aberration in the introductory memoir, but under the veil of poetic language in the long poem that follows the memoir, he explains the nature of Wilde's "disease."[51] For present-day readers, it is astonishing to discover the source of Wilde's downfall. Masked with euphemism, simile, and guilty confession, the poem "Osrac, the Self-Sufficient" reveals that Wilde indulged in unchecked masturbation as a child:

> Young Osrac, bending o'er a clear cool spring,
> Saw mirror'd in't himself, and had no room
> For other love.[52]

Masturbation is *the* prohibited category; it is a singular and well-known force, in contrast to the plurality of names for same-sex love that were circulating at the end of the nineteenth century. Wilde was "self-sufficient," and this was the cause of his "ruin:" "He reverenced to the god of self."[53] "Self drew him ever. Ah! The precious vice / Upon each sense in fascination grew. . . . His sweet abasing sin / Brought hourly on irrevocable doom."[54] Stuart-Young evokes the figure of the masturbator in its long-established position as "the archetypal image of the sex deviant," and above all else this ancient "vice" is seen to be the cause of Wilde's criminal conviction and imprisonment.[55] Masturbation is man's constant desire, or itch, and Wilde's downfall derives from his lack of the self-restraint required not to masturbate.

Queer theorists have suggested that in the years following the Wilde trials, the love that dare not speak its name did not, in fact, have a singular name.[56] "Confusion rather than covetousness" surrounded homosexuality at this time.[57] The binary homo/hetero model of sexuality is a construction that surfaced in the last quarter of the nineteenth century, but it did not dominate everyday "world maps" for several decades afterward.[58] Homosexuality emerged as one ingredient in the "rich stew" of sexualities and new identities in fin-de-siècle Britain, existing alongside a host of other labels for sexual behavior. This stew, Sedgwick writes, "has today all but boiled down to a single, bare . . . dichotomy."[59] Wilde was the axis around which many of these complex plural discourses revolved.[60] A long list of popular and scientific labels settled upon the body of this man. Near-obsolete categories from the nineteenth century, including the figure of the masturbating man, were updated and applied to Wilde; these jostled with more resilient Victorian ideas about disease and effeminacy. Emergent debates about homosexuality, adolescent sexuality, and the effects of reading on public morals also circulated around Wilde. Clearly, the world before the category "homosexual" rose to dominance was fluid, composed of multifarious designators of sexuality.

Firmly located in the sphere of everyday understandings of masturbation, *Osrac, the Self-Sufficient* is fascinating for its effort to interpret Wilde's sexuality using Victorian codes and values. The memoir also reveals Stuart-Young's obsession with masturbation and the many popular remedies for such sexual aberrations. The book helps present-day readers comprehend hundred-year-old conceptions of sexual "deviance," many of which have faded from current use or lost their relevance and emotive power. Eighteenth- and nineteenth-century prohibitions of masturbation are set on the move by Stuart-Young, put through a transition into the sphere of same-sex desire. He relocates the centuries-old rhetoric of anti-masturbation literature in the new sphere of homosexuality. For both types of behavior, popular ideas about "vice," "morbidity," "abasement," "sin," and "self-sufficiency" are set against the supposed cure, "restraint." An intense self-loathing and self-oppression is displayed in the process. The stigma and guilt of one prohibited form of desire—that is, masturbation—become mobile, crystallizing around the other desire, homosexuality.

Working within these popular conceptions of masturbation, Stuart-Young recalls, "There was something aroused within me, by the rhymes of Oscar Wilde, which savoured more of astheny than robustness."[61] The asthenic personality—characterized by hypersensitivity, low energy, and a lack of enthusiasm—was widely believed to be one of the side effects of masturbation, found alongside many other telltale signs such as pimples, irritability, consumption, and myopia.[62] As a physical type, the asthenic man would be tall and lean, with narrow shoulders and long limbs. Known for his own self-absorption and "touchiness" and for being thin, consumptive, short-sighted, and slightly cross-eyed, Stuart-Young must have appeared to himself as the prototypical masturbator and degenerate man, constantly fearing a loss of self-control.

Stuart-Young's account of Wilde is infused with the language of Victorian "purity campaigns," especially the condemnation of lust. Evangelical and bourgeois campaigners often appealed for restraint in respectable men. For example, in her pamphlet *The Hour before Dawn: An Appeal to Men*, the famous purity campaigner Josephine Butler insisted on "the sacredness of the home, and the duty of men to live and to suffer women to live in purity."[63] Replete with the language of lust and sin, this pamphlet suggests that middle-class men were "selling their strength, and health, and rank, and manhood, to Satan" when they lacked restraint and bowed before "the shrine of lechery."[64]

Stuart-Young explains the causes of Wilde's homosexuality in a way that would have been recognizable and persuasive to readers brought up on a diet of this type of moral literature. Like any uncontrolled child, Wilde is seen to have indulged in masturbation in his youth, and like any profligate husband, he lacks sexual self-control in adulthood. The surprising feature of Stuart-Young's negative diagnosis of Wilde is that he does not condemn same-sex desire itself as deviant or degenerate. Wilde's downfall relates to a combination of unchecked masturbation and lust. At the root of active adult homosexuality, then, lies a powerful passion that is neither wholly hetero-, nor homo-, nor auto-sexual. It does not discriminate between childhood and adulthood, it can possess a person wholly, and it can become abject if it remains unchecked. In its essence, therefore, the passion that caused Wilde's downfall is presented as universal, shared alike by "respectable" bourgeois patriarchs and their children and by boy-loving men in the homosexual subculture.

By the time *Osrac, the Self-Sufficient* was published in 1905, sexologists and homosexual writers had published many different accounts of human sexuality. Some of the most influential theories are absorbed into Stuart-Young's work, especially the category of "Urning" and its subdivisions, developed by Karl Ulrichs in 1869 and Richard von Krafft-Ebing in the 1880s from medical research into the congenital nature of sexual "inversion." According to these theorists, the Urning was a person whose sexual desire stemmed from having the soul of one sex locked since birth inside the body of the other.[65] While the Urning was anything but "normal" in this view, homosexuality was regarded as congenital and therefore to some extent "natural" and not the consequence of social factors such as deviant behavior or Christian sinfulness.

Many writers adopted the label of Urning, keen to find terms adequate to describe their hidden feelings. Seeking a place within the web of sexual science, John Addington Symonds, the man of letters, labeled himself a "Mittel Urning," sliding away from Ulrichs' rigid categories even as he tried to work within them.[66] Symonds does not reject homosexuality; instead, he redefines it as natural and untouched by sexual perversion. Stuart-Young also utilized Ulrichs' categories of sexual deviance in his later work.[67] In the cases of both Symonds and Stuart-Young, "deviancy returns from abjection by deploying just those terms which relegated it in the first place."[68]

Alan Sinfield and Joseph Bristow show that the Wilde trials had a lasting and definitive impact on the history of homosexuality, reverberating into the present day, causing numerous men to repudiate the qualities that came to be associated with Wilde.[69] Thus, the dominant twentieth-century queer identity was constructed in opposition to "elements that came together at the Wilde trials: effeminacy, leisure, idleness, immorality, luxury, insouciance, decadence and aestheticism."[70] Responding with disgust to the image of the effeminate aesthete, homosexual men came to adopt the hypermasculine ideals promoted by imperialist and bourgeois ideologies.[71] Thus, the "manly man" was appropriated as an object of legitimate homosexual desire. Edward Carpenter's ideal man was the opposite of effeminate.[72] John Addington Symonds also insisted on his preference for the athlete, stating plainly that "I am not effeminate."[73] Likewise, Stuart-Young, with his "morbid" and "sensitive" personality, emigrated to a part of the British empire where it was thought that a man needed the most muscular, robustly masculine physique to survive as a trader or an imperialist.

For his British critics, the quality that Stuart-Young lacked above all was integrity. "Some strange compound of compassion and respect for what remained in him of integrity" motivated Sylvia Leith-Ross to mention Stuart-Young in her memoir of 1930s Nigeria. What she describes, however, is a physically and economically broken man, a delusionist who is desperate for her to believe his "fanciful" stories about his intimate friendships with Britain's literary personalities.[74] Using similar terms as Leith-Ross, Timothy d'Arch Smith comments: "Taking his self-identification past the point of both conscious copying of literary style and his own integrity, [Stuart-Young] evolved a fictitious relationship with Wilde which he retailed."[75] In both of these instances, the word "integrity" implies moral probity and qualities of truthfulness that cannot be attributed to Stuart-Young.

Of equal significance, however, the word "integrity" also describes the wholeness of the individual, referring to a person's cohesion and unity as a subject with a proper name. It is here that Stuart-Young comes closest to fitting contemporary definitions of a queer writer. Just as the spirit-medium's bodily integrity must be put to one side before otherworldly visitors can enter and communicate, so queer writing often depends upon the openness of texts and readers to multiple, fractured voices. "It is relatively unimportant to decide how far a text presents positive images of lesbians and gay men," Alan Sinfield writes, for "textual potentiality is far more fluid than that."[76] As we saw in the introduction, "queerness" signifies a mobile identity, one that lacks wholeness or subjective integrity. In the words of Eve Kosofsky Sedgwick, "'queer' can refer to the open mesh of possibilities, gaps, overlaps, dissonances and resonances, lapses and excesses of meaning when the constituent elements of anyone's gender, of anyone's sexuality, aren't made (or can't be made) to signify monolithically."[77] Such terminology is not simply the rhetoric of a poststructuralist theorist with a loathing for ideas of origins and binaries. Sedgwick does not lose touch with issues of constraint and violence, and her work has vital relevance to the historical period in which Stuart-Young lived. Given the very real threats posed to a homosexual man's body by the state and society in Edwardian Britain, and given the plethora of different names for "deviant" sexualities, the writings of men like Stuart-Young are unlikely to "signify monolithically."[78] While his writing does make use of the constituents of identity—particularly class, race, and sexuality, as we shall see—his work steals through these existing categories of identity and difference, quietly interrogating labels and values.

Osrac seems to exemplify the queer text defined by Sedgwick. Despite its generic status as a memoir, the book is indecisive in the naming of its central players. Throughout the text, the author splits and multiplies people's names and slides between several identities. Thus, in the letters Stuart-Young produces from Wilde, he is addressed as both "Johnnie" and "Jack." Similarly, the name of Oscar Wilde is lightly transposed into "Osrac," and fake signatures and books are inserted into the photographic images in the text. The sole "real" name in *Osrac* seems to be that of the author, printed on the front cover. Upon closer examination, however, this name itself is a mask, constructed to cover the identity of John Jones of Back Kay Street, Ardwick.

These slippery, unstable names allow Stuart-Young simultaneously to hide and seek his sexuality in writing. The narrator of *Osrac* splits his main characters, and in so doing he evades the social consequences of coming out. In shifting between "Oscar" and "Osrac" and between "Johnnie" and "Jack," he opens up a multitude of potential relationships for Wilde and himself. A revealing parallel to this splitting of names can be found in the memoirs of John Addington Symonds, written in the late 1880s. Lacking a mirror to reflect his sexuality in the outside world and hounded by feelings of uncleanliness and self-loathing, Symonds felt the presence of "two selves" for most of his youth in mid-century England.[79] Oscillating between these two selves, he yearned for the stability that would result from others' recognition of him. In consequence, he writes, "I thirsted with intolerable thirst for eminence, for recognition as a personality."[80] Symonds yearns to transcend the disruption that characterized his queer subjectivity. A publicly recognized personality represents the opposite of queer multiplicity, for the personality possesses integrity, unity, and a stable name, albeit externally conferred.

Osrac, the Self-Sufficient contains a remarkably similar "thirst for eminence"; Stuart-Young writes himself into the life story of a famous personality. The difference between these two men, however, is that Symonds does not mask his desire beneath multiple names or write it out in the hand of another. His memoir strips away the masks and recognizes a singular "congenital inclination" located beneath a "composite" identity, "made up, heaven knows how, out of the compromises we have effected between our impulses and instincts and the social laws which gird us round."[81] In a manner that tends to be sidelined by queer theorists in their more celebratory accounts of fracture and multiplicity, Symonds charts the traumatic effects of the masks he wore in the 1860s and 1870s. The deceit and lies required to sustain a secret life—even the most celibate of male friendships—brings him to a point of physical and mental breakdown. In *Osrac*, by contrast, Stuart-Young seems to depend on and affirm his several masks, which allow him to court danger and evade the terrifyingly singular identity conferred on Wilde by his conviction. In both cases, however, writing plays a crucial role in expressing the hidden sexuality: "I did not keep my thoughts from running on this subject," Symonds recalls.

"I could not refrain from poeticizing the passion in a hundred forms. [Little could I . . .] distract my thoughts from unwholesome poetry-making."[82] Stuart-Young is similarly scribacious—he is a "scribophile"—obsessively writing out his passion in an effort to avoid taking sexual action and risking homophobic censure in the world.

With the failure of *Osrac* to create an impression in literary society, in 1905 Stuart-Young decided to settle permanently in Onitsha. By all accounts, he lived on the outskirts of the white community there, never able to feel completely at ease among his "own kind" or able to fit comfortably into the roles available to Europeans in the colonies.[83] Indeed, he greatly irritated the white community with his reticence toward their company. "The few Europeans then in the station would willingly have received him," the anthropologist Sylvia Leith-Ross commented of her time in Onitsha in the mid-1930s, adding caustically, "but he was touchy and difficult and preferred the society of rather shady African lawyers among whom he could feel superior."[84]

Members of the white community were ambivalent about Stuart-Young, who rapidly gained a reputation as a troublemaker with the colonial administration and a supporter of African nationalists.[85] Beyond politics, however, something else about his image seemed to disturb them. In the mid-1930s, Leith-Ross watched him "crossing the main road, head thrown back, with that peculiar walk never seen nowadays and which the Romantics called nonchalant."[86] Wearing a pale silk shirt and white linen trousers, he "carried a red 'harmattan' lily in his hand."[87] Leith-Ross's references to Stuart-Young's outmoded "peculiar walk" and "nonchalance," to his clothing and especially the flower, all evoke a distinctive homosexual stereotype recognizable to those in the know. Walking like a dandy, carrying the icon of effeminacy, a lily, Stuart-Young seems to be posing as West Africa's version of Oscar Wilde, paying bodily homage to Oscar, his "Osrac." Thus, while Leith-Ross never directly names Stuart-Young's sexuality, her use of effeminate images speaks volumes. Far from his Manchester neighborhood, this effeminate body emits loud signals of a particular type of sexuality that contests and undermines the whole host of patriarchal nineteenth-century bourgeois ideas that made up the concept of imperial Englishness.[88]

The critical rejection of *Osrac, the Self-Sufficient* may have precipitated Stuart-Young's decision to emigrate permanently to Onitsha. An alternative perspective is that West Africa made possible the written expression of Stuart-Young's homosexual identity, for the popular opinion of him in West Africa gave him the license to roam—in his imagination at least—through a range of different sexualities before settling on the lifestyle that suited him best.

4 ⌒ "Uranian" Love in West Africa

THE SMALL, DUSTY TOWN of Onitsha suited Stuart-Young, for by 1905 he had decided to remain there permanently as an independent trader, backed by a loan from the Liverpool merchant Walter Taylor.[1] As one African journalist wittily put it, unlike the colonial types who arrived in the region as administrators and civil servants, Stuart-Young "came; he saw; he settled down."[2]

In addition to the excellent trading conditions for Europeans at the turn of the century, Stuart-Young's decision to remain in Onitsha was prompted by the critical reception accorded to *Osrac, the Self-Sufficient*. The story of Wilde's passionate desire for the author brought hoots of derision from reviewers in London and helped the young man resolve that Onitsha was the best location for his future creative activities, at a far remove from metropolitan critics.

In West Africa, Stuart-Young spent a great deal of time producing an idealized written record of himself for the African newspaper-reading public, dreaming truths about himself for local consumption. Apart from his "memoir of Oscar Wilde," which was produced in Britain, all of his subsequent memoirs were published as short articles or serials in the newspapers edited by his elite African friends and acquaintances. He was held in great esteem by the Pan-Africanist businessman and editor of the *Comet*, Duse Mohamed Ali, as well as by the famous anticolonial nationalist and editor of the *West African Pilot*, Nnamdi Azikiwe, and by the Clinton family of Calabar, owners and editors of the *Eastern Nigerian Mail*. His pithy sayings and sentimental poems appeared in these men's newspapers alongside sayings from William Shakespeare, the pope, and the archbishop of Canterbury.[3]

Stuart-Young's local literary output increased considerably after 1931, when the economic catastrophe of the Great Depression meant that he could no longer afford to steer his manuscripts through private, specialist publishing houses in Britain. Nigerian newspapers—particularly eastern publications such as the *African Advertiser* and the *Nigerian Eastern Mail*—provided many inches of column space to "Odeziaku" in subsequent years, perhaps in a political demonstration to the colonial regime that not all Englishmen were writing against the ideologies of educated Africans.

In his autobiographical writings for the African press, Stuart-Young inscribed himself into a star-studded English society. "A meeting or two at the [Society of] Authors" with figures such as George Bernard Shaw were sufficient to produce lifelong friendships with our minor poet.[4] The catalogue of famous personalities whom he claims to have befriended crosses several generations and includes Oscar Wilde, "Cousin Ruddy" Kipling, Edward Elgar, Havelock Ellis, W. T. Stead, Frank Harris, and Rupert Brooke, among many other luminaries from a variety of genres.

Stuart-Young's autobiographical writings contain another discourse enfolded within the gentlemanly genre of the memoir, helping to explain his decision to remain in Africa, away from the prejudice of those who could easily decipher his codes. Many of the names cited in his memoirs are synonymous with what Lord Alfred Douglas famously described as "the love that dare not speak its name." Between 1880 and 1920, a number of homosexual writers such as John Gambril Nicholson and Charles Kains Jackson adopted the term "Uranian" to refer to this "nameless" type of love. "Uranian" describes the type of art in which an older man celebrates the youthful male body of classical Greek sculpture and expresses, in his writing, an erotic preference for adolescents and boys, particularly of the lower social orders.[5] A surprisingly cohesive Uranian alliance emerged in these decades. Poets were particularly prominent among them, drawing on the Decadent Movement and Walter Pater's aesthetics to make space for an "efflorescence of pederasty" in their writings.[6]

Stuart-Young's lists of famous friends contain disproportionately large numbers of Uranian men, some of whose names would have been known to African readers as sources of sexual scandal and court cases, particularly Casement and Wilde. Many others, however, such as Edward Carpenter, John Addington Symonds, and John Gambril Nicholson, had "come out" less publicly in their writings and would have been less familiar to Nigerian readers. Stuart-Young could thus mask the signs of his own forbidden sexuality behind the bourgeois respectability of the memoir, a genre that licenses the naming of others and explorations of their lives. In the words of Paul John Eakin, "In the memoir, as traditionally defined ... the story of the self, the 'I,' is subordinated to the story of some other for whom the self serves as privileged witness."[7] The "others" to whom Stuart-Young bears privileged witness include many boy-loving writers whose shared sexual aesthetic as Uranians contribute to the carefully masked story of the self that emerged from Stuart-Young's pen.

In one account of his early days as a trader, "West African Nights: The Bits I Remember," which was serialized in the Nigerian *Comet* in 1934 and 1935, Stuart-Young states that he marked his departure for West Africa in 1901 in the manner of a gentleman, with a grand tour of Europe and North Africa, following an itinerary arranged for him by the travel agent Thomas Cook.[8] In the tour, which was indeed grand, Stuart-Young visited eleven countries. To readers familiar with the established literary codes for Uranian sexuality, it soon becomes clear that the author is charting a distinctive homosexual route on this tour, which includes Paris, Algiers, Venice, and Budapest. "I have sat in blazing sunshine at Algiers," he writes, "while cupids in bronze, dressed in nondescript garments of yellowing gauze, have shamelessly offered themselves *pour l'amour au rebours*."[9] "I dream often of Venice," he continues, "while the starry eyes of youthful Italians . . . haunt me in my lonely tropical hours."[10] This tourist map is heavily inscribed with the adventures of other boy-loving writers, including Oscar Wilde, André Gide, John Addington Symonds, and Edward Carpenter.[11] Stuart-Young's memoirs thus mask other, less genteel possibilities for travel in the colonial period. In a textual movement that simultaneously stays in and comes out, he chooses the public genre of the memoir to exhibit this socially taboo sexuality.[12]

Whether or not these memoirs are fabricated, the false memories of a fake gentleman, it is clear that prior to his arrival in West Africa, Stuart-Young's recent past involved experiences of—or, at the very least, an artistic preoccupation with—sexual relationships between men and youths. His journey to Onitsha in 1905 and his decision to stay permanently in the town therefore raise important questions about the sexual opportunities available to British traders in the period of imperial expansion in West Africa. In leaving Britain, did Stuart-Young find a sexual identity for himself that would have been forbidden in the wake of the Wilde trials in Britain?[13] Did West Africa help to free Stuart-Young from the repressive attitudes toward homosexuality in post-Victorian England or did he enter into "sexual hiding" while living on the West Coast of Africa, masking his forbidden desires behind his self-reconstructions as a bourgeois literary gentleman?

Several commentators have examined the ways in which the extensive empire allowed European men to experiment sexually with forms of desire that were irregular or prohibited at home.[14] T. E. Lawrence, André Gide, and E. M.

Forster are perhaps the most famous examples of this sexual liberation from taboos, and, if one is to believe the "black diaries," Roger Casement's name might be added to the list of homosexual voyagers to Europe's colonies. While it is essential not to activate imperialist stereotypes and regard the colonies as places of sexual license and freedom, it may be argued that in the colonies a wide range of possibilities for homosocial friendships and homoerotic patronage became available to men for whom same-sex genital relations were not an option, but for whom conventional marriage, fatherhood, and domesticity were not feasible.[15]

The asymmetrical power relationship that is the very essence of European colonialism certainly would have given rise to coercive and nonconsensual sexual contact with the colonized. Whether as a trader, administrator, missionary, military officer, or tourist, the European man possessed a considerable economic advantage over his love object, supported in large part by the political regime. Cash relations were rarely far away from the most intimate partnership, and servants and subordinates in the colonial economy would have had a close working knowledge of this power.[16] Whatever the degree of emotional reciprocity, then, love across the colonial divide could rarely be conducted on an equal basis. The political and economic disparities conferred enormous power on the European, especially in the most common colonial homosexual couplet of adult white man and favorite local adolescent "boy." How the European made use of this power was a matter of personal choice.[17]

Stuart-Young benefited from such power in Onitsha, gaining new status as a wealthy white trader in an African society that did not recognize the minutiae of the British class system. In moving to a colonial setting when he reached maturity, this working-class "inferior" from the back streets of Manchester could take up the role of the older man in the Uranian couplet, as the social superior who legitimates his sexual attraction by sponsoring youths, partially concealing his desire behind relationships of patronage. Thus, in French Guinea between 1903 and 1905, Stuart-Young befriended and sponsored his young Muslim manservant, Ibrahim, nicknamed "Ibrahim the Unkissed" (see fig. 8). Many years later, the "unkissed" boy starred as the protagonist of Stuart-Young's novel *Soul-Slayer*, published privately by Arthur Stockwell in 1920.

This form of paternalism was common among European travelers, traders, and missionaries throughout the nineteenth century. Famously, Henry Morton Stanley took his beloved boy Kalulu to Europe and America in 1872. While in England, the youth entertained society ladies with his parodies, songs, dances, and high-spirited antics.[18] Similarly, Oscar Wilde circulated photographs of himself with his young African American valet during his tour of the United States. For palm oil ruffians, the presence of an African youth as a servant and

Fig. 8. "'Ibrahim the Unkissed' and J. M. Stuart-Young" (from *Osrac, the Self-Sufficient and Other Poems with a Memoir of the Late Oscar Wilde* [London: Hermes Press, 1905]). *(By permission of the Board of Trinity College Dublin.)*

companion increased their social status in the homeland, for a sure sign of entry to the established middle classes in Britain was the employment of a domestic servant.[19] An African servant held extra appeal as an exotic foreign body on display from the colonies.

Social aspirations aside, it is difficult to avoid a double reading of Stuart-Young's African companions: how "unkissed" were the youths who traveled and lived with this particular master? Timothy d'Arch Smith comments that it would be unfair to tarnish the Uranian poets with the label of pederast: they were certainly distinguished from other homosexual authors by their love of pubescent and adolescent boys, but their passions remained largely aesthetic and textual, unconsummated in the off-page world.[20]

Part of the problem for present-day critics relates to etymological shifts in the word "pederasty" in the course of the last century, for there is a stark contrast between historical and contemporary uses of the term. As Eve Kosofsky Sedgwick writes, a century ago, pederasty described the "relational orientation of desire by an adult toward a youth" that did not necessarily involve genital contact.[21] One did not have to be a practicing homosexual to celebrate the youthful male body, and the Aesthetic Movement of the 1890s produced a "sexless," highly textual mode of pederastic passion in which the Uranian authors participated.[22] By contrast, recent editions of the *Oxford English Dictionary* define pederasty in no uncertain terms as "sexual relations between a man and a boy; anal intercourse with a boy as a passive partner." This definition could not be more explicit or more different from its century-old usage, which emphasized desire and orientation above physical response and contact. To avoid confusion, therefore, I prefer to use the term "Uranian" in place of "pederastic" to describe Stuart-Young's complex sexual orientations and desires.

Several local historians and senior men in Onitsha testify to Stuart-Young's passionate lifelong interest in young African men. He subsidized and sponsored many local youths during his thirty years in the town; he advised and trained several bright boys in clerical skills, and he offered employment and accommodation to other youths before and after their marriages. In this way, he built up an extensive network of protégés and manservants in Onitsha. Three brief examples reveal the pattern of these relationships.

Onitsha elder Akunne Alfred Bosah reports that in 1911 the thirty-year-old Stuart-Young paid for an Igbo companion to accompany him on a six-month trip to Manchester.[23] This young man, Onwuije Hayford Bosah (uncle to Alfred Bosah), was born in Onitsha in 1888 and was Stuart-Young's junior by only seven years. Bosah was more than a servant, for his family owned the land on which Stuart-Young built his Little House of No Regrets. Stuart-Young preferred to remember him by the pet names "Bosa" and "Bosu," both of which bear striking similarities to "Bosie," the name by which Lord Alfred Douglas was known to Oscar Wilde. Bosa is described by Igbo commentators and social historians as Stuart-Young's "beloved."[24] He was the first Onitsha man ever to visit Britain, from where "he returned to Onitsha with his master and poured out his heart to Onitsha people, regarding the advanced way of life of the white race" (see fig. 9).[25]

Fig. 9. Photograph of Onwuije Hayford Bosah taken during his tour of Britain with Stuart-Young in 1911–12 (top, second from left). *(By permission of Enyi Onyeomadiko Helen Onochie.)*

Known to be a prolific, talented storyteller and hunter of leopards, Bosa lived for several years as a servant-companion at the back of Stuart-Young's Little House of No Regrets in New Market Road, Onitsha. "Stuart-Young lived upstairs, above, while my uncle and his wife and children lived at the back," reported Alfred Bosah. "Stuart-Young just landed and then perched in Onitsha. He did not like women much. My uncle consulted him if he had a problem, and he consulted my uncle. He helped my uncle, in fact he was a part of the family."[26] Stuart-Young "didn't give Onwuije any trouble," he added in 2005, "but people begin to be anxious. He doesn't mix up much. We have so many gossips. I can't say what they were accusing him of."[27] The Bosah family thus does not acknowledge an intimate relationship between the two men. Meanwhile, in solid Uranian fashion and in an echo of *Stories Toto Told Me* by fellow Uranian Baron Corvo, Stuart-Young memorialized his beloved companion in writing, producing a book entitled *Stories Bosu Told Me* in 1912.

Some years later, in the mid-1920s, an adolescent boy named Joseph Ubanyionwu Etukokwu started to pay Stuart-Young visits after school, hawking tomatoes to raise some petty cash. "Instead of buying the tomato fruits," Etukokwu recalls, "he would lure me to him, hug [me] and kiss my lips, each time trying to suck my own tongue in the process."[28] Writing about these intimate encounters in his autobiography seventy years later, Etukokwu remembers, "I often came out developing goose pimples. He would end up pulling out all the coins in his pocket and without counting, offer them to me."[29] According to the memoir, their physical contact never progressed beyond these embraces. On one occasion, Stuart-Young handed over twenty-five shillings for two shillings' worth of tomatoes; such a large amount of money would have astounded the boy and alerted his parents to a situation of favoritism and sponsorship with the white man. "I feared and detested the kissing and sucking," Etukokwu writes, repeating his striking language to describe Stuart-Young's sexual advances. But he returned to the trader's premises over a regular period, becoming his secretary in later years, and the older man tried to embrace the youth whenever there was an opportunity.[30]

In the late 1920s and early 1930s, Stuart-Young helped Etukokwu establish the secretarial business which by 1937 had become a large and successful private commercial college in Onitsha. This lucrative relationship was observed closely by Etukokwu's age-mates, who recall that Stuart-Young paid the youth "big money" to type up his numerous literary and journalistic manuscripts. The young man "walked up and down, up and down every day" from Stuart-Young's house so visibly and regularly that it became widely known around town that there was "some special connection or relationship" between the two men.[31] Stuart-Young paid Etukokwu one shilling per page of typing, and the youth was rumored to earn over seven shillings per day, the equivalent of one month's wages for an educated African wage worker at that time.[32]

Clearly, this was not a simple, one-way pederastic relationship; it was not a penetrative sexual liaison; nor was it an instance of African victimhood at the hands of a colonial exploiter. Indeed, in spite of the "detested" physical attention, Etukokwu developed such strong admiration for Stuart-Young that he named the age-grade he established "Odoziaku" (or "Odeziaku"), using the trader's Igbo praise-name to honor his role in the development of Onitsha.[33] Stuart-Young's memory is thus inscribed into Onitsha history and posterity as a result of the special connection with Etukokwu, which lasted many years.

Continuing this combination of patronage and passion in his later life, Stuart-Young is known to have fallen in love with a third Igbo youth, Solomon I. Obike from Umuahia, who lived with him as his cook at the Little House of No Regrets from the mid-1920s until the late 1930s. "Stuart-Young was in love with his cook, Solomon Obike," reported Emeka Geoffrey Olisa. "Obike started by selling groceries [and] drinks. Stuart-Young gave him everything."[34] Obike cared for the physically broken white man with such tenderness that at his death in 1939, Stuart-Young willed him all the remaining properties in his Nigerian estate, including "pecuniary rights."[35] Whereas "Bosu" was close to his master in age and possessed social status in Onitsha, "Obike was a small boy to Onwuije." Onwuije's family remains bitter about Obike's relationship to Stuart-Young, for they had been expecting to inherit the trader's property at his death.[36]

These relationships reveal a similar pattern: an older European man masks his homosexual desire through the socially acceptable sponsorship of his racial "subordinates," who benefit greatly from his interference in their lives. This was not a case of sexual tourism so much as a case of sexual masking. The colonial setting allowed Stuart-Young to relinquish his own subordinate working-class identity and take up the position of a philanthropic gentleman. This bourgeois self-image was bolstered in the case of his beloved "boys" by the production of creative writing and photographs. Stuart-Young seems to have legitimized his love by memorializing his favorite youths. Thus, the "man of letters" regulated his desire by producing novels and poems that celebrated the spiritual and physical beauty of the youths, touching their bodies with verbal rather than carnal caresses.

In 1908, Stuart-Young produced a collection of poetry entitled *Through Veiled Eyes: Being the Story of a Dead Lad's Love*. Written in West Africa and published in Britain by John Ouseley, who published other Uranian poets, including John Gambril Nicholson,[37] the collection contains no sexual guilt and no sense of social surveillance. It is astonishingly uninhibited in its presentation of the seduction and sexual conquest of a boy by an older man. Indeed, in many of the poems, sexual agency and control over the "conquest" is said to rest with the child. The development of a passionate relationship between the two males is charted in a hundred pages of explicit love poetry.

In writing *Through Veiled Eyes*, Stuart-Young entered an established Uranian tradition, filled with its own conventions and symbols of "Greek love" that were commonly used to express the intimacy between men and boys. Thus, for Uranian writers, descriptions of naked male bathers or young sportsmen on the field or photographs of naked "Oriental" boys provided an easily translatable code through which they could express their homoerotic passions.[38] True to form, in *Through Veiled Eyes* Stuart-Young includes footballing and cricketing poems featuring a white boy known as "T.O.T." Imitating and echoing better-known Uranian poets such as Nicholson and Lefroy, he also wrote poems inspired by Frederick Walker's famous painting *The Bathers* (1865–68).[39]

In the dedication to *Through Veiled Eyes*, Stuart-Young positions his desire in a realm that is untainted by the sexually active adult male body. It seems that the poet—aged twenty-seven and living in Onitsha when these poems were published—can disavow his carnal ache and his own sexual maturity by directing his love toward a prepubescent European "lad," a child who will not sully their intimacy with penetrative sex and with whom the poet can express his nostalgia for his own lost boyhood. He writes: "That this unpretentious volume of poems may be lifted from the mire of sensuality, and graced with the redeeming qualities of Youth and Innocence, I dare to inscribe it, with my fondest salutations and apologies for so fragile an offering, to my PRINCE (that was) T.O.T. Junior"[40] (emphasis in original).

Moral dirt, sensuality, and physical lust are associated with the adult body in Stuart-Young's writing: same-sex passion is "redeemed" only by its attachment to the "Youth" and "Innocence" of childhood. If the content of the poems is anything to go by, the happy couple spends most of the summer frolicking in English meadows chasing butterflies, paddling in streams, exchanging soft kisses and surface caresses, and giving one another wild flowers to celebrate their love. Each brief moment of shared delight is then reenacted in the poems, written by "the Admirer" in the loneliness of his room:

> I *dare* not speak! . . .
> For when the moon has risen I may tell
> My passion to the silence, and may kiss
> His pictured face. My bonds are loosed apart,
> And I write down in surging lines the speech
> Of my dear dreams, someday these memories
> Will meet his eyes, and I possess his heart![41] *(emphasis in original)*

In spite of its title, this collection of poems is one of the least "veiled" of Stuart-Young's literary creations. The book opens with two photographic portraits on facing pages: J. M. Stuart-Young's picture is entitled "The Admirer," and facing him through a thin veil of tissue paper is "The Hearer," a young, blond-haired boy named in the dedication as "T.O.T Junior" (see figs. 10 and 11). The striking feature of these full-face portraits—and probably the most difficult for present-day readers to accommodate—is that "T.O.T" is clearly a prepubescent boy, a ten- or eleven-year-old "tot" whose image contrasts dramatically with the mature face and receding hairline of his admirer.

Stuart-Young exhibits no reticence or secrecy in hailing this child as the object of his passions, and T.O.T is openly named in the collection as "My precious Tommy Todd." Moreover, in the poem "Gratitude," the object of the poet's desire is represented as a desiring sexual force.[42] In other poems, such as "Bathers," the poet also confers romantic agency on the child, describing how "my Prince sported with me on the beach, / Submitting when I kissed him."[43] "Indulge the thirst / Of your parched nature" is the plea in another poem.[44] T.O.T's young, smooth body is celebrated for its differences from the

Fig. 10. "The Admirer" (from *Through Veiled Eyes: Being the Story of a Dead Lad's Love* [London: John Ouseley, 1908]). *(By permission of the Board of Trinity College Dublin.)*

Fig. 11. "The Hearer" (from *Through Veiled Eyes: Being the Story of a Dead Lad's Love* [London: John Ouseley, 1908]). *(By permission of the Board of Trinity College Dublin.)*

bodies of adult males, but little or no sense is conveyed of the child's emotional and psychological immaturity or the differences between childhood and adult (homo)sexualities.

Through Veiled Eyes was produced by a specialist Uranian publisher for circulation to a specialist Uranian readership, and it required its audience to identify with an adult narrator who spends the bulk of one summer "grooming" an English boy for physical intimacy. This is the sexual scenario most likely to inspire public violence in contemporary Britain, and many readers today will feel uncomfortable with lines such as "I cannot have your kisses every day; / So rest upon my knee, and let me drink / Into my heart each feature."[45] Set in the context of Uranian art, however, it is possible to regard this as a desire fated to be celibate, if only by the status of the angelic love object in the real world as a "real boy, grubby, ink-stained, insolent, uncomprehending of Uranian passion and rebuffing its smallest manifestations."[46] Such a forgiving perspective is one of few options available to literary critics wishing to avoid the discomfort of drawing biographical conclusions from the material produced by Uranian authors such as Stuart-Young.

How "blameless," then, was Stuart-Young in his relationship with "T.O.T. Junior"? The child was a real boy, not a fictional construct. The boy was the relative and namesake of Thomas Olman Todd, publisher of occult materials and president of the British Supernaturalists' Lyceum Union, whom Stuart-Young visited in Sunderland sometime between 1905 and 1906 while on holiday from his West African business.[47] Tommy Todd, Todd senior's son or nephew, paid regular visits to the household during the school vacations, when Stuart-Young developed a strong passion for him. Biographical material from later in Stuart-Young's life suggests that his Uranian desire did not become fully sexually active until the early 1920s.[48]

Any intimacy between "The Admirer" and "The Hearer" in *Through Veiled Eyes* is, however, disrupted by another male-to-male relationship that intrudes into and transforms the romantic couple. It is here that Stuart-Young's West African location starts to infuse the European settings and characters in his verse. The portrait of the poet on the opening page, featured in fig. 10 above, has in fact been extracted from another picture featuring Stuart-Young. The full photograph, which appeared in the first edition of *Osrac, the Self-Sufficient* (1905), shows the author standing beside a smartly dressed adolescent African nicknamed "Ibrahim the Unkissed" (see fig. 8). Every hair, shadow, and line is in the same place in the later portrait of the author, but Stuart-Young has excised Ibrahim from the picture in order to extract his own portrait. What appears on the surface of *Through Veiled Eyes* to be the reproduction of lovers' portraits, exchanged in secrecy, thus becomes a matter of cutting and pasting:

one wonders who has been excised from the photograph of T.O.T in order to produce the intimacy of that portrait. As with the facsimile letters from Oscar Wilde, the poet has exercised full creative license over his visual material and forged a connection where none might have existed before.

In order to understand Stuart-Young's brand of love, the silenced, hidden African boy must be reinserted into the frame, for West Africa and West Africans exist at the heart of his Uranian writings, forming the sites of his passion. The African presence in *Through Veiled Eyes* reveals the ways in which even the most "English" of literary themes and settings were inscribed with the presence of non-English cultures and peoples in the colonial period.[49]

The "unkissed" boy excised from the photograph was the Islamic youth who worked for Stuart-Young as a servant in Conakry, French Guinea, between 1903 and 1905 and accompanied him to Europe in 1905 for the publication and launch of the "memoir of Oscar Wilde" (itself a revelation of Uranian desire). Little more is known about Ibrahim, except that he lived and traveled with his employer for approximately a year, when the two returned to Africa and parted ways.[50]

If the verse-drenched "T.O.T." was not on the receiving end of the poet's physical ardor, "Ibrahim the Unkissed" was the next most likely candidate as Stuart-Young's constant companion and servant. In *Through Veiled Eyes*, however, the boy in the original photograph is displaced by the white child, denied a presence in the English pastoral scenes evoked in the poems. Instead, Stuart-Young inserts "T.O.T." in his place. The white child stands in for the black child in the poems: the celebration of a supposedly pure and mutual love in *Through Veiled Eyes* masks the unequal balance of power between the European man and his African "boy," between master and servant, between colonizer and colonized, between patron and patronized. The poems thus carefully veil the limited choices available to the subordinate partner in the Uranian relationship.

It is possible that the poet adored both of these boys and spent his time in England loving both Ibrahim and T.O.T., albeit in the form of a purely textual passion. What is certain from *Through Veiled Eyes* is that Ibra's body is banished to the background. He makes one short appearance in the poem entitled "Bathers," quietly entering the bathing scene in the form of a servant. In the company of three others in a bathing van, Stuart-Young describes how "my Afric garçon tried to rinse / Soap and water o'er his palms." Meanwhile, "the clear tones" of T.O.T ring out, asking in the final lines of the poem, "Jack . . . Is Ibra's body black?"[51] The presence of Ibra in this poem disrupts the poet's intimacy with T.O.T. Ibra's African body comes between them in the form of a child's question that the poet chooses not to answer in the remainder of the poem.

Until now, *The Forger's Tale* has focused almost exclusively on Stuart-Young's writings and the metropolitan sexual values that drove him from his homeland. Over the decades of his residence in Onitsha, however, the "unlettered" masses of market women, local traders, residents, and children had a great deal to say about his character, work, and lifestyle. As the next chapter will reveal, they produced a number of Igbo names through which it is possible to chart the variety of popular interpretations of Stuart-Young from the first moment of his arrival in Onitsha. These local naming practices provide a rich source of information about the history of homosexuality in colonial Igboland and offer a useful starting point for culturally sensitive research into Africa's queer histories.

5 ～ The Politics of Naming

Igbo Perspectives on Stuart-Young

> Every European has his nick-name, which hits him off to a T. The one amazing thing is that hundreds, thousands, tens of thousands of us, spend our lives here without becoming aware that we are "the man with the twisted smile," or "the woman whose ears are hard as iron."
>
> —J. M. Stuart-Young, "Tribute to Tom"[1]

ONITSHA RESIDENTS, particularly those closest to Stuart-Young's protégés, were not ignorant of his Uranian desires, but unlike most British people in the era after the Oscar Wilde trials, they showed a great deal of tolerance toward him. The explanations for this forgiving attitude are explored in this chapter, for by the time young Joseph Etukokwu experienced his mentor's physical advances in the mid-1920s, a body of highly charged local Igbo names had emerged in and around Onitsha to describe Stuart-Young. Taken together, these names form a kind of memory bank, preserving different aspects of the trader's biography in mnemonic form.

In precolonial and colonial Igboland, as in other parts of Africa, names carried great descriptive weight, providing commentaries on cultural or economic events in the locality and expressing views about an individual's personal achievements and genealogy. Such compression and expressive economy on the part of Africans often brought out the most flowery reactions from colonial anthropologists. In his book *The Lower Niger and Its Tribes*, for example, Major Arthur Glyn Leonard describes the significance of Igbo names in the following terms: "There is more in a name—more joy and more sorrow, more pathos and more passion, more tragedy and more comedy, more humanity and inhumanity than it is possible for the civilised unit to realise."[2] Concluding with a literate man's metaphor for orality, he writes, "These names are but the pages, and the proverbs are the chapters, in the life-history of every house."[3]

Igbo praise-names and nicknames were not stable in the manner of European names given at birth or taken at marriage, however; they could shift and multiply during a person's lifetime in response to an individual's achievements or transformations in personal status.[4] Thus, a market woman who amassed great wealth might become known by the praise-name Oliaku ("eater of wealth"), an epithet reserved for extremely wealthy individuals.[5] A miserly white trader would come to be called "Oganah" ("presents have ceased"), while a colonial officer who sent his troops into a town on a punitive raid would be named "Ozumbah" ("a fighter or breaker of towns").[6]

Stuart-Young was regarded as an extraordinary European from the outset of his life in Nigeria. Within a short time of settling in Onitsha in 1905, he earned the first of his locally conferred names: "Odoziaku," meaning keeper, caretaker, manager, or arranger of wealth. Conferred on him by the Igbo market women with whom he conducted the bulk of his trade in palm oil—but who were never allowed into his domestic space—this praise-name referred to the immense private fortune he accumulated as a trader and to the manner in which he displayed and distributed his cash and goods in the community.[7]

Stuart-Young enthusiastically adopted this name, with one significant alteration from the market women's usage. Almost immediately upon receiving the name, Stuart-Young transformed "Odoziaku" into "Odeziaku," and he and his elite African friends misspelled the appellation for the rest of his life. "Odeziaku" was adopted and endorsed without comment by African newspaper editors until Stuart-Young's death in 1939. One practical explanation for this apparent error is that in the early twentieth century, Igbo orthography was more flexible and less finalized than today. A second, equally feasible explanation, however, is that Stuart-Young and his friends cleverly built an additional layer of meaning into the praise-name: by adding "ode"—meaning to write, or writing—to the accepted connotations of "Odoziaku," they extended the conventional acknowledgement of individual wealth to include Stuart-Young's passion for writing. "Odeziaku" thus names his capacity to generate literary wealth as well as material wealth.

Misspelled as "Odeziaku," this name was Stuart-Young's favorite, standing in for the double-barreled gentleman on many occasions: it appeared on his letterheads, shopfronts, and houses. He also used it in the 1920s and 1930s as the nom de plume for many of his poems and articles in Nigerian newspapers. "Odeziaku" itself went through further transformations when Stuart-Young wrote for a short period under the pseudonyms "Jack O'Dazi" and "O. Dazi Aku": the former reveals his preference for Celtic names and the latter for an Africanized identity. In this way, he appropriated the salute of Onitsha market women into his own literary orbit, making it a part of his self-image and transcribing it onto the printed page for the consumption of African readers.

"Odeziaku" was also used on several of Stuart-Young's shopfronts and to promote certain products in his stores, all of which were connected in one way or another with the act of writing. "There was no Onitsha schoolboy that had not bought 'Odeziaku Exercise Book' or 'Happy-Go-Lucky-Johnnie Note Book,' etc from Odeziaku Bookshop," recalled S. I. Bosah in an essay for the *West African Pilot* composed immediately after Stuart-Young's death.[8] Another Onitsha youth remembered that the trader used to "spend his leisure [time] . . . cutting letters of wood which he used in labelling his shops."[9] These young men's vivid memories show how Stuart-Young literally incarnated himself as a "man of letters." He printed his name onto stationery products and he cut out characters in order to fix his local identity to his shop fronts. "Behold some of the names of 'Odeziaku's' buildings," wrote Bosah: "'Ye Little Wonder Shop,' 'Half Way to Bush,' 'Upper New Market Road View,' 'JMSY,' 'Odeziaku' . . . etc."[10] Both "JMSY" and "Odeziaku" thus possessed a distinctive textual materiality on the streets of Onitsha, looming above Stuart-Young's properties as literal signs of his presence in town.

One can view these displays as a blatant form of self-production, for Stuart-Young used "Odeziaku" as a brand name in order to compete with fellow European palm produce traders and win the hearts of Igbo clients. "Odeziaku" became the African double of "JMSY," an equally manufactured name that functioned in a similar way to enhance (or to mask) the status of plain "John Young." He wrote proudly in 1933, "[T]he name was conferred upon me by the Africans of this district over a quarter of a century ago, and . . . I am better known by it to-day than by my birth-name." Stuart-Young defined "Odeziaku" as a material and spiritual "trade repairer" or "trade adjuster"; in the same essay from 1933, he remembered having been "regarded by the people of Onitsha district as a sort of 'governor' upon the machinery of commerce" in the first two decades of the twentieth century.[11]

With or without its self-promoting owner, and when correctly spelled, the name Odoziaku is intimately connected with the manipulation of trade wealth—the "governorship of commerce"—by skilled entrepreneurs. Alongside Stuart-Young's appropriation of the name as an advertising tool, "Odoziaku" therefore powerfully signifies his adoption into Igbo Africa, representing, in his mind at least, a grassroots seal of approval for the town's favorite European man.

"Odoziaku" conveyed an array of further more complex and ambivalent commentaries, however, that either circulated beyond Stuart-Young's comprehension or that he chose to ignore in his positive interpretation of the name and his clever insertion of a reference to writing. First, "Odoziaku" describes "a woman recognised as having distinguished herself in looking after her husband's wealth and landed property."[12] A hint of gender ambiguity thus infuses the application of the name to Stuart-Young: who was *his* earthly or spiritual "husband"? Second, and more seriously, a hint of hoarding and individualism is conveyed by "Odoziaku," moderated only by the suggestion that its owner was keeping, or managing, his wealth on behalf of the community, "arranging" his money with the welfare of others in mind. "Miserly rich men are despised" by the Igbos, writes S. I. Bosah in his history of Onitsha. "A rich man is expected to be a free giver because his wealth is ordered by God."[13] This particular praise-name therefore served as a reminder to its carrier of his—or, more often, her—responsibility to redirect the hoarded wealth into social investments, including marriage and the production of heirs.[14] Stuart-Young did not, however, have any children through whom to circulate his wealth; as he stated in one interview, "I shall die without issue, in any part of the world."[15]

A further, more complex meaning of "Odoziaku" relates to the way this praise-name was used by Igbo women traders as a comment on shifts in the sexual division of labor that governed their relationships to commodities and labor in the colonial period.[16] Increasing numbers of white palm oil traders and entrepreneurs like Stuart-Young arrived in Onitsha in the early twentieth century with the explicit goal of personal enrichment and early retirement back to Europe. As chapter 2 demonstrated, their trade closely involved Igbo women, who controlled the supply of palm products and often profited from their dealings with white traders, acting as links and envoys along the trade routes to the interior. That one of these white entrepreneurs chose to live locally in defiance of the get-rich-quick mentality earned him great respect among these women. At the same time, however, their praise-name for him functioned as an index of economic changes occurring in the colonial period in that it gauged precisely who accumulated great personal wealth and closely monitored how this wealth was managed. In naming the trader Odoziaku, therefore, the Igbo market women were not commenting solely on issues of sexuality; they were exercising what Patricia Hayes describes as Africans' own "forms of integrity which were resistant to colonial force and cultural manipulation," forming their own matrix of meanings from the evidence before them.[17]

Other Igbo names were produced for Stuart-Young that he neither wished for nor memorialized in his textual self-production. Stuart-Young's success in inscribing himself for posterity as Odeziaku was supplemented by another, more ambivalent set of names that also stemmed from those with whom he traded and mingled in Onitsha. "Fabulous tales were in the air," wrote C. A. J. Onwuegbuzia two years after the trader's death, and many people believed "he possessed some super-natural means of amassing wealth."[18] "There was something mysterious about him and people didn't understand what gave him money," commented Akunne John Nworah in 2005.[19]

From the outset, people were struck by Stuart-Young's standoffish manner with women. "He was not known to be associated with women except strictly on business," commented Chike Akosa. "If he was ever married back home there was nothing to show for it."[20] Of particular significance to the Igbo onlookers was the fact that not once in his entire residence in Onitsha did Stuart-Young allow an African woman into his house as a wife, as a "concubine," or simply as a maid. No English woman visited him from home. Many other European traders along the Nigerian rivers embarked on formal and informal liaisons with African women, and, as the twentieth century progressed and colonial disapproval intensified toward interracial relationships, more European men brought their wives out to join them in the colonies.[21] As the last chapter suggested, however, Stuart-Young rejected the company of women and preferred to develop friendships with local men and boys. He thus remained ostensibly unattached in a society where "the act of getting married is regarded as a fundamental ritual which serves as a religious definition of adult existence,"[22] and he remained childless in a culture where one of the cardinal proverbs was "children first, wealth follows."[23] Indeed, he lived in a society where, when people "assess the career of a person, their primary criterion is the number of children he has raised to support and survive him."[24]

To this day, Stuart-Young is remembered as a "woman-hater."[25] This term must be contextualized to be understood, however, for as Paul Gordon Schalow demonstrates in his ethnographic study of early modern Japan, in some cultures "woman-hater" connotes a great deal more—or less—than its contemporary western sense of misogyny. In seventeenth-century Japan, for example, where it was socially normative for men to desire boys as well as women sexually, the term *onnagirai* ("woman-haters") emerged to describe men who preferred to have sexual relationships exclusively with boys; attitudes toward women were not the defining characteristics of *onnagirai*.[26] Likewise, in Gilbert Herdt and Robert J. Stoller's study of the Sambia people of Papua New Guinea, a different type of woman-hater describes his fear of women and his preference for erotic contacts with pubescent boys who are small, quiet, and hairless.[27] After several sexually unconsummated marriages to women, this man, Kalutwo, is left culturally stranded and derided by his community for his effeminacy; he yearns for "the trappings of marriage," especially children and property, but is unable "sexually and psychologically [to] . . . bear intimacy with a woman" because he feels that erotic contact with women is "dirty and dangerous."[28] One might see Stuart-Young as like Kalutwo, more gynophobic than misogynistic in his attitudes to women.

Stuart-Young stated his sexual preferences and fears in a remarkably candid letter to celebrated scandalmonger and sexually explicit author Frank Harris. Dated 11 April 1925, the letter confesses to the occasional "homosexual embrace" with "my boy lover" and gives a clear statement of sexual identity: "I am an Urning—woman love frightens me" (fig. 12).[29] In a maneuver that typifies his tendency to narrativize his life story, Stuart-Young offers his autobiographical details to Harris in the form of the synopsis of a novel, *Broken Interludes*. As with his later novels, *Johnny Jones Guttersnipe* and *What Does It Matter?* (discussed in chapter 7), this novel contains a hero who is "myself" and a relationship that "tears me to pieces" with the autobiographical memories it arouses. Indeed, so emotionally difficult is his subject matter that Stuart-Young invites Harris to take on the project with its original, "wonderful plot," and asks him to "remould it" for publication.

This short letter is a rare surviving example of Stuart-Young's correspondence, and it reveals more information about his sexual biography than any other document in existence. Perhaps its most surprising disclosure relates not to his active homosexuality but to the existence of a wife, called Nellie, whom Stuart-Young describes as "the first (and the last) woman in my life." According to the letter, the couple married late in 1919 and separated "by mutual consent" shortly after the end of their honeymoon. Nellie's miscarriage of their child provided the opening for Stuart-Young to tell her that he found "the physical act with her . . . bestial and repulsive to my nature." It is unclear whether Stuart-Young also disclosed his homosexual inclinations to Nellie, but her husband's description of sex with her as "bestial and repulsive" must have caused enormous distress at the end of a difficult voyage. Clearly, Nellie had "insisted on coming" to live in Africa with her husband, a practice that was becoming increasingly normative in the colonies at the time. Such a move, however, made Stuart-Young miserable, disrupting his carefully negotiated, long-established bachelor lifestyle in Onitsha. Nellie's pregnancy prevented such a scenario, to Stuart-Young's relief, and her miscarriage gave him the opportunity to repudiate her.

The dramatic marital disclosures contained in this letter to Harris are not simply an example of Stuart-Young's fabrications, designed to shock and impress a correspondent who, in his own memoirs, expressed repulsion for homosexuals and distaste for Africans and boasted excessively about his heterosexual promiscuity.[30] A marriage certificate held by the General Register Office of England confirms that at the Parish Church of Shirley, Southampton,

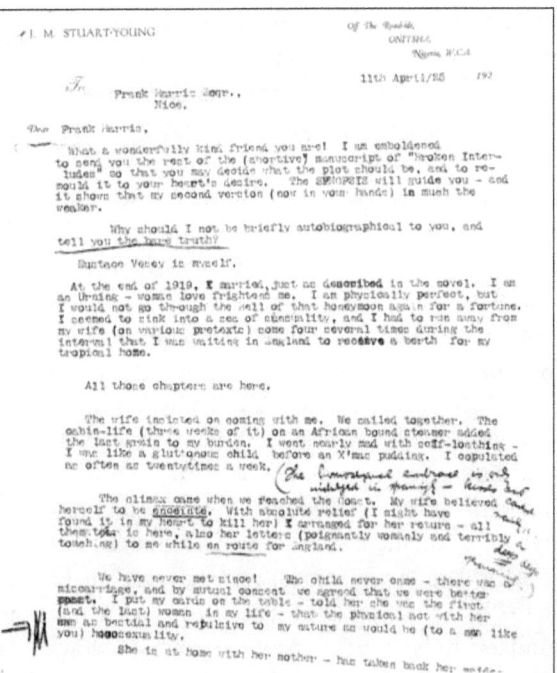

Fig. 12. Letter from Stuart-Young to Frank Harris, dated 11 April 1925. *(By permission of the Harry Ransom Humanities Research Center, The University of Texas at Austin.)*

on 18 October 1919, one "Jack Young," a merchant aged thirty-eight, did indeed marry Nellie Gibson Etheridge, aged thirty-three, a spinster. Nellie's father is listed as a "gentleman," while Jack's deceased father had worked for the Manchester Railway.

More surprising still is the husband's marital status at this wedding, for he is listed on the marriage certificate as a "widower." Stuart-Young's statement that Nellie was "the first (and the last) woman in my life" is therefore inaccurate, for while Nellie certainly was the last woman in his life, in marital terms she was not the first. A marriage certificate from 25 March 1908 records the union of "John Stuart Young," who describes himself as a professional "correspondent," with Annie Knight, a spinster, in the Parish Church of St. Luke, Chorlton-on-Medlock, Manchester. This marriage lasted only two years, however, for Annie died of pulmonary tuberculosis in Manchester in May 1911, aged only thirty-one and without any children. On her death certificate, her husband's occupation is described rather differently from the marriage certificate, for he is now listed as "a commercial traveller (foreign)."[31]

In his letter to Harris, Stuart-Young provides no context or explanation for his improbable marriage to Nellie Gibson Etheridge. Nellie was a qualified schoolteacher and was unlikely to be loitering near the Southampton docks or in the vicinity of the Southampton West Hotel to liaise with the wealthy commercial travelers who disembarked from the West African steamers.

As we have seen, Stuart-Young had a firmly established "Uranian" lifestyle in West Africa by 1919 and had already brought at least two African youths to Britain for "grand tours." Given the details of his life prior to this marriage, one wonders how the couple met and fell in love at all and why Stuart-Young—who clearly did not wish for Nellie's companionship at the Little House of No Regrets—desired a second marriage. Perhaps he wished to disguise his increasingly active Uranian passion in Africa behind the cover of a conventional bourgeois marriage, in the manner of many other homosexual men, including Oscar Wilde, in the nineteenth and twentieth centuries.[32] Another possible explanation is that the couple were cousins through the Gibson line: Stuart-Young's father, John Pultney Young, was born near Southampton to a mother whose maiden name was Gibson. Cousin-to-cousin marriages were quite common in the nineteenth century. Indeed, one such union may have occurred already in Stuart-Young's family, for his mother's maiden name was also Gibson. With this connection in mind, Nellie's father and Stuart-Young's father may have conferred about the union and agreed that for different reasons their offspring would benefit from the marriage.

Stuart-Young's letter to Harris, with its passionate, scrawled annotation, greatly contrasts with the sense of sexual perversion, sickness, and self-loathing to be found in his memoir of Oscar Wilde, published twenty years earlier. Against the image of the "homosexual monster" found in that text, monstrous sex is defined as vaginal and heterosexual in this letter of 1925. Like the woman-hater Kalutwo in Herdt and Stoller's study, Stuart-Young represents heterosexual contact as polluting and dangerous. Unlike Kalutwo, however, he cleverly uses this sense of heterosexual revulsion to redefine boy-love as natural, clean, safe, happy, and healthy. Over and against the monstrous self who indulged in vaginal sex with Nellie, Stuart-Young sets "deep deep yearning" and the true lover's "kisses and caresses," which are reserved for "my boy lover." After a youth filled with guilt at his unstoppable "perversion," Stuart-Young seems finally to have achieved the emotional freedom for which he yearned. In the process of admitting the naturalness of "my nature," he redefines perverse and grotesque sex in terms of heterosexual vaginal contact. Intimate boy-love and the "homosexual embrace" thus become permissible precisely for their nonvaginal status.[33]

Without any knowledge of the dramatic marital events described in this letter to Harris, members of the Igbo community accurately labeled Stuart-Young a woman-hater in the early twentieth century. Interestingly, in using this term, Igbo commentators located the trader's sexuality outside discourses of effeminacy; the term preserves his masculinity, unlike the many available labels attached to men in other sexually transgressive groups in West African cultures, such as cross-dressers.[34] Stuart-Young's homosocial domestic life and his financial sponsorship exclusively of boys are thus accommodated by the Igbo term woman-hater. The naming did not stop there, however, for a further, equally perceptive array of names accrued to the trader from different sectors of Onitsha society.

In spite of his own failure to produce children, "Odeziaku" was known to love boys: he would attract them to his stores with gifts, tricks, and amusements. Schoolboys often gathered outside his largest store to play with the two magic mirrors he fixed there for their entertainment.[35] Outside this shop each Christmas, he distributed biscuits, free pencils, and "Odeziaku" exercise books to the boys and girls of Onitsha.[36] This connection with the children earned Odeziaku another of his locally conferred names, "Eke Young." Used half-jokingly, half in fear by the children, "Eke" (or "Ekke") is the name given to the sacred python in Igboland, and as a nickname it would have carried a variety of powerful connotations.[37]

In many parts of precolonial and colonial Igboland, the Eke python was addressed as "Mother" and was allowed to come and go freely from people's homes. Eke pythons were reputed to crawl into the beds of children and women as a sign of blessing from the supreme deity. Even if terrified, the occupant of the bed was forbidden to move or cry out because of the immense good fortune such an occurrence would bring.[38] Accidental killings of Eke pythons in the early twentieth century required rituals of exoneration, including a period of mourning and an elaborate formal burial ceremony.[39]

Stuart-Young aroused similar feelings of fear and good fortune in the children: he was widely known to have taken "Bosa" to Britain and to sponsor local boys, bringing them great wealth in the manner of the python. It is possible that as a white man, like the sacred snake, he also held a degree of untouchability in the children's eyes: none wanted to harm or come in contact with the body of the white trader.[40] As with Odoziaku, a degree of gender ambiguity also attaches to the Eke title in Stuart-Young's case, for the python is regarded in parts of Igboland as "a symbol of female beauty and gentleness" and is connected with the earth goddess, Ala.[41] Such maternal gentleness is tempered, however, by a recognition of the python's danger to children. For instance, in 1906 Major Arthur Glyn Leonard noted "the occasional unruliness of these pampered creatures in attempting to swallow infants and young children."[42] Each of these complex associations adds to the powerful local interpretation of Odeziaku in his manifestation as Eke Young.

The trader's romantic love of boys also gave rise to this nickname from the children of Onitsha. As Misty Bastian points out, "Eke" might have been a code word among local boys to signify Stuart-Young's sexuality.[43] The obvious connection between the snake and the phallic male certainly struck Talbot in his extensive anthropological research among Igbo and Ibibio communities in the 1920s and 1930s. He refers to it repeatedly in *Tribes of the Niger Delta* (1932) in his references to spirit marriages between priestesses and Eke pythons and to images of "phallic snake" shrines and carvings in southeastern Nigeria. Talbot includes numerous illustrations of the phallic snake symbol, including the one seen in fig. 13: here the snake is represented as a male stranger who has traveled upriver from the sea wearing a European hat. Stuart-Young's Eke status with the children may therefore have signified the young people's ambivalent feelings about the foreigner's capacity both to sponsor and seduce. The nickname would have offered a word of warning and foreknowledge about the trader's proclivities.

In local recollections of Stuart-Young, the Eke nickname contains a variety of inflections. Writing in 1941, C. A. J. Onwuegbuzia stressed the financial and occult aspects of the name: "They gave him the 'Eke' . . . as they thought he charmed one that produced him money."[44] In referring to "they" rather than "we," Onwuegbuzia establishes a distance between himself, as a member of the educated Igbo elite, and the "illiterate folk" who, he says, generated these names and spiritual associations.[45] To S. I. Bosah, who wrote a "memoir of

Odeziaku" from a young boy's perspective in 1939, "Eke" means simply "'the keeper of boa-constrictor' because of his zoological interest in keeping boa-constrictors and other creatures."[46] After offering this empirical explanation, however, Bosah hints at a further meaning that echoes the unwritten views of the "illiterate folk" reported by Onwuegbuzia: "In every home at Onitsha, 'Eke Young' was a great watchword," Bosah writes, giving the "close connection" with Onwuije Hayford Bosah as an example of Stuart-Young's behavior.[47] As a watchword, the name required local residents to be attentive to the trader's movements around youths. Bosah uses Eke both to describe a prepubescent child's perception of Stuart-Young as the eccentric keeper of snakes and animals and to describe the powerful combination of wealth and favoritism that accrued to Stuart-Young's favorite adolescent boys.

By 1921, Stuart-Young was widely recognized as the wealthiest European trader in Onitsha, if not in the whole of Nigeria. He seemed to attract and breed money, especially during and immediately after the Great War. The names Odoziaku and Eke insinuate that he had entered a spiritual agreement with an entity in the other world on whose behalf he was managing large quantities of money and commodities. Money "stuck" to him, even though he gave a great deal away in the sponsorship of Igbo youths and appeared, to many observers, to do little to generate wealth. "He was an enigma," stated Akunne John Nworah. "We stayed outside his house and looked at him after school every day. All day he sits in the same position, reading and writing, no visitors, nothing. His way of life compelled attraction and interest."[48] The broader local community also watched with great interest as Stuart-Young leased land from Onitsha chiefs and built additional properties around the town center. It was rumored that he held séances in these houses and taught his male protégés

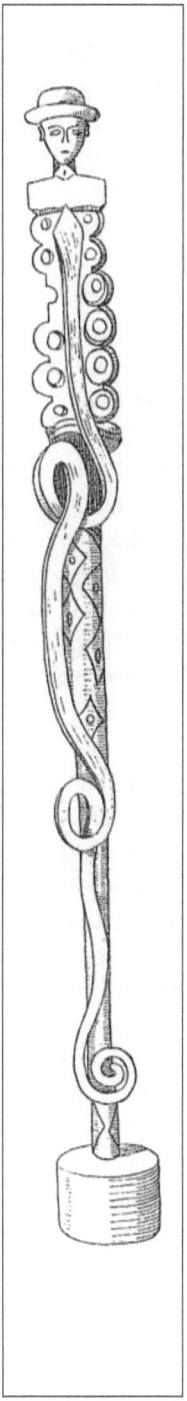

Fig. 13. Carved staff in the form of the python as foreigner (from P. Amaury Talbot, *The Peoples of Southern Nigeria*, vol. 2, *Ethnology* [London: Oxford University Press, 1926], 101.) *(By permission of Oxford University Press.)*

the secrets of the occult. As Chike Akosa wrote of the trader's first beloved Onitsha boy, "It was Stuart-Young who imbued Hayford Bosah with the knowledge of the ancient and modern occult lores and practice. He was taught elementary metaphysics, and the art of divination, levitation and the cabala."[49]

Stuart-Young always denied such activities, but his lifestyle furnished a torrent of proofs to local people. His connection with the nether world was assured when in 1938, toward the end of his life, he lost his voice for a full year. His laryngitis—in fact caused by throat cancer—signaled at the very least a strong link, and probably a "marriage," within the spirit world, for aphasia was one sign of possession. What caused a great stir among observers was the way in which Stuart-Young would "build and tear down houses," frequently changing his mind about the position of walls, adding rooms and balconies, or, for no apparent reason, replacing entire buildings with differently shaped structures.[50] Alongside his reclusive lifestyle, such "eccentric" activities sent loud and clear signals to the Igbo community, and Stuart-Young rapidly earned his third and most important local name, closely connected to his Eke Young nickname, as a votary of the water spirit Mami Wata.[51]

Mami Wata (or Mammy Water) is a powerful spirit throughout West Africa, but her precise characteristics are as slippery as the fish scales on her tail. Intimately connected with the rise of international slavery and external trade along the rivers, she is known to be surrounded by Eke snakes and to "marry" chosen mortals to whom she brings great wealth. No man can be her husband, however, so her male spouses are often considered to be her "wives."[52] Apart from this, she is a plural and shifting force, signifying different things in different places and times and along different West African rivers.[53] Such fluidity makes it especially difficult to obtain historically accurate information about how Mami Wata was interpreted in the early twentieth century, for her meanings cannot simply be extrapolated from the contemporary Nigerian narratives and shrines in which she currently appears.

Mami Wata would have represented a historically located and specific fusion of meanings relating to modernity, money, trade, consumption, and production in the early twentieth century. Oral accounts of Stuart-Young's life, recorded with the oldest men of Onitsha in 2002 and 2005, assist in the effort to piece together a picture of the socioeconomic debates and spiritual beliefs that were expressed through Mami Wata in this period, but their memories contain biases, particularly the biases brought by their gender, elite social status, and membership in Christian denominations. What is striking about these recent interviews is the elite men's reluctance to endorse the Mami Wata connection. "Stuart-Young was restless. He was individualistic and a loner," Chief Patrick Ekwerekwu remembered, adding, "People said he was married to

Mami Wata, but this was speculation and a bad story, suspicion."[54] Chief Chike Akosa said, "People saw him as a mystic, or jujuman. They called him a jujuman due to ignorance and superstition."[55] Barrister I. I. Ekwerekwu drew together the threads of Stuart-Young's various nicknames into one coherent identity: "Always he was pulling down houses and rebuilding them. Really, what people believed was that he was married to Mami Wata, and the children called him 'Eke Young.'"[56] In a similar vein, Chief S. I. Bosah recalled, "He was fond of the boa constrictor and he was given the name Eke, that is, python. They said he married Mami Wata. They said he was a spiritualist. Those interested in spiritualism would go to his house."[57] In commenting on his spiritualism, these interviewees disavowed any personal involvement in the trader's séances. According to the men I spoke to, Stuart-Young's adolescent male protégés and his European male palm oil ruffian colleagues were the primary participants in his occult activities rather than mission-educated youths, market women, or his elite professional friends in the community.

One after another, these educated and elite male commentators circled around Mami Wata, presenting the mermaid as other people's explanation of Stuart-Young's peculiarities. "We didn't understand him," stated Nworah, "he was almost akin to a spirit."[58] Considerable embarrassment surrounded the Mami Wata and spiritualist connections; these elite men, who mixed with Stuart-Young as youths, freely recalled the children's name of Eke Young but distanced themselves from the mermaid or rejected the connection altogether as the "superstition" of illiterate adults. Yet, taken together, the connections they drew between the python, the mermaid, the occult, and wealth all signaled that Stuart-Young was one of the rare men to be chosen by the mermaid for marriage, on whom were conferred great wealth and spiritual gifts, including the power to prophesy.[59]

The elite men's reticence about Mami Wata may have been caused in part by Stuart-Young's financial near-ruin during the Great Depression in the early 1930s, which decreased local curiosity about the sources of his wealth. In large part, however, their ambivalence signals that the Mami Wata name and all it implied was a popular designation from grassroots women traders and farmers in the 1910s and 1920s rather than from the educated Christianized elite of Onitsha, especially those men whose current status, wealth, and connections could be traced back to Stuart-Young's sponsorship. The elite men's aloofness from the "illiterate" masses may explain why there is so little mention of Mami Wata in the many obituaries to Stuart-Young published in the Nigerian newspapers in 1939. Referring to him instead as "Dr" Stuart-Young, this class of African preferred to use the title that had appeared in the 1930s in newspaper articles by highly educated West African editors such as Nnamdi Azikiwe.

Nevertheless, publications by Onitsha citizens contain many references to these popular "rumours," "myths," and "legends" of Stuart-Young's spiritual alliances. The Nigerian novelist Chinua Achebe remembers Stuart-Young as "a legend among the Igbo even in his lifetime; for was he not a lover of the wealth-giving but fiendishly jealous mermaid-queen of the Niger River? They called him *Eke* (python) which he disliked and *Odoziaku* (Arranger of Wealth) which he didn't."[60] Chike Akosa writes, "Legend had it that he was married to mammy water or the mermaid who paid him nocturnal visits and was said to be the source of his vast wealth."[61] "Rumour was," wrote Onwuegbuzia, "he contacted the 'mermaid' who brought him an inexhaustible supply of wealth."[62]

The most revealing published account of the power of Mami Wata as a spiritual connection can be found in the autobiography of Joseph U. Etukokwu, one of the adolescent boys whom Stuart-Young attempted to seduce in the 1920s. "I was naturally afraid to go to him again for the sale of tomato fruits," Etukokwu writes, recalling the physical advances that the white man made when, as a youth, he first visited the Little House of No Regrets.[63] It is curious to note that while Etukokwu gives no name whatsoever to Stuart-Young's Uranian desire—neither condemning nor condoning "homosexuality"—he is particularly keen to deny any association between himself and the mermaid: "I know that many people associate me with worshipping or invoking the *mammy water* or mermaid like they associated same with late Odoziaku, more so as pictures of the mermaid are conspicuously displayed at my hotels. This is far from the truth. I have never been fetish [*sic*] or occultic or believed in anything in life like juju."[64] In response to people's surveillance and public discussion of his own rise to wealth and prominence, assisted at the start by Stuart-Young's sponsorship, Etukokwu sees no need to defend himself against the charge that he is a "homosexual." Homosexuality does not signify an identity in itself. Rather, if it is recognized at all in a singular sense, it is simply one of several signs of a spiritual association with the water deity: homosexuality is less socially recognized as an identity than an imputed "marriage in the water."[65] It is therefore his rumored marriage to the mermaid that Etukokwu is most keen to deny while setting the record straight in his autobiography.

Although he was hailed as a wise man and a merchant prince, Stuart-Young was not a man of status in local terms: he obtained no local titles or kinship ties within the community. In this, his wealth was typical of a Mami Wata worshipper, being "acquired rather than inherited and . . . therefore outside the kinship system."[66] As a white trader and, more important, as an unmarried, childless man, he could not transform his wealth into social investments in the manner of local big men and merchant queens.[67] His wealth "vanished" in service to the African community, and his investments reaped no long-term rewards. According to local criteria, the trader might even be labeled "mad" for allowing his money to disappear in this way.

It is as a "madman" filled with cultural otherness that Stuart-Young features in a short story by Chinua Achebe. "Uncle Ben's Choice" is set in 1919 and features a young African clerk in the Niger Company at Umuru.[68] The clerk is faced with a choice one night when a strange woman with long soft hair invites him into bed: he knows that to have sexual intercourse with Mami Wata will make him extremely wealthy but render him infertile, and he flees from the room to seek refuge with a friend. "'For where is the man who will choose wealth instead of children'?" he asks, and adds by way of a moral:

> The same night I drove Mami Wota [sic] out she went to Dr J. M. Stuart-Young, a white merchant and became his lover. . . . Oh yes, he became the richest man in the whole country. But she did not allow him to marry. When he died, what happened? All his wealth went to outsiders. Is that good wealth? I ask you. God forbid.[69]

Achebe's story sets the African clerk against the European trader in an explicit comparison that assesses Stuart-Young's biography from within Igbo social values. "Uncle Ben's Choice" offers an alternative obituary in which Stuart-Young is seen as an isolated figure on the margins of the community who has, in Henry John Drewal's terms, exchanged progeny for profit, died without status, and transformed his money into "bad" wealth.[70] The story reveals how despite his local praise-names and celebrity status, Stuart-Young remained a failure by some people's cultural standards, becoming immensely wealthy but remaining disconnected from the formal structures by which wealth and success were recognized in Onitsha.

Offering fair prices for palm oil and kernels, Stuart-Young attracted many Africans to his factories on the riverbank, and it is from within these communities that his Igbo names arose. "His palm oil and palm kernel buying stations were among the busiest in town," S. I. Bosah recalls, and "goods sold in his shops were of rock-bottom prices, invariably cheaper than their counterparts offered by the commercial firms."[71] People knew that in his stores in town, the trader always had new and bizarre lines of imported goods to exchange for their produce or cowries. Female entrepreneurs, who dominated trade in Igbo areas, made straight for his stores because Stuart-Young's unusual commodities could fetch high prices when taken along the river to be exchanged for palm produce in distant communities.[72] His stores "were a melting pot of toys, footwears, vehicles," plus "haberdashery, hats, shoes, ready-made suits, frocks, singlets, shirts, tinned food, building materials, household utensils, books, school materials, gun-powder, matchets [sic], etc."[73] The books on his shelves included *The Bumper Book for Boys* and *The Convict Ship*, as well as his own publications.[74]

Outside his largest store, Stuart-Young placed two mirrors flanking the entrance: "Two large looking glasses in front of his shops were a great amenity to children," remembered S. I. Bosah. "One of the glasses would make a tall man look short, whilst the other would make a dwarf look gigantic. Every evening we boys would congregate there to make fun of ourselves [i.e., each other]."[75] Paradoxically, given his outright rejection of the Mami Wata association, by placing these mirrors on either side of the commodity-filled store, Stuart-Young had set up what could have been regarded locally as a large-scale version of a Mami Wata shrine. "Mami Wata devotees consider the mirror as one of Mami Wata's most prized possessions, and thus an instrument essential for communication with her," writes Drewal.[76] Her liquid medium is symbolized through the mirror, and her shrines are filled with commodities, including "popular imported prints . . . foreign literature, trade goods."[77] The reflective surface of the mirror provides a passage, or threshold, between land and water, past and future, surface and depth, waking and dreaming, allowing votaries to move into a state of possession.[78] Stuart-Young's distorting mirrors that threw the body into ripples would have increased this symbolic "wateriness."

Further transforming his stores into shrinelike sites, he would be seen on many occasions "moulding effigies, which he employed to allure customers to his shops."[79] Other shopfronts were decorated with panes of brightly colored glass with a small square hatch through which the children could peep to see the trader.[80] These marketing and advertising techniques, probably learned from British department stores, would have been resymbolized and reinterpreted in Onitsha, where many different types of shrines were filled with effigies and figurines. At other times Stuart-Young would be observed sitting alone on his balcony, oblivious to the street, surrounded by writing materials. To the unlettered passerby looking up, here was somebody "writing notes" to Mami Wata or rendering a "spiritual account" for her inspection.[81]

Taken together, these written and oral testimonies help to build a composite picture of the ways in which Mami Wata functioned in the social imaginary of different classes of Onitsha citizen in the 1910s, 1920s and 1930s. Putting the numerous pieces of Stuart-Young's identity together, nonelite Igbos would have seen unmistakable associations with the water spirit. Most obviously, he was childless, lacking a spouse, wealthy, in possession of occult knowledge, successful as an entrepreneur, and popular with children. His white skin probably helped these connections to cohere, evoking an archaic "Mami-Wata-as-European," or "Mami-Wata-as-Foreigner" image.[82] In addition, the votary's voice is frequently distorted or contorted, silenced, or "electrified" in communications with Mami Wata, who often speaks to her worshippers through spiritual "telephones."[83] Stuart-Young's frequent bouts of laryngitis, particularly his prolonged illness in 1938, would have confirmed the rumored connection, alongside the secretive séances he was rumored to hold at his house. Finally, the water spirit is frequently symbolized by the boa constrictors or Eke pythons surrounding her as companions or entwined in her hair. Drawn from Indian and German images of snake charmers and from Hindu prints, which occasionally featured a male rather than a female figure, this image would have strengthened people's association of "Eke Young" with Mami Wata.[84]

Several questions remain unanswered within this story of Stuart-Young's "marriage" to Mami Wata, however. When was he initiated and by whom? If he was not initiated locally, why was there such a pervasive perception—and memory—of him as a "wife" of the water deity? Why did he deny it when it served as an acceptable, persuasive explanation for his sexual eccentricity?

Stuart-Young's three Igbo names—Odoziaku, Eke Young, and "wife" to Mami Wata—are connected by their shared emphasis on the generation of wealth, and the latter two names highlight the ways in which wealth can be harnessed through spiritual or occult forces. For Onitsha townspeople, the trader's everyday behavior exceeded the boundaries of conduct for an ordinary colonial businessman. Through their range of names for him, people could study and debate Stuart-Young's spiritual and earthly biography. Many of the ambiguities and outright violations of community codes that were observed in Stuart-Young could be explained, if not actually resolved, through these names, especially the connection with Mami Wata.

Here was a powerful case of the reversed gaze in the colonial encounter. Stuart-Young was regarded anthropologically by West Africans. His life, his work as a trader, and his writings were interpreted in terms of what the literary critic Simon Gikandi describes as "a reversed gaze at the culture of Englishness."[85] The African nicknames for Stuart-Young gain additional significance in this context, revealing the process of "Africans gaz[ing] at Englishness" even as the Englishman gazed back at them.[86] As a self-conscious representative of British culture, Stuart-Young helped Igbo market traders and local people to understand the metropolis in their own terms; his conversations and dealings with Igbos enabled the localization of discourses about Africa and imperialism. In this, he helped Africans to comprehend the terms in which European configured them and formulate their own "grammar of difference" in response.[87]

Whether he knew it or not, his association with the sacred python and the water spirit made Stuart-Young's life a great deal easier in Onitsha. In particular, his "marriage in the water" made it possible for this single, childless, boy-loving man to live a Uranian lifestyle without being labeled perverse or abominable. His desire was re-centered—some might say shrouded in myth—through Mami Wata, taken out of his body and deposited in the River Niger. This is not to say that he could live without comment in this colony, however: his behavior both as Eke Young and as a "wife" of Mami Wata was closely monitored and discussed by an expectant, observant local community, who studied and discussed all the signs of his sexuality without necessarily isolating it as a singular phenomenon.

The story that emerges in this chapter through the recollections of Onitsha townsfolk reveals the success of Stuart-Young's efforts to produce himself for posterity. Stuart-Young asked to be remembered as a bourgeois literary gentleman and philanthropist, especially after the failure of his business in the Great Depression. His Igbo names, which continue to circulate today, supplement these self-representations, adding layers of meaning to the names he produced for himself.

The African community's names for Stuart-Young are replete with markers of his difference from the norm. They reveal the efforts and negotiations of local adults and children as they sought to understand the foreign body in their midst. The people of Onitsha opened up powerful alternative identities and realms of interpretation for Stuart-Young, accommodating him even as they carefully marked his violations of local social norms. As a result of the careful local naming procedures described in this chapter, Onitsha gave Stuart-Young the opportunity to explore his Uranian desires. Given the intimate connection between writing, naming, and (homo)sexuality in his case, it is possible that the stream of memoirs, articles, poems, and novels he produced in his lifetime could not have been written from any other location than Onitsha, a town positioned *outside* the hegemonic sexual and social identities of industrial imperial Britain.

The ways in which the different strata of Igbo society responded to Stuart-Young offer vital insights into local constructions of the intimate encounters between Europeans and Africans in the early twentieth century. An important moment in the history of imperial sexualities is marked by the naming processes described in this chapter. What emerges from this diverse oral archive of names is that Stuart-Young's self-naming was a form of masking, a way of not remembering his own social and sexual biography. Such forgetfulness, or self-forging, reveals much about the constraints of class and sexuality in imperial Britain at the turn of the twentieth century. Meanwhile, his Igbo names are a way, albeit ambiguous and allusive, of not forgetting. These names serve a vital function in the reconstruction of eastern Nigeria's cultural history in the colonial period, complementing textual sources of information such as Stuart-Young's own writings for the elite, African-owned newspapers, to which the next chapter turns.

6 ⌇ The Strange Toleration of Stuart-Young in the African-Owned Press of Nigeria

STUART-YOUNG USED HIS STATUS as an author and local personality to enter West African newspaper culture center stage. For two and a half decades between the 1910s and late 1930s he occupied numerous spaces in African-owned newspapers, including letters pages, poetry corners, occasional columns, and columns of his own.[1] A turning point in his writing career occurred between 1921 and 1923, when he left his thriving palm oil business in the hands of Igbo staff and spent sixteen months lodging with African friends in Tinubu Square, Lagos, as a full-time writer.[2] His output increased so dramatically in this period that *every* English-language Nigerian newspaper, and most Ghanaian newspapers, received a large volume of submissions on an almost daily basis, and a political voice emerged in these articles that reached far beyond the walls of the aesthete's ivory tower. So pervasive was his presence at this time that on several occasions letters from the more politically engaged and confrontational palm oil trader Odeziaku appeared side by side with letters signed by Stuart-Young in his capacity as poet, philosopher, and intellectual.[3] Indeed, Odeziaku seems to have had a rather ambivalent relationship with J. M. Stuart-Young, referring to him in one letter to the *Nigerian Eastern Mail* as "the little J. M. of Onitsha," author of "clinching couplets."[4]

Much of this work, however, expresses racially derogatory views about Africans. Probing the reasons why so many of these articles and poems were accepted for publication by African editors, this chapter considers Stuart-Young's role in the newspaper culture of the period and the reasons why this white man was able to carve out a niche market for himself in the West African press. How did his writing mesh with, or stand apart from, the burgeoning anticolonial journalism of the 1920s and 1930s?

In his descriptions of local communities in the 1920s and 1930s, Stuart-Young's writing abounds with negative Eurocentric stereotypes of Africans: "For they are children, / Frank children one and all," he wrote in the poem "I Love the Forest."[5] Changing his viewpoint very little over the years, he commented in 1937, "I might best compare the Black man's realm of the unconscious to a child's money-box. That many of the coins are base metal, we know too well—[they reveal] hideous forms of superstition and juju, and all the horrors of fetishism."[6] An early poem, "African Nights," which was reworked and reprinted many times in succeeding decades, described African dancers as "Poor dusky children! Moving to the beat / Of clam'rous tom-tom and the heated song."[7] Requiring the poet's paternalistic moral intervention for their improvement rather than the palm oil trader's cheap imports, these dancers "chant the lust of gain, / Clap hands for baubles and to dross propend."[8] Another anthropological poem that Stuart-Young republished regularly was entitled "The Great Ju-Ju of Ibo" (also published as "The Great Fetish of Ibo, Southern Nigeria"), whose opening lines were "Look upon this loathsome Thing, / Hideous in its Grovelling!"[9] "Afric, awake! Awake!" the poet cried repeatedly,[10] dismissing the very ceremonies and dances West African cultural nationalists worked so hard to accommodate in the newspapers that carried Stuart-Young's verse.

Stuart-Young remained on the side of Englishness and empire in much of his newspaper writing, firmly believing in Africa's need for "the benevolent supervision of European Government," over and against what he referred to as the "satanic" fetishism of precolonial Africa.[11] The lands under British control are "all for the mere 'taking,'" he wrote, seeing the empire from a typical trader's perspective as containing "undreamed of wealth of Nature's Bestowing!"[12] Showing little sense of Europe as a repressive force in West Africa, he believed in the ideal of a cosmopolitan empire and that "our rule has brought peace and security, where once there was unrest and war."[13]

These negative representations of precolonial Africa are informed by Stuart-Young's belief that "individually, the Negro is eminently tolerable. In the mass . . . he becomes primitive man at primitive man's worst. He may then be devilishly cruel, and he may take fire at a spark. Lacking leadership, there is a genuine Negro menace in West Africa."[14] Many of his poems and articles describe the backwardness and childlike qualities of African communities. Praise for the "loyalty" and "innate cheerfulness" of such people is accompanied by infantilizing statements such as "[The African] is very like the little dog that comes waddling toward you with both tail and rump eagerly squirming, in an earnest desire for recognition,"[15] or "He is a child, and is taking a long time to grow up! Maybe, like Peter Pan, he will never grow up!"[16]

Stuart-Young's use of the common Victorian concept of imperial authority as parental seems designed to emphasize his own identity as a literary gentleman in the colonial world in order to enhance his status as a writer who represents Africans to themselves. Given his self-proclaimed sexual identity as a boy-loving man, however, his construction of Africans as "children" and his references to the character Peter Pan reveal the way in which his discourse accommodates imperial control within his own youth-oriented form of sexuality.

Many of his articles for the West African newspapers are filled with similarly patronizing cultural and racial stereotypes, all of which seem out of place in these African-owned publications. One wonders how local editors could have tolerated these opinions, especially in the affirmative, Pan-Africanist atmosphere of Nnamdi Azikiwe's *West African Pilot* and Duse Mohammed Ali's *Comet* but also in regional newspapers such as the *Nigerian Eastern Mail* (Calabar) and the *African Advertiser* (Calabar). Rarely, however, was Stuart-Young castigated by African editors or readers in their responses to his deluge of articles and poems. Quite the reverse. Indeed, on one occasion, after an item in the *African Messenger* on the topic of African education in which Stuart-Young described literate youths as forming a criminal fraternity, an African reader named "Reform" wrote from Lagos: "I wish to thank Mr Stuart-Young from the bottom of my heart for his able article in your last issue . . . on the failure of the present system of education."[17] This letter-writer added, "Our hatred of manual labour and our love of sensuality and luxury habits we have copied *in toto* from Europe, are the cause of all our trouble."[18] What prevents "Reform" from total subservience to Eurocentric racial stereotypes in this example is that he locates the source of the problem not in a "primitive" Africa but in a decadent, degenerate Europe whose influence must be resisted in the colonies. A cultural nationalist reading is thus enabled by Stuart-Young's work.

In 1926 and 1927, Stuart-Young wrote several articles that contributed to the lively ongoing debate about changes to colonial education policies, particularly regarding the teaching of the English language in elementary schools.[19] Stuart-Young took the side of most African participants in the debate, who supported the use of the English language in classrooms rather than the vernacular education the British government supported; he insisted on English-language instruction in all schools. His reasons, however, were somewhat different from those of his African counterparts, who believed that vernacular education would exclude them from the white-collar workforce. Stuart-Young wished to ensure that Africans continued to gain access to the beauties and poetry of a "superior" language over and against their own "hideously narrow" and "tribal" languages. "It is contact with a higher culture which can alone broaden the outlook," he wrote, describing the literature of local cultures as a "sorry exhibition of parables, animal-stories, sexual-babblings and senily [sic] inconsistencies."[20] Subjected to such stories, Africans would remain "not far removed from Neanderthal man . . . always subject to Devil Worship, witchcraft, 'ju-ju.'"[21]

Rather than offering a defense of the cultures and civilizations represented by Nigeria's vernacular languages, the editor of the *African Messenger* intervened at the end of this opinionated, dismissive article, not to comment on Stuart-Young's negative image of Africa, but simply to correct Stuart-Young on a factual error: "We are afraid our correspondent has gone a little off the track," he wrote, "and has repeated the mistake which many people have made in confusing the Education Bill with the Memorandum issued by the Colonial Office Advisory Committee."[22]

The lack of censure for Stuart-Young's assertion of cultural superiority derives from the way in which African-owned newspapers functioned in the early to mid-colonial periods. From the 1880s onward, African editors defined their publications as organs for public debate and education rather than simply as vehicles for the communication of news or editorial ideology. Many newspaper columns were specifically designed to trigger discussion among readers, while others were aimed at educating readers in grammar, logic, mathematics, and history, shadowing the secondary school system for those who wished to sharpen their minds but lacked the resources to stay in school. "The Press deserves its name," ran a reflective editorial in the *Nigerian Eastern Mail* in December 1937: "(1) It gives a chance to all to voice out their feelings. (2) It corrects some of our defects. (3) Its weekly publications are of the great[est] interest and educative value to the general public. A real instructor and director to the Africans."[23]

This self-conscious definition of the newspaper exemplifies the role of the African-owned press in colonial West Africa.[24] Operating in a triple role as conveyer of news, educator of autodidacts, and platform for public debate, the African-owned press could fairly ask its readers, "Now, dear ladies and gentlemen, are these articles not interesting and educative when properly considered and put into practice and not just for mere reading sake?"[25]

Concord with this position came from the readers' side throughout the 1920s and 1930s, for articles were expected to be "interesting and educative" at all times. In 1930, a letter to the *Nigerian Observer* of Port Harcourt from one "Jack Never Fear" insisted that readers subscribe to the journal "for the purpose of gathering better informations [sic] than theirs for the formation of their character whilst they also have got important subjects to forward to you for publication and general discussion which at the end may tend as pathway to moral and intellectual advancement."[26] In 1931, a reader in Aba wrote to thank the *Observer* for "the great help I have derived by reading your valuable journal," particularly for the weekly "Tutorial Course" in English and arithmetic, which had "inspired me with new hope and purpose."[27] Another reader of the same journal offered a long list of positive qualities in the newspaper, including: "(3) That the 'Brain Rousers' week by week afford all classes valuable lessons on General Intelligence. (4) The cable news [from England] makes one feel as if he were in England or on the continent."[28] Reader participation was thus a defining principle of the African press: editors encouraged readers to put their literacy to good use and write in on a wide range of issues. This, in turn, sustained the sales of particular newspapers, for readers became involved in textual communities, purchasing newspapers in order to follow and participate in the progress of topical debates.

Two topics, marriage and education, fueled a greater amount of literary activity than any other in the African-owned press throughout the colonial period. These topics drove the pistons of local print cultures and formed the primary themes of early West African novels. As Ann Laura Stoler and other "new imperial historians" have shown, both of these topics were vehicles for the expression of tensions between local and imperial codes and values in the colonial period.[29] Stuart-Young's social and political writings must be interpreted in this context if we are to explain the apparent anomaly of the local accommodation of his dismissive views. While there were occasional complaints against his racially superior attitude, rarely was he perceived to be anti-African. Indeed, his deliberately controversial statements on the themes of monogamous marriage and the education of Africans were probably included by editors precisely because they inspired debate and discussion in the letters pages, attracting subscribers to the journal and involving people in the emergent civil society of their country.

Rather than causing dismay among local African readers, Stuart-Young's articles set him on a collision course with two important European institutions: the Catholic Church and the colonial administration. As a local poet and prominent "personality," he conferred on himself the authority to comment publicly on any matter of morality, ranging from African marriage patterns to the intricacies of Christian doctrine, from changes in the colonial education syllabus to the ethical values that should underwrite British imperialism. Stuart-Young used the African-owned newspapers to elaborate on all these topics and more, and, to the excitement of African readers, again and again he fell foul of the Church and the imperial government. He openly supported the ideas of the race activist and leading Pan-Africanist thinker W. E. B. DuBois, and he opposed racial discrimination against Africans in the colonial civil service.[30] He vocally opposed the imposition of produce taxes on

Nigerian consumers and traders and complained persistently against government bureaucracy and the "parasitism" of white civil servants who retired early on fat pensions.[31] He often also rejected racial categories in favor of the "brotherhood of man" and "our *oneness*, our identity . . . our common humanity."[32] These views earned him great prestige, not only among West Africans but further afield, to the extent that in 1925 one reader in Dominica submitted the following eulogistic poem to the *Gold Coast Leader*, entitled "To J. M. Stuart-Young, Esquire, Poet and Author":

> Greetings I send to thee, broad-minded Englishman,
> Greetings kind and true, from Afric's lowly son;
> Honour you well merit, honour you have won,
> Fairly you plead the case of the down-trodden African.
>
> Oh, so many abuse the "Children of the Sun,"
> As if we are the scums [sic] of this poor earth;
> Few Englishmen like you admit our worth,
> But we with hearts quite stout go marching on.
>
> Care not one whit about those who look with disdain
> At you while you labour for the unfortunate,
> Your work is just, therefore never from it refrain.
>
> Go onward still, ever follow the cause that straight
> Your deeds however small be they won't be in fain [sic]
> Rewarded surely thou wilt be sooner or late.[33]

As an individualist in West Africa—an individualist, moreover, who had fled British sexual codes and prejudices into the "open air" of Nigeria—Stuart-Young opposed the institutional presence of the Church and its apparent interference in local people's sexual relationships. By the late 1920s he defined himself as a "Free Thinker," from which platform he suggested that "the black man would have been weaned from superstition" far earlier had it not been for the Christian missionary, who "makes utterly unsupported statements" about God and marriage.[34] In a direct attack on Roman Catholicism in the late 1930s, Stuart-Young stated, "The African, taken by and large, has no conception of what monogamy means," adding that church marriage contributes "heavily to crime."[35]

In exasperation, Father William L. Brolly, principal of Christ the King College between 1933 and 1937 and member of the Roman Catholic Mission in Onitsha, wrote articles for the *Nigerian Daily Times* and the *African Advertiser* in which he attempted to dampen Stuart-Young's confidence about his commentary on theological issues. "No subjects are more filled with pitfalls for the dilettante dabbler than Religion and Philosophy," Father Brolly snapped at the end of 1937, attempting to close the exchange but also unwisely labeling Stuart-Young an "Orange bigot" for his anti-Catholic opinions.[36]

One can sense an undeclared class struggle occurring between the Irish priest and the English trader over the same patch of African territory. Their public clash reveals both men's struggle to create themselves in colonial Onitsha and to produce the ethnographic category of "the African" for African readers. Brolly embarked on a typically Christian interventionist approach to African cultures, urging people's transformation away from old customs. Meanwhile, Stuart-Young adopted a romantic stance in which Africans were regarded as childlike and innocent, living like Peter Pan in a static Neverland.

For local readers, however, most of whom came from the mission-educated elite and sub-elite, the two men's struggle highlighted the ideological fractures separating European men of different professions or classes from one another. Their public disagreement would have revealed to readers that European "knowledge" of Africa was not stable or coherent and that imperialism was not a monolithic discourse but one ruptured by disagreements about the very definition of "Africa."

To the great delight of these readers, who fueled the debate and took sides with letters and follow-up articles in subsequent months, Stuart-Young refused to back down. In response to one of Father Brolly's articles, he went on the offensive against the same target once again, asking "What a celibate priest can know, by personal experience, of the state of marriage?"[37] Accusing the Catholic Church of "inflexibility" and "hypocrisy" and declaring that "Rome reeks of superstition [and . . .] Mumbo Jumbo," he reiterated his opinion that the African was incapable of sustaining monogamous unions "at this period of his development."[38] Stuart-Young sent copies of these personalized attacks on Brolly and the Catholic Church to newspapers throughout West Africa, exploiting his extensive, well-established network of journalistic contacts from the Gold Coast to Nigeria.

The "Odeziaku versus Brolly" argument provided great entertainment to Nigerian readers for many months, and it helped sustain and spread the debate about monogamous Christian marriage, which flared up repeatedly throughout the 1930s in the pages of West African newspapers. The *Nigerian Daily Times* supported Brolly, earning an accusation of pro-Catholic bias from Stuart-Young.[39] The *Nigerian Eastern Mail*, by contrast, carried correspondence praising Stuart-Young as a "freethinker," an antagonist of the Church, and a role model for Nigerians.[40]

Stuart-Young's place in West African newspaper culture as a trigger for discussion among readers and an antagonist of colonial institutions helps explain why there were so few complaints about his assertions of English cultural superiority. In the wake of his articles on education, for example, in which he dismisses African languages as incapable of expressing beauty, one reader's letter to the *Gold Coast Leader* hailed Stuart-Young as "the highest man above all others staying in this country West Africa."[41] Instead of complaining about the white man's patronizing descriptions of educated Africans and his labeling of them as "criminals," the writer, "Ofidendewah," points out that "Stuart-Young has become a household word in West Africa, and deserves to be so," for he is "one of the luminaries of this spiritually and morally dark age."[42]

The forgiving local assessment of Stuart-Young also included additional nontextual considerations alongside factors relating directly to the contents of his articles and poems. To appreciate the enthusiastic local reception of Stuart-Young in the colonial context, it is necessary to understand the ways in which he figured as a literary "personality" in West Africa, for he did not exist simply as words on a page. Rather, he was featured in newspapers as an exceptional white man who was openly "for the Africans." Known to be a friend of African political leaders, a regular public speaker at African clubs, and an opponent of repressive colonial legislation, his very appearance on the pages of the anticolonial newspapers sent out signals of his pro-African political alignments. In addition, he regularly made statements in which considerations of social class erased racial categories, replacing essentialist labels of identity with class as a starting point for progress and transformation. Class is a vital element in the way Stuart-Young connected with the elite African community. For example, he wrote:

> I am with the Negro race, to the death, in an effort to break down these rotten traditions of superiority! Until the Ruling Classes recognise that they share the same blood as the Poor; and until they realise that they are in a position of *Trust* and not one of Power; I shall continue to assault their stronghold by every means at my command. . . . It is absurd for the white man to hold that the mere colour of skin makes a difference.[43]

This reading of race through the vector of class enabled Stuart-Young to engage with Pan-Africanism by identifying Africans as an exploited class and to urge a "hand-in-hand" approach to liberation rather than a racially separatist path to independence. The problematic sentiments in his articles on African education and marriage may therefore have been interpreted locally as challenges designed to stimulate debate and stir up colonial categories rather than as racist assertions of African inferiority.

For readers who ardently disagreed with Stuart-Young's sentiments, he was simply sidelined or ignored as an irrelevant voice. "The space granted to Mr Young in our local papers could be used by him to show his talent as a reputed fictionist and lyric-writer," suggested Charles Ndaguba in a nonaggressive expression of opposition to Stuart-Young's position in the marriage debate.[44] The ardent cultural nationalist and contributor to the Gold Coast press Kobina Sekyi never once mentioned Stuart-Young in his many articles, despite Stuart-Young's public admiration for him and the frequent appearance of their poetry side by side in the "Poet's Corner" of the *Gold Coast Leader*.[45] A striking instance of their uneasy juxtaposition occurs in the *Gold Coast Leader* of 19 November 1921, where Stuart-Young's music hall–inspired poem "I Go Down into My Garden" describes how "Ev'ry dew-drench'd spray of lilac shines blue-black against the sky," while on the same page Sekyi's anticolonial poem "To Albion" repudiates England for its imperial "pride o'ergrown."[46] The organic garden of one becomes the "overgrown pride" of the other. On this day, Sekyi's work is followed by two poems by Stuart-Young, for "I Go Down into my Garden" and "A Winter Love Song," with its line inspired by Sir Harry Lauder, "Yet you're dreaming in the gleaming," occupy the remainder of the column.[47]

For other West African journalists, the maverick white man of Onitsha was simultaneously given a place in the region's literary culture and positioned outside the most important current debates. In an article entitled "My Friend 'Odeziaku,'" Zik (the *West African Pilot*'s Nnamdi Azikiwe) cleverly dismissed the social and political commentator by praising the abilities of the poet. "As a poet Dr Stuart-Young is one of the leading poets of the century," he wrote, grossly overrating the literary abilities of his friend; but, he continued, "as a student of international politics 'Odeziaku' is miles away from the realities of diplomacy."[48] In this manner, Stuart-Young was placed firmly back into an ivory tower and cautioned not to emerge from it too rapidly in future.

Similarly, in an article for the *Gold Coast Times*, the anticolonial journalist Kobina Kwaansa carefully negotiated between Stuart-Young's position as a white man who could not fail to be implicated in an imperialist mentality and his positive local reputation as "adept in interesting himself alike in local journalism as in journalism elsewhere . . . all alone out of many others of his colour in these parts."[49] Kwaansa contrasted Stuart-Young's reputation as pro-African and a promoter of the "brotherhood of man" with a recent article in which Stuart-Young wrote a paragraph "purposely deriding the 'educated African,'" whom he accused of criminality, arrogance, laziness, and corruption.[50] Nevertheless, Stuart-Young is accommodated by this most Pan-Africanist of journalists, who wrote, "If memory serves, it was this same Mr Stuart-Young himself who once wrote that the African can do without the white man, and not vice versa."[51]

Kwaansa's reference to Stuart-Young's previous publications demonstrates that he collected back issues of newspapers and may have formed his own archive of cuttings. He is probably remembering Stuart-Young's series of articles inspired by Marcus Garvey, entitled "The Negro at Home," published in the *Gold Coast Leader* throughout the second half of 1922. In this series, Stuart-Young inserted short paragraphs in which European colonialists were addressed directly and critically: "The genuine aboriginal negro," he wrote, "does not need you. Most certainly he has no parasitic intentions."[52] In another contribution to the series, he wrote, "I, for one, am proud to call [the African] friend and brother."[53]

Kwaansa was not alone in his use of the press as an archive, for West African newspapers served as proto-libraries for many readers. Newspapers were far more than fleeting texts for readers, to be disposed of once they were out of date. From the earliest days of African newspaper production in the 1880s, the press would serialize books on topics relating to the region as well as articles and stories culled from the English-language press in Britain and neighboring West African countries. Lengthy publications by Pan-Africanists and by anthropologists and colonialists would be serialized—sometimes stretching over a two-year period—alongside British popular novels such as Amy Baker's *Never Laugh at Love*, which was serialized in the *African Advertiser* throughout 1937. A broad range of political opinion was represented in these serializations. With little apparent conflict of interest, fiercely Pan-Africanist publications from West Africa and the United States, including work by Kobina Sekyi and W. E. B. DuBois, would appear alongside pro-colonial publications from Britain, such as Sir Harry Johnston's offensive anti-Liberian piece "Why a Nigger Republic Must Fail."[54] In this way, regular subscribers to the newspapers could build up their own collections of a wide range of texts from diverse ideological perspectives relating to their history and region.

Readers did not simply compile their own private libraries from newspaper serializations. Keen students of the press also retained occasional articles and correspondence that had been published many years before in a wide array of journals. For instance, in a letter to the *Nigerian Observer* in November 1930, one reader called "Manu" makes reference to an article by Stuart-Young published in the *Nigerian Daily Times* nine years earlier, on 21 October 1921, that exposed the "hard facts" about the European trade combines.[55] Stuart-Young had recommended that African producers and consumers boycott the combines in 1921, and the time had come, Manu concluded, to implement Odeziaku's wise idea.[56] This practice of retaining quotable items for future reference was common in the 1920s and 1930s, revealing the ways in which West African readers processed and carefully filed what is regarded in the West as the most ephemeral of printed forms. Newspapers thus fulfilled a vital intellectual role in West Africa, providing factual information that readers used as reference material to research and write their own articles.

Taken together, Stuart-Young's three decades of journalistic writing reveal the rise to authority of a spirited public intellectual. From his earliest literary productions, including *Osrac, the Self-Sufficient* in 1905, a loud cry for recognition reverberates through his writing. He finally achieved this goal in the West African press. Whether he incited rejection and anger, as in the case of Father Brolly, or applause, as in the many tributes to him published by African readers, for nearly three decades Stuart-Young operated at the center of West African newspaper culture. Here, in the space of the African newspaper column, he achieved his passionate lifelong desire for acceptance as a poet and an intellectual. Increasingly opinionated and maverick in his views, he was neutralized and toned down by tolerant African readers, who absorbed his contributions into their own discursive frameworks and made use of his racial polemics to activate debate. As the next chapter will reveal, however, Stuart-Young did not write exclusively on African topics, and as the years passed, he became increasingly preoccupied with the circumstances of his birth and upbringing in Manchester, returning repeatedly to the back streets of Ardwick in an effort to reimagine and comprehend the intersections between social class and male sexuality.

7 ⌁ A Class Apart

"Johnny Jones" of Back Kay Street

> Here is John Jones growing more impatient than ever because hungrier, who wonders if he is to wait for a dinner until the Social Revolution has arrived. What are we to do with John Jones? That is the question. And to the solution of that question none of the utopians give much help.
>
> —William Booth, *In Darkest England and the Way Out*[1]

STUART-YOUNG LIVED A SOLITARY creative existence on his rural West African trading posts. Surrounded by the forests that had so impressed Henry Morton Stanley, the aspiring author finally claimed the social and intellectual freedoms denied to him at home: he set himself up as a scholar with houseboys and cooks to tend to his domestic needs, and in the cool evenings after work he wrote copious novels and memoirs in addition to poetry. What is striking about the narratives he produced is the way in which they are permeated by Back Kay Street. Stuart-Young may have escaped his urban environment for the supposed simplicity of Africa,[2] but his Manchester birthplace features in many of the prose texts he composed in West Africa.[3] On each occasion, his narrator comments that this mean, cramped little street has nothing to redeem it from the soul-destroying "drabness" of working-class life. Each time it is evoked, this place is shown to stifle the imagination of children, killing their creativity.

As the years passed, Stuart-Young produced a steady stream of slum writings, including two supposed "autobiographies" by his alter ego, the palm oil trader Jack O'Dazi, and two novels, *Johnny Jones Guttersnipe* (1926) and its sequel *What Does It Matter?* (1927). In these publications, as this chapter will suggest, Stuart-Young's exploration of the psychological damage that afflicted British working-class children is unusual for its sexually explicit detail. Nevertheless, reviewers praised the "strangely moving" and "sympathetic," "arresting," and "truthful" portraits of 1880s and 1890s working-class Manchester in these novels.[4]

In each of these narratives a formula emerges that barely changed with the decades and the different genres he chose. Stuart-Young writes the life story of a gifted, ambitious boy who is born in the slums of industrial England, rebels against his father, and rejects the city before reaching maturity. His intense sensitivity to noise, smell, pain, and sexual indecency make him unsuitable for city life, marking him out as an artistic genius and an innocent child. Here is a boy who "loves Beauty and . . . instinctively shrinks from all that is vile and brutal," although by the psychological labels that dominate these novels, this hypersensitivity also signifies his "degenerate" sexual type.[5] Having struggled in adolescence against an array of weaknesses caused by his genetic inheritance and sustained by his physical environment—including a tendency toward morbidity, homosexuality, onanism, and astheny—the boy realizes his potential as an individual only by leaving the slums behind and emigrating to the tropics. As the narrator of *What Does It Matter?* comments, "[f]ree will" can be obtained only by fleeing "those two mighty influences, heredity and environment."[6] The colonies thus contain far more than the promise of gold for this working-class youth.

In Stuart-Young's representation of Britain, the maxim is "You are going to be what society *lets* you be," for British class society prevents the poor boy's rise from the streets into the ranks of the literary elite.[7] This template occurs again and again in Stuart-Young's writing. In each case, Africa features as a redeeming pastoral force, a paradise found after the sexual innocence of childhood has been forcibly taken away in the city. Healthy English manhood, it seems, can be achieved only in a space that is both rural and imperial, radically opposed to the inner-city slum. A degenerate adult man can regain the purity of childhood only in the "simple" surroundings of Africa, exchanging his own lost world of childhood for its living equivalent among the people of the tropics.

In representing Africa's childlike innocence, Stuart-Young radically inverts the logic of the "darkest England" discourses discussed in chapter 1. Rather than regarding the "savage" as William Booth does, as the negative pole for comparisons with British slum-dwellers, Stuart-Young regards the *British* urban environment as the source of immorality, brutality, coarseness, and uncleanliness. Its antithesis is rural Africa: "People in England had asked me whether I do not feel sorry for the benighted condition of the West African savage," the fictional trader Jack O'Dazi comments in his "autobiography."[8] Turning the nineteenth-century discourse on its head, he cries, "Pity them? O fools and blind! The negro is morally clean—it is we 'civilised' guttersnipes, who are cursed with uncleanliness from the cradle to the grave!"[9] Such sentiments concur with the African cultural nationalist view of a degenerate Europe that was briefly discussed in chapter 6.

The first visual image to confront readers of *Johnny Jones Guttersnipe* is a carefully drawn map of the streets surrounding Ardwick Green in the 1880s and 1890s. In order to locate the protagonist in this "real" world, an arrow directs viewers to Back Kay Street, the birthplace and home of Johnny Jones (see fig. 14). This map accords perfectly with Ordnance Survey records for the period, where Back Kay Street is tucked into the narrow plot behind Kay Street like the afterthought of a Victorian town planner (see figs. 15–17). Back Kay Street, like Kay Street and the surrounding roads, was finally demolished in the sweeping slum clearances of the 1960s that left the map bare of all

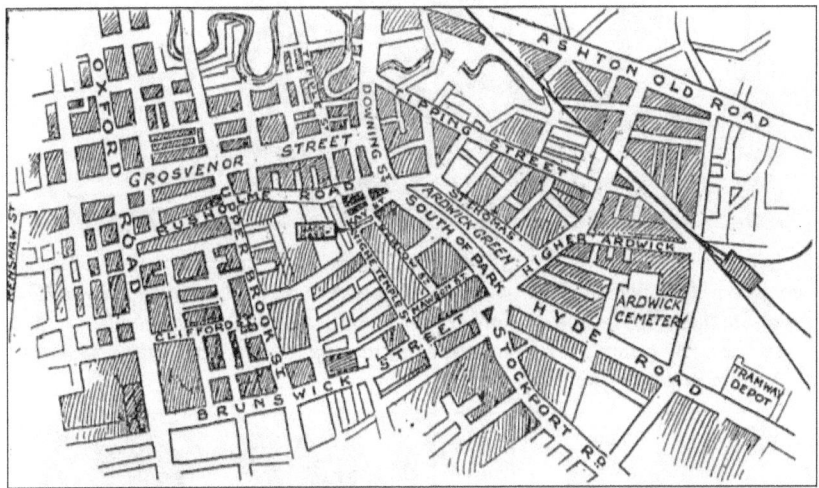

Fig. 14. *(above)* Map of Back Kay Street drawn by Stuart-Young *(from Johnny Jones Guttersnipe [London: C. W. Daniel, 1926]); fig. 15. (below)* Ardwick and Back Kay Street in 1932 *(reproduced from the 1932 Ordnance Survey map with the kind permission of the Ordnance Survey).*

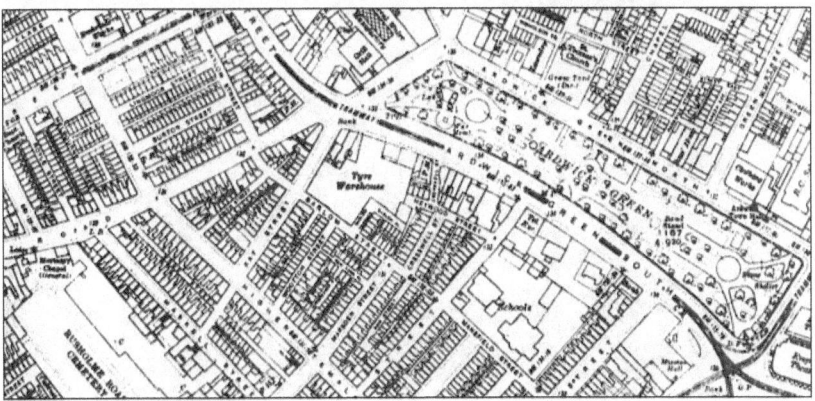

A *Class Apart* ⌐ 121

Fig. 16. (above) Typical dwellings in Ardwick, Manchester: Back John Street, 1902. *(By permission of Manchester Library and Information Service: Manchester Archives and Local Studies.)*; fig. 17. *(below)* Street scene from Ardwick, Manchester: 4–8 Union Place, 1902. *(By permission of Manchester Library and Information Service: Manchester Archives and Local Studies.)*

buildings until new housing estates and warehouses were built on the plots in the 1980s (see figs. 18 and 19).

Stuart-Young's map is remarkably accurate, helping to establish the parallel universe in which Johnny Jones moves, shadowing his author's biography. Like a clone of Stuart-Young, Johnny Jones is born on 3 March 1881 and raised at 13 Back Kay Street. He attends St. Thomas's School in Ardwick, a board

Fig. 18. (above) A view of Stuart-Young's neighborhood as it is today: Kale Street, which replaced Kay Street. *Fig. 19. (below)* Buildings on the site of Back Kay Street in 2005.

school for slum children with separate entrances for boys and girls (see figs. 20 and 21). His father is a middle-aged railway worker born in 1837; his mother, a washerwoman, dies in 1912; and his elder sister, born in 1879, dies of consumption when she is only fourteen years old. Upon leaving school, Johnny works in a series of tedious jobs animated only by his thefts and embezzlements of money. The young man is finally found out while working as a clerk at a mantle manufacturer's and sentenced to six months in Strangeways, from May to November 1899.

The Johnny Jones novels help us to piece together the life story of an enigmatic writer whose own memoirs remain wholly unreliable, filled with forgeries and exaggerations. By a curious inversion, the novels provide vital clues to major dates and events in Stuart-Young's life, competing with his memoirs for their accuracy.[10] Birth and death certificates for the Young family, as well as census and court records, reveal the historical accuracy of the information furnished by the novels. Given the reliability of the data, is it possible that these novels are authentic autobiographical accounts, the sole surviving documents of their kind from a life distinguished by its mass of forgeries, dreams, distortions, and fabrications?

Fig. 20. St. Thomas's School, Ardwick. (By permission of Manchester Library and Information Service: Manchester Archives and Local Studies.)

Fig. 21. Photograph of the boys' entrance, St. Thomas's School, Ardwick.

Unlike Stuart-Young's nonfictional publications, *Johnny Jones Guttersnipe* and *What Does It Matter?* contain no claims to great and illustrious friendships and no upper-middle-class school environments. Instead, they follow the story of one working-class boy in his efforts to break away from a script that is predetermined by his social background and location. No Oscar Wilde or Rudyard Kipling steps into the frame to whisk the young hero away on fantastic voyages. He grows into adolescence alone, with a guilty sense of his own sexual abnormality and an escalating loathing for his father.

Johnny Jones Guttersnipe and *What Does It Matter?* offer a realistic account of working-class life in late Victorian Manchester. Crammed with local detail, these novels present one of the most factually correct portraits of the author's life prior to his departure for West Africa. Stuart-Young emerges from behind his forger's mask into the light of autobiographical disclosure; he writes his own life story at long last, filled with sociological and domestic details about his experiences at home, school, and work in the 1880s and 1890s. Of all his published writings, these novels appear to confess *through* fiction to the author's experiences.

Described as "autobiographical novels" by the few critics who have commented on them, the Johnny Jones books positively reverberate with personal detail and disclosure, to such an extent that Timothy d'Arch Smith regards them as memoirs.[11] "The best source of information on his early life is his autobiographical novel, *Johnny Jones Guttersnipe*," agrees G. D. Killam, suggesting that this novel "offers, once we allow for its heightened dramatization and emotional hyperbole, a convincing re-creation of his growing up."[12] Reviewers of *Johnny Jones Guttersnipe* in 1926 expressed rather more ambivalence about its generic status. "It reads as though it were autobiographical, as *David Copperfield* was autobiographical," wrote one suspicious reviewer.[13] Reading through the lens of social science rather than fiction, a second reviewer commented that "it should be of interest to the sociologist and the psychologist."[14] The *Times Literary Supplement* review declared that while "this story makes no attempt at anything in the nature of a plot . . . yet it grips one nevertheless by virtue of the author's obvious sincerity and knowledge of his facts."[15] Given the absence of any diaries or reliable memoirs by Stuart-Young, it is certainly tempting to read these novels as fictionally encoded descriptions of the author's own childhood.

The task of unpicking fact from fiction is highly problematic, however, requiring the "unpicker" to act as an authority on precisely which strands are true and which have been fictionalized, to separate and straighten each narrative thread like an oakum picker working at a piece of rope. Additionally, at no stage did Stuart-Young invite readers to interpret the Johnny Jones novels as autobiographies. Even had he done so, his many memoirs testify to the unreliability of the life stories he narrated. We cannot simply trust the tales and read Stuart-Young's biography into his fiction. These novels occupy a hybrid status in between genres: they are ambiguously situated "factual fictions."[16]

Despite the multifarious markers of autobiographical authenticity in these novels, it is essential not to confer on Stuart-Young an authentic working-class identity and thereby situate him outside the ideological frameworks of his time. Whether fictional or autobiographical, working-class writing cannot be regarded as a pristine discourse offering unmediated access to an author's lived experience. Such an assessment would mistakenly and romantically situate working-class texts in a realm of lived experience, as if they were untouched by genre, popular culture, and the narrative techniques deployed in all writing. Rather, we should read Stuart-Young's so-called autobiographical novels as narratives that *enable* him to write his life story within the popular genres of his day.

Johnny Jones is an idealized version of the author, mediated by a nostalgic narrator who continually asserts the right of his protagonist to forge, fake, and thieve his way out of the slums. Thus, Johnny Jones cleverly embezzles money from his employer. Unlike Stuart-Young, who was tried for similar activities in 1899, Johnny uses the stolen £200 for benevolent ends, to pay for the upkeep of a Nonconformist mission hall on Nelson Street.[17] Previous embezzlements have been used in a similarly charitable manner, to purchase medication for his dying sister.[18] Thus, when Mr. Jones insults his son at the trial in the novel, calling him "tainted goods," a "disgrace" to the family, and a blot on his own "stainless" name, readers are likely to sympathize with Johnny junior, for his crimes have a wholly altruistic foundation.[19]

In court, Johnny is told by the magistrate that he should be proud of his hardworking father, whose name he has brought into disrepute.[20] If the two novels prove anything, however, it is that John Jones senior is the one who is "tainted" and "stained," a "disgrace" to his progeny who is personally responsible for both the hereditary and the environmental causes of the son's degeneracy. Johnny's soul, the narrator insists, has been "slowly murdered— murdered by the man who should have loved and protected him . . . !"[21] (ellipses in original).

The charitable use to which Johnny puts his stolen money adds layers of moral vindication to Stuart-Young's own real-life thefts, and in a final enlargement of his heroic status, the hero is placed into cell number C33, from where he takes on an uncanny resemblance to another, rather more famous "C33" who contemplated the Christ-like life from Reading Gaol.[22] Represented as Wilde in prison, incarnated through quotations from The Ballad of

Reading Gaol and *De Profundis*, Johnny is placed in a separate moral category from his fellow convicts.[23] In both clothing and manner he is marked out from them by his "deep hunger for th[e] spirit of Beauty."[24] Surrounded by "wholly repellent, wholly evil" working-class men in court and prison, he delights in the solitude of his cell, shut away from the "repugnant... automata" who surround him on all sides.[25]

By deliberately playing with the ambiguities between fact and fiction, Stuart-Young sets up a protective mask from behind which he debates and discloses the details of his youth. Justifying and idealizing his biography, the novels turn full circles around the axis of Stuart-Young's life, spinning new tales around the far less salubrious details of the author's Manchester youth.

The artistic rationale for his choice of the novel as a genre is offered at the end of *Johnny Jones Guttersnipe*, where the hero muses that "autobiographical self-expression whether in prose or verse, would be a sure way of assimilating the past into Art—the past, with all its privations and pains."[26] Constantly attempting to transcend poverty and pain in his art, Johnny Jones, like his creator, dismisses the genre of working-class autobiography for precisely the reasons that make it attractive to social historians. In Johnny Jones's view, the unrelenting descriptive realism required by autobiography locks an author out of the realm of the beautiful and prevents him or her from "creat[ing] one deathless song."[27] For the slum-born writer, the loyalty to facts and the past required by autobiography inhibits the "slowly lifting horizons" of the writer's ideals for a better future. Autobiographies from the slums therefore serve only to block the possibilities for their authors to break free from the past.[28]

In this, Stuart-Young acknowledges that social class is, in historian Peter Hitchcock's words, "not a thing but a relation and one that puts a heavy burden on representation."[29] To this idea that class operates within, not in isolation from, systems of representation, Stuart-Young adds that if writers choose naturalistic or autobiographical techniques, they confine themselves to the realm of mechanical reproduction: they exclude the artist's right to interpret and modify material, to explore the differences between "ideality and reality," thus preventing the introduction of passion and morality to Nature.[30] "Storytelling is not merely a matter of transferring information," the narrator of *Johnny Jones Guttersnipe* insists; "rather [it is] one of imposing 'atmosphere.'"[31] In a postscript to his earlier novel *Soul-Slayer* (1920), Stuart-Young makes a similar point, hailing fiction as the perfect form with "a striking difference from autobiography," for in fiction "the tedious ego is left out, and the reader is asked to sorrow or to joy before the fascinating shrine of Fancy instead of before the chilling altar of Fact."[32]

Situated in the context of working-class literature in the late-Victorian, Edwardian, and Georgian periods, Stuart-Young's novels reveal a great deal about how social class informs and generates modes of writing, ways of reading, and attitudes toward genre. The Johnny Jones novels contain fascinating details of one working-class autodidact's reading matter, and they constantly salute authors such as Dickens for crossing the boundaries of class, gender, and education by portraying "the other side of the shield."[33] Aged only twelve, the precocious Johnny Jones "already had dipped into the pages of Darwin's *Origin of Species* and *Descent of Man*. He had even tried to read Swift's *Tale of a Tub*. And Herbert Spencer's *First Principles* had held him literally spellbound."[34] Participating in the popular British debate about "good" and "bad" reading matter among the newly literate classes, Stuart-Young shows how his hero's degeneracy is fed by texts, for young Johnny Jones goes so far as to read what others regard as "immoral and harmful" literature, including the decadent poets of the 1890s.[35] In Strangeways, by contrast, the prison librarian provides Johnny with a steady stream of wholesome and uplifting nonfictional texts, including *Bacon's Essays*, *Macaulay's Prose Works*, a volume of *Good Words*, W. F. H. Lecky's *Map of Life*, and novels by R. L. Stevenson and J. M. Barrie. While the former texts—presented as immoral and harmful—contribute to Johnny's degeneration, the prison books help to morally "regenerate" the lad, preventing him from succumbing to sexual immorality.[36]

Teeming with literary references stretching from Dickens to Darwin, Charles Booth to Baudelaire, Tom Paine to Samuel Pepys, and describing many ordinary people as they read and respond to literature, the Johnny Jones novels disclose far more than the life story of a single boy. Debates about literary realism and the function of fiction subtly inform characters' comments. The prison librarian, for example, points out in response to Johnny Jones's request for slum fiction, "I would be censured by the committee if I requisitioned Realism for our heterogeneous readers in Strangeways Gaol."[37] Instead, he provides prisoner C33 with a steady stream of didactic literature containing maxims and religious tableaux for the young man's edification.[38]

Stuart-Young's refusal to write autobiography may also be explained as a refusal to be an object of study to others. In creating the characters of Jack O'Dazi and Johnny Jones, he can treat them as his own sociological specimens for dissection and analysis in the manner of a Victorian commentator. Thus, in his role as Jack O'Dazi's "editor" and as narrator of the Johnny Jones novels, Stuart-Young can analyze his protagonists and prescribe moral cures. "Johnny was not a really healthy specimen of the physical boyhood of slumland," the narrator-cum-sociologist interjects in an early scene-setting chapter of *Johnny Jones Guttersnipe*; "only half a dozen genuinely 'normal' traits would emerge in our hero's character."³⁹ "The reader has already spent several intimate hours inside this guttersnipe's home," the narrator continues, adding to the distancing effect by asking, "But has he quite understood the implications of what has been described? Has sufficient emphasis been laid upon the degrading restrictions of this poverty-stricken household?"⁴⁰

As Johnny's narrator, Stuart-Young can wear the mask of a middle-class sociologist and engage with popular theories of degeneration and redemption, showing how the removal of a "degraded" youth from society—to prison, or, preferably, to the tropics—effects a moral cure for sexually deviant behavior. Thus, within three months of his transplantation from Back Kay Street into Strangeways Prison, Johnny's feelings of abjection and enfeeblement transmogrify into a state of grace and liberty: he finds prison "inspiring and even stimulating."⁴¹ Paradoxically, "this calamity" of prison in fact "sav[es] him from the coils of his slum environment."⁴² Inside Strangeways, Johnny manages to achieve the class position that was denied to him outside; surrounded by books from the library trolley, plus paper and pens, with the luxury of "a room to himself" from where he can translate French lyrics and write his own poetry, he experiences "a wonderful joy" and can "breathe with open lungs" at last.⁴³ Peacefully picking oakum and cotton, he contemplates life, death, poetry, religion, and philosophy, musing on the meaning of his favorite poems by Wilde, Shelley, and Wordsworth and his favorite poets Robert Bridges, William Watson, and Arthur Symons.⁴⁴ In this manner, Stuart-Young mobilizes the story of working-class degeneracy found in Victorian slum-writing: he cuts it free from its fixed poles and demonstrates how congenital weaknesses can be corrected by a new environment.

Many of the ideas and explanations in these novels—including the hero's pervasive sense of self-disgust at his onanism—derive from nineteenth-century publications on sexual deviance. In an echo of the anti-masturbation discourse that characterized *Osrac, the Self-Sufficient*, Johnny "was continually tempted by the evil voices of the night to take a secret 'way out'—that 'way out' being one which might make of him a sexual pervert."⁴⁵ The novel also implies that masturbation is associated with the state of moral "dejection" that precedes homosexuality in adulthood, which itself leads to "mental instability—and the ward for imbeciles."⁴⁶ Johnny is a vivid illustration of the effects of Victorian moralists' sexual prohibitions, revealing the ways in which ordinary people's attitudes toward the male body altered in response to changes in popular morality.

Separated by thousands of miles and several decades from industrial Manchester and the 1890s, Stuart-Young looked back on his birthplace from Onitsha, and what he saw confirmed the views of nineteenth-century moral commentators, particularly their theories of childhood development in the slums. As the nineteenth century progressed, writings about poverty and class gained impetus from popular theories of degeneration. In particular, Stuart-Young's favorite plot line and vocabulary show the influence of Max Nordau's best-selling study of fin-de-siècle society, *Degeneration*, which was translated into English in 1895. Nordau launched ideas of morbidity and evolutionary regression that persuaded many readers that a physical and moral sickness was pervading urban society in Europe. He equated living in the modern city to "living on the edge of nervous collapse" and said that Europe's "decadent artists," including Oscar Wilde, derived their genius from their sexual abnormality.[47] Unhealthy, oversensitive specimens like artists and homosexuals were products of modern urban living, in Nordau's view, for the city flushed out an individual's inherited weaknesses.[48]

With a boldness that must have shocked many contemporary readers, Stuart-Young rejects innuendo and does away with prudery and shame. Influenced perhaps by the new sexual psychology of Sigmund Freud, his modern 1920s narrator explores childhood neurosis through scenes of parental intercourse as witnessed by the child. Stuart-Young looks behind the veils that Victorian sociologists placed over references to the copulating body in the slums. In so doing, he exposes what takes place at night behind closed doors in "darkest England."

Working-class children are shown to be morally and sexually corrupted from the outset of life, destroyed by their fathers, and denied the emotional head start enjoyed by middle-class boys whose private bedrooms protect them from their parents' night-time "horrors."[49] The narrator of *Johnny Jones Guttersnipe* comments:

> Only very poor children, cursed with some measure of sensitiveness and a reluctant familiarity with the leper-spots of life, know the terrible agony of waking in the night,—of waking to listen . . . to what should be a sacrament; a thing holy and mysterious as Creation itself: but which has, now and for evermore, degenerated for the hearer into a crime! It is Hell . . . ![50] (ellipses in original)

Fully conforming to the gender and degeneracy theories of his day, Stuart-Young paints a portrait of an introspective young man with a "tendency to girlishness and sentimentality" that is not checked in childhood, as it should have been.[51] The individual responsible for these traits is not the individual who manifests them, for John Jones senior has forged his son's soul. With the sexually active John Jones as his father, by the age of ten, young Johnny Jones has developed "an evil and unnecessary habit of squinting," "no instinct for play," and "the evil habit of private immorality," indulged in each time he overhears his parents having sexual intercourse in bed.[52] Immersed in this "cesspool" of adult sexuality and stricken with guilty self-loathing about his masturbation, the innocent boy is transformed from "a sensitive, dreamy and poetical child, blessed with the hope of genius, into a dull, devil-may-care, disenchanted sensualist, in revolt against he knows not what."[53] As in the O'Dazi autobiographies, published ten years earlier, there is no escape for the "guttersnipe" from the sexual taint surrounding him. Nature and nurture conspire to corrupt and ensnare the innocent slum child and distort the healthy sexual morality of the adolescent boy. He is rendered "soft" by his environment and by continual masturbation. As the narrator points out, "to be 'soft' in the vernacular of the class into which Johnny Jones had been born meant utter unfitness for the struggle of life. It implied, although it did not understand the word, degeneration."[54]

With an innocent Adamic child at the center of the narrative, the concept of working-class respectability is overthrown in these novels, replaced by degeneracy as a category. Alcoholic drink symbolizes and symptomizes the moral state of this family, for when he is drunk the head of household wastes scarce resources and indulges in noisy sexual intercourse with his wife. Contrasting with those neighbors in Back Kay Street who have taken the pledge, "the dissolute habits of the head of the house" ensure the family's position on the wrong side of the thin line separating the upper working classes from the lower middle class.[55] Crucially, the father's alcoholism drains scarce household resources to such an extent that the mother is forced to take in laundry in the manner of a "lower working-class" woman, shutting herself in the cellar for ten hours' washing each day.[56]

Operating in territory where most middle-class moralists feared to tread, Stuart-Young's slum writings blow apart the myth of working-class respectability and deny the existence of "good character" among many working-class families. The household portrayed in the Johnny Jones novels is headed by a sadomasochistic and alcoholic man who, to put it mildly, lacks the "good character" ascribed to the upper working classes by observers in the nineteenth century. Bragging about his own honesty and respectability, with a jug of beer in his hand and a lecherous eye on his wife's body, John Jones senior is one of the most abusive adult men to appear in Stuart-Young's work; he seems to have been created specifically in order to ridicule the previous era's romantic representations of working-class decency and family life. Nevertheless, at his son's trial for embezzlement he rages:

> Have you thought of the disgrace that you have brought on me—on *me*, who have kept my stainless name throughout my life? A felon— my son a common felon! And with my example before you! Haven't I always trained you in the right way? Haven't you always been shown, both by precept and example, that honesty is the only policy?[57] (emphasis in original)

As readers see, however, the "real" Mr. Jones is the opposite of his self-representation, for even as Johnny's sister lies dying in the bedroom, "his father's sensuality found audible indulgence only a few yards away."[58]

In conjunction with the narrative of parental sexual intercourse, in *Johnny Jones Guttersnipe* and *What Does it Matter?* a less straightforward and more problematic arena of bodily contact arises: the contest between man and boy, or father and son. In both novels, the mature sexual body of the adult male is contrasted with the slender frame of the innocent boy, the former bearing down on the terrified latter. From the outset, Stuart-Young establishes the adult male body as grotesque, a source of contamination: "The child always remembered a gigantic body, with heavily rounded shoulders, and a massy red face," comments the narrator of *Johnny Jones Guttersnipe*. "The forehead was slightly bald at the temples; and the lips, brightly red, were generally pursed into a mocking smile. But the voice—the voice was one that never seemed to be anything but angry and scornful."[59] On each occasion, the child's-eye view of the mature male body is that of a threatening figure, repulsive for its size, color, and odor. John Jones senior is continually presented as a "gigantic figure . . . towering above him" and "a very mountain of humanity" from whom the boy shrinks in fear.[60]

To some extent, the power struggle between father and son takes place, in true Oedipal fashion, over the body of the mother. Johnny junior longs only "that his father should die," leaving son and mother together in solitude.[61] For Johnny, however, heterosexual desire can occur only in the abstract: "Woman, in the abstract, seemed to him like snow—a spotlessly pure white element, just so long as it lay untrodden and untouched. . . . But how dubious was its cleanness, when coarse hands had taken it into their grasp and heavy feet had trodden it into the mire!"[62] (ellipses in original). Judged by Johnny's "snow test," Mrs. Jones is always already contaminated because she is his mother. Rather than physically desiring his mother in Oedipal style, the son is repulsed by the female body, believing it to be contaminated once touched by the male. The active force in his fantasy is the father, not the mother. Mrs. Jones remains an entirely passive, unsexed figure in both novels, idealized as a worker and family carer but endowed with no separate qualities as a woman. Indeed, in her many sexual encounters with John Jones senior, witnessed in the bedroom by the son, Mrs. Jones is represented as a mere vessel for her husband's eroticism.

A disturbing narrative emerges around the competitive father-son couplet in which the older man physically and—symbolically at least—sexually abuses the boy. *Johnny Jones Guttersnipe* contains vivid descriptions of the corporal punishment meted out by the father to the son. With "malicious delight" and a "pout" on his lips, Mr. Jones approaches the prostrate boy in a long-drawn-out scene that does not require much decoding to take on sexual meanings:

> The bed-clothes were swept aside. The boy placed a protesting arm across his back. It was pulled viciously apart, and then both hands were pinned together at the top of his head, while a heavy knee fell across his feet. He was completely at his father's mercy, and the blows began to fall. . . . Johnny kept his face buried in the bed-clothes. . . . Then it appeared as if every inch of the flesh he possessed was on fire. He turned his head aside, and looked up at the underside of his father's face. . . . [H]is father had given himself over to the pleasure of his lust, and he would not leave off until his time was spent and his strength exhausted.[63]

Much of this disturbing scene is drawn verbatim from Stuart-Young's overtly sadomasochistic novel *The Soul-Slayer* (1920), in which the white father of a "half-caste" African boy indulges in such regular, pages-long, abuse of the son that the boy—disturbingly named Ibrahim after Stuart-Young's first African protégé—dies from his injuries. As with John Jones senior a decade later, the father in *The Soul-Slayer* is characterized by his lust as he symbolically enacts the rape of the boy. Both fathers are said by the narrator to have succumbed to a passion that is "wholly sensual and violent."[64] What shines through Stuart-Young's representation of these fathers is his extreme repulsion for the postpubescent male body.

In spite of the morally outraged tone of the narrator, the passages discussed above can be taken for a contribution to that which they overtly condemn, for the recurring scenes of adult male desire cannot easily be contained within the established genre of slum writing. Indeed, it is likely that they are included in Stuart-Young's novels as offerings to the group referred to by his alter ego, Jack O'Dazi, as "my paidophil friends," and hailed by Stuart-Young in the postscript to *The Soul-Slayer* as the Uranian subculture for whom he initially conceived that novel.[65] Aged forty-five when *Johnny Jones Guttersnipe* was published, Stuart-Young was so passionately committed to the ideal of boyhood innocence and boy-boy love that he deliberately ignored, or covered up, the potential of a more sexually active adult readership whose desire was precisely for the childish body of pubescent boys. Despite his frequent declarations of a nonphysical pederasty that revolved around textual admiration rather than carnal intervention, Stuart-Young succumbs to a sadomasochistic inclination in these repeated scriptings of men's violence against boys. In addition, it is impossible to ignore the fact that *The Soul-Slayer* and the Johnny Jones novels were written by a mature adult, a man effectively in possession of the body of the father.

So forceful is Stuart-Young's response to the father that in all his writing he rejects adult masculinity and spurns the intimacy and privacy of family life per se. The heterosexual family model is represented as an indecent institution, permanently degraded by the phallic, drunken patriarch. Its replacement is an asexual, classless form of man-boy and boy-boy companionship, a celibate version of the ideas of "comradeship" developed by Edward Carpenter and other Uranian writers.[66] In an imperial, class-conscious twist, Stuart-Young's narrator also suggests that had Johnny Jones attended one of the British public schools at which the curriculum included sports and games as well as art, he might have survived his morbidity to become an athletic male, "eager for Adventure" and fit for imperial service overseas.[67] As if in preparation for his own departure for the tropics, Johnny takes up cycling in an effort to exhaust his body and prevent the enervation he experiences as a result of his masturbation. Saved by the bike, the lad can now sleep through his parents' sexual intercourse, and "purity" reigns once again in his mind.[68]

Contrasting with the scenes of brutality by the father are scenes of nonpenetrative romantic passion between adolescent boys. In the course of *Johnny Jones Guttersnipe* and *What Does It Matter?*, readers are presented with three major relationships of the "beautiful" and "innocent" type: at age eleven or twelve, Johnny's "yearning went out to a boy, some six months his senior" at school, who had "fresh-coloured cheeks, curly brown hair, and the clearest of grey eyes," to whom he sent a "daintily flowered" Valentine's card.[69] Unlike his classmates, who indulge in homosexual "dirtiness," Johnny's difference is insistently marked out by the narrator, for "our hero stands apart from all in this group."[70] Johnny next feels a passionate attachment to a charismatic child-preacher with "flaxen curls and great wide blue eyes [with] a comic resemblance to the boy blowing bubbles, in Millais' canvas, which advertisements of Pears soap had made world-renowned."[71] A final moment of youthful passion occurs behind bars in Strangeways Gaol, where Johnny espies a "golden-haired child" named Rigsby, aged sixteen, with "curls [which] seemed to radiate the sunlight."[72] Upon discovering that Rigsby's crime is the rape of an adult woman, Johnny impulsively "kissed him full on the mouth."[73]

The narrator revels in describing these boy-boy romances between youths whose sexuality is confined to kissing and cuddling. Of course, the fact that these romantic scenes are written by a fully mature man disturbs the fine line between aesthetic appreciation and voyeuristic adult desire. Nevertheless, each of these relationships revolves around the aesthetic category of the beautiful, which is applied to the smooth frames of the adolescents and counterpoised to full adult masculinity. An idealized, aestheticized love is explored in these passages, which draw so heavily from Uranian celebrations of the youthful male body that the issue of the rape of women is glossed over. Thus, in the kissing scene with Rigsby, Stuart-Young is preoccupied with developing a sexual ideology in which "homo-passivity" is promoted. In their kiss, Rigsby's and Johnny's "two souls had spoken with the eternal and fearless language of love."[74] This moment marks the outer limit of male-male physicality for Stuart-Young, the point beyond which beauty and desire are made sordid by sexual penetration.[75] However, given the offense for which Rigsby is in prison, Stuart-Young's choice to describe the perfection of Uranian passion through him shows a myopia that verges on misogyny. He does not resolve this issue when he has the prison warder describe Rigsby as "the victim of some girl's wiles."[76] "In many of these rape cases," the Warder continues, "any fool of a judge might know it was the woman who tempted!"[77]

Spiritually uplifted by his period of joyful solitude in Strangeways, transformed into a "regenerate" man, Johnny Jones is thrust back into the world that revolted him when he is released.[78] He wanders the streets of Manchester in a state of alienation and purchases a newspaper in which he discovers the details of the Boer War, which has erupted in previous months. Meditating upon Africa on his way home, Johnny finds, "strange paradox! His heart was stirred by the enlargement of the British Empire," yet "this bloody quarrel with the Boers could not be called just."[79] Given Stuart-Young's rejection of industrialization and urbanization as corrupters of boyhood innocence, it is hardly a "strange paradox" that Johnny identifies with the white farmers of South Africa rather than the mining magnates and urban industrialists whose interests Britain was protecting in the conflict.[80] In this scene of newspaper reading, Stuart-Young shows how the colonies entered British people's imaginations in diverse and unpredictable ways. A new country and a new continent enter Johnny's mind through the newspaper he buys, giving the impression that this lad from the industrial midlands has a stronger sense of South Africa than of the imperial metropolis, which remains a remote location cut off from people's daily lives.[81]

Stuart-Young echoes the Victorian moralists' solution to the problems of poverty and degeneration in Britain by endorsing the popular rationale for emigration to the colonies. "Perhaps over there," Johnny enthuses, "he could find a new chance of prosperity and peace!"[82] "Father, I know that I am destined for Africa—to a country where the sun is warm and the skies are open and free," he announces upon reaching home. Africa is "a country [*sic*] where Nature is the motive power of action and where pretence is not called for; a country, moreover, where life is sane and healthy!"[83] Clearly, the moral regeneration of Johnny Jones cannot be carried out in Manchester. Siding with the white farmers of "darkest Africa" and leaving degenerate England behind, Johnny knows that he needs to inhabit "the peaceful and ample surroundings of a rural and undeveloped district" of Africa.[84] If this is a prescription for urban dwellers generally, Britain's morally and physically unhealthy white stock must be removed en masse and transplanted elsewhere, in a manner that conforms to William Booth's colonial "solution" for the inhabitants of "darkest England."[85]

Johnny Jones leaves for South Africa just as his author left for West Africa, carrying a suitcase containing books and manuscripts, a dinner jacket, and the photographs and autographs of the famous personalities he wrote to as a fan. A portable typewriter and a camp bed complete the African outfit.[86] Given the strength and passion of his exposure of the effects of the slums on children, it is hardly surprising that Stuart-Young grasped the first available opportunity to leave Britain.

It was only after many years in West Africa that he wrote the full story of Johnny Jones. In the novels discussed in this chapter, Stuart-Young sets up his own imperial version of the nineteenth-century moralists' scheme for the transformation of the working classes and their deliverance from sin. He severs each of his fictional heroes from his birthplace and "rescues" each one to Africa. This, perhaps, is Stuart-Young's most subversive gesture, for even as he benefited from the opportunities offered by colonial trade and imperial expansion, he inverted the logic of the European intervention in "savage" places, saving his degenerate heroes again and again by transplanting them to this purer place.

8 ⌇ The Production of a Poet

Stuart-Young's Verse and Its Readers

> The fake is often made worse by the theft of small turns of speech which though not in any sense irregular or grotesque, the poet has somehow made his own; it is like stealing marked coins, and it is a dangerous practice when posterity is policeman.... [T]he wise [poets] melt down the stolen coin and impress it with their own "character."
>
> —Graves, On English Poetry[1]

IN THE EARLY 1930S, just as his palm oil business crumbled under the impact of the Great Depression, Stuart-Young created yet another duplicate or substitute personality for himself. This figure may be regarded as the final and perhaps the most successful of his forgeries or multiple incarnations. Named "Dr. J. M. Stuart-Young" and appearing for the first time in print in 1934,[2] this character shares Stuart-Young's date of birth and address at the Little House of No Regrets in Onitsha, but he claimed to have been educated at Manchester Grammar School and the University of Durham, from where he held a doctorate in Rationalism (or Naturalism).[3] Additionally, he said he had held newspaper appointments on the *West African Review* and *West Africa*, belonged to the "Royal Society of Authors," and had expertise in "Occultism and African folklore."[4] This chapter explores the African responses to Dr. Stuart-Young's forged self-constructions and the ways in which Stuart-Young deployed his doctorate to try to control the direction of Nigerian literary culture.

One of the most striking features of Dr. J. M. Stuart-Young is the way he echoes, but also resolves, some of the most troublesome areas of Stuart-Young's previous incarnations. His maturity in years and his literary experience are asserted at every turn, and in this he may be seen as the polar opposite of the youthful author of *Osrac, the Self-Sufficient*, whose tentative self-vocalization depended on the idea of childhood genius awaiting recognition. A veritable English gentleman, this new manifestation presents himself as scholarly, mature, gifted as a poet, highly articulate, and sensitive to Beauty, Literature, Love, and Nature.[5] In this, he echoes the poet laureate Robert Bridges' famous statement that "the artist or poet is the man possessed by the idea of Beauty."[6] Such a man is anything but a palm oil ruffian in colonial West Africa.

In particular, Dr. Stuart-Young assimilates and reprocesses British and Igbo discourses about sexual deviance; he describes himself as disinterested in women, detached from society, interested in spiritualism, and emotionally sensitive.[7] Several of these qualities attracted laughter in court in 1899 for the young "John Mount Stewart Young" when he stood trial for forgery and embezzlement. These terms had added further layers of anxiety and guilt to the youthful narrator of *Osrac*'s sense of his own sexual abnormality. Later in his life, local people interpreted many of these attributes of Odeziaku of Onitsha as proof of Mami Wata's intervention in the trader's life. Now writing as a poet and an intellectual, Dr. J. M. Stuart-Young utilizes the very terms by which his deviance had been named in previous years. He transforms the signifiers of difference into the very definition of literary genius and describes how "repression of all natural desires, and abstention from sexual gratification may reasonably lead to [poetic] inspiration."[8] The true artist, he writes, is "a visionary character," a dreamer capable of discovering "something new and strange."[9] For Stuart-Young, the greatest poets are isolated outsiders, sexually inactive, sensitive souls who wander through natural landscapes and, in their poems, inspire readers with glimpses of exquisite beauty and inner truth.[10] This figure is anything but a man who cannot escape from carnality, guilt, and squalor.[11]

Stuart-Young's self-projection into the celibate Dr. J. M. Stuart-Young in the mid-1930s fulfilled his lifelong dream of standing a class apart from others. His Englishness is crucial to this self-construction. For many years he had held firmly to the view that "[w]e look forward with exultant pride to the rapidly-approaching hour when the whole world shall think and speak in our golden tongue."[12] Inspired by a host of "immortal" English poets, he developed this long-standing belief into a distinctive personality for himself and offered it for the consumption of West African readers, stepping forth as a public lover of literature, a sponsor and cultivator of local creative talent, and an enthusiastic and prolific poet.

The success of Stuart-Young's self-construction is revealed by the range of new praise-names he attracted from African admirers, especially in Nigeria. Responding to his daily deluge of poems in their newspapers, amounting to many thousands since the First World War, African audiences accorded Dr. Stuart-Young of the late 1930s the status of "West Africa's Poet Laureate."[13] As early as 1914, he had been labeled "the West African Kipling."[14] While he modestly rejected these accolades on grounds of inferiority to the masters,[15] Stuart-Young nevertheless enjoyed considerable public recognition in West Africa, and his stature was undoubtedly enhanced by his supposed educational achievements and his claims of personal friendships with "Cousin Ruddy" Kipling and poet laureate Robert Bridges.[16]

One sign of Stuart-Young's public success in West Africa was the fact that he was hailed by readers in precisely the terms he conjured up in his own descriptions of the ideal poet. "A tall, sleek, silky person is Mr Stuart-Young, with an air of distinction altogether his own," wrote M. O. Kodit Onwuh in the *African Messenger* in 1925, adding that "purity and goodness hang about him like an exquisite aura."[17] "This brilliant author," stated an editorial in the *Gold Coast Leader*, is "a genius" and "one of the best known literary personages of the day. . . . [He is] a household word throughout the literary world," and his work is "expressive of the highest idealism which moves mankind."[18] His fame did not escape the notice of the editors of *West Africa* in London, who as early as 1917 hailed him in one of their "Men of the Moment" columns as "a fine scholar, brilliant journalist, successful merchant, and true friend of the Negro."[19]

Many similar tributes appeared in other West African newspapers. By the mid-1930s he was recognized by the editor of the *West African Pilot*—nationalist leader Dr. Nnamdi Azikiwe (Zik) and personal friend to Stuart-Young—as a man of genius with an international reputation, a poet to enter eternity with Shakespeare. At his death in 1939, the editor of the *Gold Coast Times* added an MA to Stuart-Young's PhD and described him in glowing terms as "a philosopher and a poet—a traveller and a journalist—an Astrologer—and a mystic as well as an occultist."[20] Two years later, in 1941, he was remembered fondly by friends on the *Comet* as the "poet genius" who "inspired the Nigerian Youth, and . . . encouraged the African's efforts."[21]

The identity of "literary gentleman" fitted Stuart-Young so well in the eyes of others that his authorial voice remained firmly in this mode until the shocking exposure of his false qualifications by *West Africa* and the *Nigerian Daily Times* immediately after his death. Even after these revelations, respected leaders of "renascent Africa" such as Zik honored Stuart-Young as the "one man who has helped us usher in a revival of learning, which has been responsible for the transformation of the mental life of West Africa in general and Nigeria in particular."[22]

Here was one of the few white people known to be "fully for Africans."[23] He became a local hero in the eyes of elite (and sub-elite) men, "protecting the economic interests of the people," for "with his trenchant pen he fearlessly opposed and condemned the amalgamation of certain commercial firms" into trading monopolies.²⁴ Inspired by Stuart-Young's literary talent and his presence in Africa as a noncolonial white man, local readers expressed a sense that the location of their town had edged away from the periphery. In the view of "Olomu," writing in the *Nigerian Pioneer* in 1917, the presence of O. Dazi Aku in Onitsha had diminished "Onitsha's position as an 'appendage.'"²⁵ Twenty years later, Zik wrote in the same vein that "his presence in Onitsha has helped in developing that community to be arriving at a stage when it might become the cultural centre of Nigeria."²⁶ No longer relegated to the cultural margins of the British Empire, Stuart-Young's Igbo admirers in Onitsha positioned themselves, through him, at the heart of English literary culture, as readers and also as scholars and writers who were encouraged by their resident poet to work hard for their Cambridge Senior Examinations and "take up a literary career."²⁷ Through their famous Englishman, the people of Onitsha thus recognized their place on the world map.

This positive relationship worked both ways. In colonial West Africa, Stuart-Young could resolve many of the problems posed by his personal heritage. Surrounded in Onitsha by admirers and acolytes, in receipt of a large postbag filled with fan mail and letters seeking guidance from young West African poets, he could rely on others to reinforce and verify his identity as a PhD and literary gentleman. As early as 1924, he started to develop this public personality, corresponding with aspiring poets and, on occasion, publishing utterances on the quality of their efforts. In one article entitled "Teaching the Novice to Know," written from Onitsha but published in the *Gold Coast Leader* of Accra, Stuart-Young wrote an open letter to one "Percy Bysshe Shelley Coker."²⁸ Young Coker's pen name shows clearly and magnificently that he positioned himself within an English Romantic tradition.²⁹ The maestro rapidly alerts the novice that the contrary is the case, however, firmly situating him outside English letters. "For an African of seventeen," he writes, "handicapped by the weakness of using a language which is only artificially his own, I repeat what I have said of former efforts from your pen—you improve!"³⁰ Stuart-Young then prints Coker's poem, "Nature's Arts," in its entirety before commenting on its flaws and rewriting it as a sonnet. Coker's poem opens, "The rolling clouds, the pledge of years, / The proudest fields, the loving tide / The minute worm, the *role* of tears / Are Nature's Arts and earthly pride."³¹

In rhyme and theme, this verse shadows Stuart-Young's own material, revealing one African reader's response to the Englishman's lyrical poetry. Coker has sent his mentor a verse modeled on the poetry Stuart-Young submitted to the West African newspapers. When he responds to this ventriloquistic shadowing, however, Stuart-Young is keen to put a distance between himself and the youth, writing an extensive damning critique of the poem: "As a description of the tide, *loving* will never do!" he commences (emphasis in original), and, taking "Nature's Arts" line by line, proceeds to dissect and dampen the young man's literary pretensions.[32]

In writing a sonnet from the young man's poem, Stuart-Young situates himself within an older poetic tradition than that embodied by Percy Bysshe Shelley Coker. Using Coker's central images, he composes a verse that opens, "The clouds, high-poised in stately pomp and pride / O'er rolling fields that pledge ungarnered years, / Or stilled on lonely shores where human ears / Have never heard the slow incoming tide."[33] Pleased with this achievement, he tells the youth, "There, as clearly as simple words can express it, seems to be what you tried to say; and did not, because you have not yet sufficiently mastered the English tongue."[34]

Several levels of ventriloquism, mastery, and rejection operate in this short exchange of verse forms. Inspired by Shelley and Stuart-Young, Coker finds his voice as a poet, expressing himself through these mentors. Rejecting Coker's use of his own poetry, Stuart-Young returns to a pre-Romantic model and, using a verse form that harks back many centuries, demonstrates his own prowess as a "master of the English language." In this manner and on several levels, the English mentor "eats up" the younger poet.

Stuart-Young often performed the role of teacher and master in a less cruel manner, inspiring young writers to work hard on their grammar and assisting people in "How to Speak in Public."[35] He also offered "Tuition by Post" on behalf of "a famous college in Australia," teaching subjects ranging from English Literature to "Electricity" to Nigerians who wanted to prepare for higher qualifications.[36]

In spite of his success as a public intellectual, the enthusiasm of African readers for Stuart-Young's poetry is difficult to understand by contemporary standards, for his rhyme schemes and themes are suited to century-old popular verse. Even at the time of publication, his volumes received mixed, often negative reviews in Britain. One critic wrote, "We are staggered and much amazed by such serious traffic in the commonplace."[37] Reviewers at *West Africa* described his poetry as "sugary and slight."[38]

There can be no doubt that Stuart-Young was a minor poet whose work appealed to tastes far removed from present-day literary standards. In consequence, it is difficult not to deride the quality of his verse. A small but representative sample of his poetic limitations may be found in lines such as "Will you tell me, Little Lady, where your small feet are a-going, / All alone and unattended where the evening sun is glowing?" with the refrain, "Heigh ho! Heigh ho! / I am one of those who are bound to roam, / Though fire gleam bright on the Hearth of Home."[39] From a later period, there are these William Watson–inspired lines:

> Dancing and glancing and sparkling,
> Great river, with waters of brown,
> As you rush by the rolling hillside,
> And dash the deep valley adown—
> . . . .
> Dreaming and beaming and streaming
> By meadow and fields at rest,
> With the flow'rs and sweet tender blossoms
> Lying asleep on your breast. . . . [40]

Two years later, there is this music hall ditty:

> Oh, a rose, a rose is a lovely flow'r,
> And rich as it is rare:
> For its white or crimson petals perfume the summer air;
> Yet too well we know that the rose must go,
> When its transient beauties pass,
> For when all is said a flow'r once dead
> Has fill'd its hour, alas![41]

Stuart-Young selected many such poems, which had been published in book form in Britain, for resubmission to West African newspapers, where they found enthusiastic African audiences and were reprinted regularly over the years.

The poems quoted above reveal the limits of Stuart-Young's creative powers, yet they must be multiplied by approximately 10,000 if we are to appreciate the full extent of his literary output, for he produced at least thirteen volumes of verse in Britain between 1905 and 1934 and wrote approximately one poem per day for a period of thirty-five years in West Africa. Thousands of his poems found publication in the African-owned newspapers of colonial Nigeria and Ghana. Illustrating Edmund Gosse's statement that "there is nothing in which fashion alters so rapidly as it does in poetry," the majority of these poems would be dismissed today as laboriously rhymed and sentimental, covering a range of hackneyed Victorian themes.[42] Did the sheer abundance of Stuart-Young's verse in combination with his many essays in the newspapers on the interpretation of poetry somehow seduce West African readers into a false sense of the man's poetic merit?

What is lacking from this representation is a sense of the cultural values and contexts that inspired Stuart-Young and motivated his readers. Fashioned in an era when music hall lyrics were still immensely popular and widely performed in theaters, public bars, and private parlors, many of his verses were written both to be read aloud and to be set to music and performed.[43] Additionally, many of his lyrics are in the style of famous music hall singers, particularly Sir Harry Lauder, whom Stuart-Young adored and whose melodious lyrics achieved wide circulation between 1901 and 1933. Each published volume of Stuart-Young's poetry carries a statement inviting composers and performers to set the words to music, and he performed his own lyrics at private gatherings in Nigeria, playing his accordion to accompany his voice. Several of his poems are marked as "reserved" by composers and music hall performers, and from his own account it appears that lyrics such as "My Little Garden World" became popular with British music hall audiences.[44]

The simple choruses, clockwork rhyme schemes, and incessant repetition of words such as "golden," "dreaming," "silvery," "roses," "moonbeams," and "dew" in his poems must therefore be "set to music" and historicized in order to be understood by present-day readers. As Stuart-Young himself stated, "The constant use of these (and similar) epithets is, in greater or lesser degree, inevitable to the song writer. . . . The whole human race calls for these three epithets (*golden* and *little* and *dreams*) with an insistence which cannot be denied!"[45] Unafraid to write in simple rhymes, he drew freely upon the familiar vocabulary of an English music hall tradition. Thus, one frequently finds him "dreaming in the gleaming," a phrase that parodically echoes Sir Harry Lauder's household hit, "Roaming in the Gloaming."[46]

In a similar vein, if Stuart-Young's sonnets, nature poems, and epigrams are taken in isolation and read only for their content, they appear to be sentimental and clichéd, filled with too many "hast thous," "wherefores," and "didst thous." Situated in their own time, however, they can be seen as perfectly acceptable examples of a non–avant-garde or counter-Modernist poetic tradition. An example of this counter-Modernist poetry—in fact, one that compares very poorly with the lines from Stuart-Young quoted above—is "Spring Arrived," by Henry Newman Howara, one verse of which runs, "And the Springtide cometh in / With a very merry din / Of the birdlets in the groves— / Little gossips with their loves."[47] The tradition of which this poem forms a part valued simplicity above complexity and lyrical, rhyming verse forms above experimental challenges to convention. Robert Bridges (master of the "hast thou" poem) and William Watson were the figureheads of this loose configuration of popular poets that emerged in the late-Victorian period. Other accomplished members of the group are A. E. Housman, Alfred Noyes, Lawrence Binyon, Norman Gale, Stephen Phillips (Binyon's cousin), and Alfred Hayes (known as "Happy Mr. Hayes" for his ecstatic rural rhymes).[48]

Ordinary British readers sought out these poets and avidly consumed their work. Sales of Housman's *Shropshire Lad* (1896), for instance, topped 5,000 in

1918 and 21,000 in 1922, achieving a domino effect during the First World War, when the poem's English pastoral scenes evoked powerful feelings of nostalgia for a prewar idyll.[49] Likewise, Watson, Bridges, Gale, and Hayes were highly rated by ordinary readers in the Edwardian period for their images of rural England, especially compared to the racy colonial verse of Rudyard Kipling. Each of these men looms large in Stuart-Young's utterances in the Nigerian newspapers on the subject of poetic value, and his tendency to cluster them together into a group of mentors helps magnify a neglected pattern in English literary culture.

Stuart-Young aligned himself with these mainstream poets, who were publicly recognized and honored in their time by mass readerships as well as by the literary elite but who have subsequently fallen into a vacuum because they do not belong to definitive schools or literary movements. Perhaps the characteristic feature of Stuart-Young's mentors is their status as individuals who are located outside the self-conscious "isms" that emerged to label the dynamic, complex changes in literary productions in Britain between the 1890s and 1930s. This was a period—which has since been labeled Modernist— when writers created aesthetic labels to accommodate their literary experiments and fragmented literary forms.

While Stuart-Young's mentors cannot be forced into an aesthetic straitjacket or "ism," it is possible to chart a common trajectory in their work, for all of them rejected Decadence and harked back to older poetic styles, forms, and themes. In all of their verse a pre- or nonindustrialized English countryside looms large as the setting for the expression of love and nostalgia. Additionally, most of them express feelings of joy rather than despair. As Peter Brooker and Peter Widdowson state, one can find in the work of these poets "the collusion of aestheticism and literary pastoral with patriotism and the construction of a myth of rural England."[50] Regarded by David Perkins as "cultivated traditionalists," these poets lacked a sense of irony and possessed in its place a "simple but earnest devotion to ideals," especially the ideals contained in Nature and in Love.[51] The poets' images of an ideal unchanging Englishness were simple, unified, rural, and utterly intertextual, located in a tradition of pastoral poetry rather than in actual places.[52] Thus Bridges wrote, subtly acknowledging the familiarity of his subject matter, "Clear and gentle stream! / Known and loved so long, / That hast heard the song / And the idle dream / Of my boyish day; / While I once again / Down thy margin stray."[53] Located in both nature and in poetry books, the much-loved stream gives the poet a long "margin" in which to inscribe his feelings.

Again and again in the West African newspapers, when commenting on "good" poetry Stuart-Young praises Bridges, Watson, Gosse, and Hayes for their "healthy" and joyful view of life, expressed through their robust, nature-loving themes.[54] By contrast, he criticizes the 1890s Decadent vision of nature because it is infected with immorality, to the extent that in his view, Swinburne's "denial of Beauty" declassifies his writing from the label "poetry."[55] Rejecting Swinburne's morbidity,[56] Stuart-Young reserves his highest praise for the following type of lyric by Watson: "Oh, England is a darling, / And Scotland is a dear, / And well I love their faces / At any time of year; / But on a summer's day / My heart went astray / And I gave it all away / To bonny Ireland."[57] Promoted by Stuart-Young for its song-like simplicity and naturalness, this lyric is anything but cynical and urbane. The simple ditty must have appealed to his musical ear without introducing troubling thoughts of sex or death, and for this he gave it the label "beautiful," revealing, in the process, his primary criteria for the judgment of poetry.[58]

Nevertheless, the Uranian influence can still be found at the heart of his verse in the 1930s, for the outdoor African setting Stuart-Young chose relaxes gender boundaries and renders them fluid. True to Uranian conventions, Stuart-Young explores the development of what is repeatedly presented as passionate Love between "comrades." Interestingly, it is often difficult to ascertain the sex of the romantic couples Stuart-Young describes in his poetry and prose. Writing in celebration of the "open air" of Africa, he exclaims in one essay, "what joy it was to stroll on a moonlit night into the forest, amid a silence made magical by starshine and dew! The occasional movement of a bird in the nest made our linked hands come more intimately together. . . . [Our] kisses and caresses led no further than kisses and caresses."[59] In his verse we find African lovers of unspecified gender and age who are addressed only as "you" in poems that may be performed equally by male or female voices. The beloved is not gendered in the majority of his poems, and love is cut loose from a single-sexed body. Located and expressed in the African forest, these genderless nature poems play out Rictor Norton's argument that "[i]f any particular genre can be called a homosexual genre, the evidence would point most convincingly to the pastoral."[60] When the addressee is definitely male in these nature poems, Stuart-Young slides out of sexual accountability by offering the song to female vocalists for performance on English music hall stages.[61]

These strategies enable same-sex passion to exist in a submerged, carefully encoded form in Stuart-Young's representations of African nature. In one less-than-subtle moment of coding, it is referred to as "the love that dare not speak its name."[62] At other times, however, it is only through our supplementary knowledge of the common themes and symbols of Uranian poetry, or of Stuart-Young's biography, that we can read his love poems as declarations of "lad-love" rather than heterosexual passion. The amorous poem "Reverie," for example, contains a genderless addressee but is dedicated to "O. Bosa." We know O. Bosa to be Onwuije Hayford Bosah, or "Bosu," the poet's beloved manservant and companion who traveled with him to Britain in 1911. The poem runs:

> You give yourself to me in close embrace:
> I . . . seek your soul!
> You loan your beauty to me for an hour:
> I hold it in my hand . . .
> . . . .
> While brain and body, soul and senses mate
> With you, with you![63]

At other times Stuart-Young repudiates "the secret story of our Shakespeare's soul" by inscribing female lovers into the sonnets, reinforcing the image of the poet as a heterosexual man who asserts heterosexual codes of love.[64]

Stuart-Young moved away from the sexual anxieties of his youth by reinventing himself as a celibate English literary gentleman who is dedicated to poetry. From this platform, he wrote, "We dream of a better Utopia, a state where men and women shall be 'comrades,' without this wretched smear of sex, sex, sex over everything."[65] Placing "palship" above sexual passion, he reinforced his message that for the true lover of beauty and literature, sexual relations with *either* sex are out of bounds.[66] In this manner, Stuart-Young absorbed the figure of the Uranian into that of the nature poet and accommodated those who manifested "divergence from type" into a "School of Platonics, of Friendship, of Camaraderie—and sex is a side-issue only."[67] These ideological repositionings on the subject of sex allowed him to conclude, with Edward Carpenter, that "what is abnormal may be the only future normal—because it is nobler and better!"[68]

With the impact of Modernism in Europe, Stuart-Young found it increasingly difficult to place his essays and nature poems in the London periodicals. A steady stream of his work, carried on the mail boats from West Africa, had appeared in British publications ranging from the *Westminster Gazette* to *Chambers's Journal*, *The People's Friend*, and *John O'London's Weekly* since the early 1900s. In an article written shortly before his death in 1939, however, in which he criticizes editorial policy at *John O'London's*, it emerges that the periodical had accepted only one or two poems in the course of two decades.[69] It also emerges that Stuart-Young argued with the editors on the subject of poetry and defended Longfellow to these "egregious moderns . . .

who would exclude [Longfellow] from the name of poet."[70] Except for the occasional verse published in the *Westminster Gazette* and *West Africa*, Stuart-Young had lost his foothold as a poet in the British literary journals by the early 1920s, probably as a consequence of the changes in aesthetic values after the First World War. On a more practical level, with the onset of the Great Depression, he ran out of resources to continue the private publication of his poetry in volume form in Britain, and the distribution of his volumes for review in the London periodicals dried up. It was under these cultural and economic constraints that Dr. J. M. Stuart-Young took to the platform of the West African press.

What makes this colonial white man's essays—and their poetic consequences—worthy of attention is the fact that in his role as literary authority in West Africa and intercultural arbiter between Britain and the colonies, Stuart-Young undertook the task of ensuring that European avant-garde writing would not find a place in West African literary culture. Between 1924 and 1939, he produced a multitude of articles on the subject "What Is Poetry?" each one arguing that "I am inclined utterly to disclaim the iconoclast in his gloomy prophecy that a renewal of Poesy will be possible only when we forsake the past, and continue this stumbling re-beginning."[71] Addressing himself especially to "African readers, especially to boys," he condemned D. H. Lawrence, James Joyce, and other Modernist writers to a prison term about which he knew a great deal: the authors of this iconoclastic literature, he wrote, "should be penalised. Six months hard labour."[72] No space for nerve-ridden, "sex-obsessed" writers was permissible in the African literary territory patrolled by Stuart-Young: these writers represented everything he had fled England to avoid.

Given Stuart-Young's self-confessed susceptibility to "nerves" and "morbid sensitivity," it is easy to understand why he should wish to keep Decadent and Modernist literature out of his African refuge: the former literature carried charges of effeminacy and homosexuality and the latter carried charges of "immorality," albeit of a heterosexual variety. Ironically, however, the majority of boys to whom his comments were addressed struggled to comprehend Stuart-Young's difficult, polysyllabic prose. "His writing was high-sounding, difficult," complained Akunne John Nworah. "You must have your dictionary about you when you read him."[73]

Clearly, Modernism was not allowed into the world outside the Little House of No Regrets in Onitsha. In rejecting the "moderns," Stuart-Young went so far as to codify his own aesthetic and present it for the benefit of African readers. He quoted and commented on the power of his own lyrics, giving himself a central place in tradition. The following verse is offered as an instance of perfection: "Once on a golden strand / We wondered, dear, apart; / I captive took your hand, / You captive took my heart."[74] Resisting the way in which Modernism rattled the integrity of the subject, he explained that lyrical poetry such as this is an example of an "earnest" expression of "the ache of sentimentality in the heart" and the manifestation of "what mortals loosely call 'the soul.'"[75]

Stuart-Young's poetry and essays on art thus require explanation in terms of cultural values and attitudes that are disconnected from the European avant-garde and its opponents. While his essays reacted to developments in European literature, he formulated his ideas at a far remove from metropolitan culture. His reaction against Modernism occurred almost entirely from West Africa, within the pages of the African-owned newspapers. In particular, his ventriloquistic quotation of other poets must be explained within the context of West African literary culture in the colonial period.

Renowned as a local personality, Stuart-Young received, and replied to, large quantities of letters from aspiring poets across the territory of "British West Africa." From his Little House of No Regrets in New Market Road, he remained in continual dialogue with these correspondents. He also engaged with local aesthetic and cultural values in Onitsha, for he gave regular speeches at African clubs and societies, at which his comments had to remain relevant to local interests in order to secure the attention of audiences. Likewise, as a palm oil trader, he was a cultural broker in Nigeria, learning about and adapting to local tastes for particular commodities. It is therefore highly probable that Stuart-Young's sheer locatedness made him keenly sensitive to local responses to his poetry. Indeed, as we shall see, his literary values and models of inspiration were influenced by these local standards in ways that are at a far remove from the literary experiments and debates occurring in Britain and Europe at the time.

Stuart-Young's joyful poems, and the sentiments that inspired them, are so outmoded by contemporary standards that it would be easy to dismiss the enthusiastic African responses to his work as naive or ignorant. How could the author of such lines as "I climb the steep: and lo! a feeble flock / Of cattle grazing; and the music flows / . . . / A youthful shepherd sits upon a rock, / And sings his 'Lura, là, là, là'" be compared to Kipling, or indeed to Shakespeare, by political and intellectual leaders in West Africa?[76] However, it is unhelpful to dismiss the many African admirers of Stuart-Young as lacking the ability to distinguish between good and bad English verse. Such assumptions disallow the possibility that African readers followed their own cultural directions and interpreted Stuart-Young according to their own well-formulated criteria.

In one particular area Stuart-Young can be placed firmly within West African aesthetic models. His ventriloquism of lines and forms from his mentors bears a striking similarity to the long tradition of "inspired quoting" by which eloquence and wisdom are defined across many culture groups in West Africa. Established long before British rule in the region, local quoting techniques accommodated the expansion of the colonial education system in the late 1920s and 1930s, absorbing Shakespeare, Dickens, and other European writers encountered in schools and local newspapers, including Marie Corelli and Hall Caine.[77] These foreign authors would be redeployed in new ways by local audiences, cut adrift from their textual moorings, and launched into local discourses. African readers and writers would extract pithy quotations from poems or novels, or they would condense and summarize a paragraph of prose and introduce it into their own discourse in innovative ways. Resituated across genres, the quotation would be put to a new use, functioning to reveal a core of wisdom or truth in the discourse of the user.[78] The quotation would also function to reveal the user's eloquence and intelligence, for the appropriate quotation of a proverb or the application of an impressive new saying would create approval and satisfaction among listeners or readers.[79] Local literary evaluations of the "good" and the "beautiful" in West Africa were therefore finely tuned to the extraction and redeployment of material as well as to the invention of new forms.

Stuart-Young's own work was frequently treated as a storehouse of proverbial quotations and epigrams by African audiences. A strong example of this process can be found in the *Nigerian Eastern Mail*, which regularly culled quotations from his work and republished them as maxims in the column Sayings of Yesterday and Today. Couplets extracted from his verse and lines taken from his essays frequently appeared in this column alongside quotations from the archbishop of Canterbury, the pope, Zik, George Bernard Shaw, and others.[80] On one occasion, a short story by "Odeziaku of Onitsha" was instantly rendered into Sayings of Yesterday and Today. Four pages after the end of this short story, which featured European palm oil traders and an African hero who opposes the monopolistic European combines, a quotation from the protagonist was reprinted in which Europeans are condemned for making Africans into "underdogs who cannot rise up."[81] This defictionalizing process—whereby a pertinent quotation is hooked out of a stream of narrative—illustrates the rapidity with which new and relevant quotations could be coined in West Africa.

So quotable was Stuart-Young's output that the *Nigerian Eastern Mail* once ran a column entitled "*Ex Ore Infantium*: Some Sayings of Odeziaku," which included an epigram that was itself a composite quotation: "Faithfully kept and steadily followed, a noble aim is as good as a noble deed. The effort counts more than the price, the race more than the goal!"[82] At other times, Stuart-Young's verse was quoted from the pulpit in local churches, redeployed for religious ends. On at least one occasion it was quoted in the inscription on a gravestone: walking in a Nigerian graveyard with friends, Stuart-Young was surprised to encounter his verse, "Yes, we shall meet again, / And all past pain / At meeting be forgot; / I said Good-bye but you / Made answer, friend and true, / Forget Me Not!"[83] Each of these examples illustrates the ways in which lines from Stuart-Young's newspaper articles and poems were extrapolated by readers, redeployed as maxims, and put to new local uses. These local quoting practices greatly assist in our understanding of the reasons why Stuart-Young's sentimental and apolitical poetry remained popular with African readers in the stormy 1930s of anticolonial protest and emergent African nationalisms.

A powerful instance of the way a particular quotation could take hold locally was Stuart-Young's "coining" of a maxim in a long newspaper article on the subject of poetic inspiration, entitled "Genius, Talent or Mediocrity." On 9 February 1924, he wrote:

> There is the man who knows not, and knows not that he knows not—he is open to instruction; teach him! There is the man who knows, and knows not that he knows—he is asleep; awaken him! There is the man who knows, and knows that he knows—he is a wise man; follow him![84]

At this stage Stuart-Young did not claim to have invented this saying, correctly attributing it to Arabian oral tradition. What is ironic is that the quotation is used in order to illustrate the need for "individual thinking" rather than derivation.[85] In promoting individuality, this man of multiple name changes, masks, forgeries, and ventriloquistic personae draws upon an Arabian quotation to illustrate his point. In so doing, and against his manifest argument, he anticipates poststructuralist theories of the impossibility of an author ever achieving authenticity or pure self-expression in print.

Nevertheless, by West African aesthetic rules Stuart-Young's innovative and frequent reuse of the Arabian saying in different contexts rendered it his own, for his constant repetition of the quotation in coming years caused it to migrate from its folkloric source and attach to him as its user, or "owner." Within days of its first appearance in print in 1924, the saying had entered popular discourse, attributed to Odeziaku. Pleased to have initiated the saying, Stuart-Young repeated it many times in his articles. Fourteen years after its first appearance in print, he continued to quote it. Thus, at the reception to welcome Zik home to Onitsha in 1934, an occasion on which Stuart-Young played the prestigious role of chairman, he reused his saying to describe Zik's academic achievements in the United States. Again, in 1938, the saying appeared in the form of a riddling poem in the *West African Pilot*:

> The man who knows not
> And knows not that he knows not—
> Avoid him
> For a stupid fool is he!
> The man who knows not
> But seems aware that he knows not—
> Enlighten him,
> He may be glad to see!
> The man who knows
> And knows not that he knows—
> Arouse him,
> For he's dreaming: fast asleep!
> The man who knows,
> And himself knows well that he knows—
> Follow him,
> This man of knowledge deep!
> Yea, follow him,
> Who Wisdom's Gates unbars:
> Although the Path be steep.
> "I will lead you to the stars!"[86]

To this day, the saying remains a favorite in Onitsha. "He who knows" is one of the last surviving traces of Stuart-Young in the town. Appropriately enough, given his creativity as a forger, this memorial to him is an echo of an echo, a ventriloquist's projection.

In a similar manner to West African innovators of wise sayings, Stuart-Young borrowed and creatively adapted material, simultaneously displaying his own wide knowledge of English literature and absorbing the quoted texts into his own discourses. As with his famous saying "He who knows," Stuart-Young reused his borrowed lines so regularly that they slowly broke away from their original authors and attached to himself. Thus the opening lines from "Celibacy"—"Think not the poet loves like common clay: / He woos his Art, and to his muse is wed"—are reused so regularly in new versions of the poem that they become simultaneously "Shakespearean" and Stuart-Young's own innovation.[87]

Stuart-Young's mode of writing may also be related to his lifelong interest in the occult. In Onitsha as well as Manchester he remained a practicing spiritualist with the power to summon up voices from the other world and project those voices on the page and in the séance room.[88] In one powerful account of his spirit possessions, he wrote, "[A]t many a séance I would . . . assume half a score of different personalities inside the one evening, and I could be in the course of a few brief hours of communal 'sitting' both man and woman, child and valetudinarian."[89] Some of these voices found expression in a written form, including, as suggested in chapter 3, the supposed letters from Oscar Wilde. While further demonstrating Stuart-Young's "queer" lack of a stable identity, what is striking about this account of his mediumship is the way it can also be used to describe his creativity as a poet. His poetic output shares many features with his spirit possessions: in both expressive modes he summons up voices, ventriloquizes, and moves ambiguously through open gender doors, encountering and hosting other voices that provide inspiration for his own lines. As he wrote at the start of one poem, summoning his mentors, "Inspired bards of older times, / Help a minor poet's rhymes!"[90] The sheer derivativeness of Stuart-Young's poetry can therefore be seen not only as a sign of homage to the forms perfected by his mentors but also as a sign of his trance-like submission to their possession of his voice.

In some instances, particularly in his earliest published poetry, Stuart-Young grafted his own words directly onto his mentors' verse forms. As chapter 4 suggested, one early volume of verse, *Through Veiled Eyes*, echoes the work of John Gambril Nicholson, Edward Cracroft Lefroy, and other poets from the British Uranian subculture so closely as to fall into the category of plagiarism.[91] In the manner of the Uranian poets, Stuart-Young chose swimming scenes and lads on the sports field as his themes.[92] Similarly, the ghostly voices of Shakespeare, Milton, Swinburne, Bridges, Watson, Kipling, and many popular music hall singers echo through Stuart-Young's verse as inspirational forces, guiding his selection of themes, words, and images.

The sheer excess of imitative quotations in Stuart-Young's poetry can be explained in part through the concept of spiritualist inspiration and possession, which helped, in chapter 3, to explain his otherwise preposterous decision to include facsimiles of *faked* letters in his memoir of Oscar Wilde. In the spiritualist view of this behavior, the poet functions as the medium for the other's voice, which manifests itself ventriloquistically through the pen.[93] Stuart-Young manifests poetic inspiration through imitation rather than through innovation. An illuminating instance of this poetic mediumship can be found in the sonnet entitled "Sebastian Melmoth (died in Paris 30 November 1900 aged 46)," published in one of the last volumes Stuart-Young produced in

Britain.[94] The sonnet reveals that two decades after the death of Wilde, the poet continues to receive the sound of his voice, albeit speaking under the pseudonym Wilde adopted upon release from prison.[95] In the sonnet, the narrator is visited in a dream by Melmoth, who communicates in "Fragments of Faëry, peerless without flaw."[96] Acting as receiver and translator of this "peerless" language and reporting back the words of Wilde, the narrator's soul is possessed to the extent that the voice of the other within himself takes possession of his critical faculties and causes him to "read awry / The tender meaning of Love's greater law!"[97] So enchanting is "This 'lord of language'" that the poet has to wait for the visitant to select his own moment to "hasten . . . back to Hell."[98]

This model of ventriloquistic inspiration, whereby the self is rendered passive and open—suspended puppet-like until it is animated by the other—does not easily conform to the mainstream Victorian literary values within which Stuart-Young worked. Loyalty to literary tradition may have been condoned by the critical establishment, but excessive imitative modeling by individual poets was often frowned upon as a sign of fraudulence.[99]

The spiritualist perspective offers a persuasive explanation for Stuart-Young's serene attitude toward imitation, but other important motivations played a part in his poetic choices. In particular, his compositions developed out of his ongoing desire to express his homosexuality in an encoded form. Of course, an "encoding-decoding" model is too simplistic when applied transhistorically to all readers of a particular text, for all readers cannot decode the *same* message from a text regardless of their own locations. The encoding-decoding model is a great deal more persuasive, however, when it is applied to subcultural or minority groups within specific historical contexts, especially those for whom social exclusion necessitates the development of shared symbols and secret codes for the expression of a collective identity. The iconic "bathing boys" scenes in homoerotic art of the late nineteenth century, as well as the development of Hellenism in art and literature, are exemplary instances of an "encoded" homosexuality.[100] Interpreted through this encoding-decoding model, Stuart-Young's close revocalizations of other poets' verse forms can be regarded as part of a secret discourse of homosexuality, expressed in a displaced form through his use of the Uranian poets.

Whether we regard him as spirit-possessed or as one who expressed an encoded sexuality, the image of the "poet-outsider" permeated Stuart-Young's writing, allowing him finally to accommodate that other, sexually unacceptable outsider figure who stalked him through childhood and youth, whispering of Uranian love and Decadent poetry and taking the form of the boy-loving man with natural but misdirected passions. The poet's supposed sensitivity and tenderness provide legitimate channels of expression for Stuart-Young's suppressed double, whose physical desires were surrounded by guilt and anxiety.[101]

Albeit composed on a remote Nigerian trading station, his poems about love and nature are strikingly familiar and domestic, embedded in the verses of well-known English poets dating back to Shakespeare. Where one might expect such verse to express an expatriate's feelings of nostalgia for the English countryside, however, Stuart-Young makes a surprising move: he transplants the vocabulary of English nature poetry into African soil.[102] Anything but wild and dangerous, the jungle around Onitsha becomes a flowery woodland in his verse, providing scented camouflage for secret lovers. Echoing the work of Alfred Hayes, he writes, "Gladly seize the fleeing minute in the forest's scented gloom, / While the bud has honey in it, while the blossom is in bloom; / In this fervid Christmas weather rest we softly in the grass, / And in warm embrace together count the moments as they pass."[103] African mud huts become cottages in his poems, jungles become lark-filled orchards, and the "savages" of colonial discourse are tamed into rustic peasants singing "Lura-là," armed with scythes rather than spears.[104]

Images such as this can readily be interpreted as a colonization of African landscapes, for they display the trader's typical inability to envisage difference and imposition of similitude upon distinctly other worlds.[105] Stuart-Young creates a gentle, tame African nature that sweetens and beautifies the jungle evoked by writers such as Joseph Conrad, to the extent that this forest would not be out of place in Edmund Spenser's *Shepheardes Calendar*. Stuart-Young universalizes the poetic vocabulary for rural England and relocates it to West Africa. In the process, he thoroughly denationalizes the rose-covered cottages, meadows, pastures, shepherds, plowmen, and woodlands in the poetry of rural Englishness. "What value an English harvest, or the glamour on glade and hill," he asks, "when the spirit eternally broods on a Winter that knows no chill? / We *cannot* forsake the tropics . . . each night brings us music and mirth, / So the land that was Home of our childhood no longer remains on the Earth!"[106] So pervasive is his universalization of his models that when he imagines English rather than African landscapes, he includes phrases such as "'Tis summer-time in England" and adjectives such as "English grass."[107]

What distinguishes Stuart-Young from his Modernist compatriots, whose work is probably more acceptable by our contemporary standards, is that he works within the trader's economy of similarity rather than in the Modernist economy of cultural relativism and difference. Viewed sympathetically in the context of colonialism, this style can be seen as having some radical potential. In seeking a voice to convey his love for the African countryside, he blurs the undivided Englishness contained in his models. If Bridges and his Edwardian contemporaries offered an "unchanging England" for public consumption, as critics have suggested, then Stuart-Young erases the social and national differences upon which those poets depended.[108]

The poem "Interior Warfare" provides a remarkable example of this process.[109] It describes the death of the narrator's African lover when her village is raided by hostile African neighbors. Rather than rendering the scene in the style of Edgar Wallace's *Sanders* novels, where "tribal warfare" is bound to occur between "savage," spear-wielding populations, Stuart-Young adopts a sentimental, romantic voice that disallows racial difference and situates his love within a benign natural environment:

> The cuckoo haunts the forest, dim and shady.
> 'Tis here we lay, where sunshafts mark the grass;
> This lonely bird has often seen my lady.
> And heard our whispers where the swift hours pass.
> . . . .
> You, darling one, had come from sunslope tender;
> Your lips were rosy as your eyes were black;
> Your skin was satin-soft; your body slender;
> And I possessed them all, nor gave them back.
> . . . .
> And wood doves cooed to see us meet together.[110]

This tranquil scene might be found in any volume of English nature poetry by Watson, Hayes, or Le Gallienne. Simultaneously working within and subverting his English models, Stuart-Young universalizes the Edwardian nature poem and makes it available for descriptions of African landscapes. If he colonizes African nature with images culled from late Victorian poetry, he also decolonizes, dislocates, and dehistoricizes his poetic models. As he writes self-consciously in the postscript to his collection of poetry, *The Seductive Coast,* "I have sought to render the South—and the most morbid and unhealthy of the known Tropics, be it added—in terms of the North."[111]

Stuart-Young finds in "the terms of the North" a way to render the tropics without recourse to the equally "Northern" discourse of Africa's uncontrolled sexuality and savagery. The dominant model at this time to describe love between the races can be found in Stephen Phillips's poem "The Black Peril," which feeds popular fears of degeneration through miscegenation and adds to colonial fantasies of uncontrolled black male sexuality. In words of racial loathing, the poem warns, "Beware the black blood with the white! / The skull of brass, the hands that tear! / The lecherous ape, not human quite, / The tiger not outgrown his lair."[112] The final couplet of the poem reinforces the racist aggression: "Restless he crouches day and night, / Leaps! And a woman is his prey."[113] Poems such as this cannot simply be put to one side as an embarrassing residue of imperialism in favor of Phillips's more sentimental nature poems and love poems. Rather, such poems serve to highlight the ground-breaking potential of Stuart-Young's investment in a common humanity and a shared poetic vocabulary.

In a perceptive appraisal of his poetry by Adisa Williams in the *West African Pilot*, Stuart-Young is seen to "breathe that spirit of common humanity that binds mankind together."[114] "It is the distinguishing charm of his verses that they do not rely on the glorification of the imperial spirit for their appeal," this African critic writes. "Rather, they reveal a genuine sympathy for the West African coastland, the hinterland and its people."[115] Williams has diagnosed Stuart-Young's difference from the norm. In the process of seeing Africa through English pastoral spectacles, the Englishman writes against a long tradition of colonialist representations of Africa. In addition, the figure of the lonely wandering poet-lover allows Stuart-Young to conceptualize his own presence in West Africa outside the framework of colonialism. Rather than acknowledging his position in the imperial economy as a palm oil trader protected by the colonial regime, his status as a poet allows him to present himself as a nature-loving antagonist of civilization, a natural man who is the literate European brother of the "noble savage." He has stepped into the African forests as if fresh from the pages of Rousseau's *Emile*, and he finds in West Africa "a land of Fruit and Flowers."[116]

This process of pastoralizing Nigeria had special significance as the stormy 1930s progressed toward the nationalist 1940s in West Africa. In poem after poem, it becomes clear that Stuart-Young's rejection of the British industrial environment did not lead him into the English rural landscape of the Edwardian pastoral poets. As with his slum-land novels, where the sexually corrupted protagonists are transported to the open air of Africa, his nature poetry locates moral health and goodness in rural African settings. Time and again "the care-free and healthy life of the people of West Africa" is contrasted with "the artificiality of European City Life" in which people become "restless, neurotic, impatient of convention."[117] "We love thee well, West Africa," the poet cries, years later, never deviating from his nature-loving message.[118]

In return for this egalitarian vision, Stuart-Young's West African fans found in their poet "a character who is worthy of emulation."[119] His passionate celebrations of African nature contributed—albeit indirectly and in a highly mediated form—to the Pan-Africanist project to build "renascent

Africa" by constructing positive uplifting images of the continent.[120] Verses that might otherwise be dismissed as sentimental doggerel or romantic cliché can therefore be re-viewed through this alternative lens, in which the cardinal themes of European Romantic and post-Romantic poetry—Nature and Beauty and Love—have been radically disconnected from white bodies and European settings, universalized and made generic. Stuart-Young's most ventriloquistic verse thus holds an important position in relation to the increasing anticolonialism in the newspapers of "British West Africa."

An unsympathetic view of this poetry is that it represents the cultural wing of British imperialism, for Stuart-Young reacts against avant-garde literary movements in favor of the very pastoral Englishness that fed and sustained the imperial ideology, fueled its imperial masculinities, and sent colonialists to far-off lands in the certainty of their superiority. As I hope I have shown in this chapter, however, the manner in which Stuart-Young Africanizes his mentors and their themes serves to denationalize "English Nature." In the process, West Africa becomes, in his words, "This level paradise, / Where Shepherds pipe and woodland fairies dance," an idealized place for the expression of genderless love and the development of an African nature poetry.[121]

CONCLUSION

"Tales That Lie Awake"

STUART-YOUNG DIED FROM throat cancer at a hospital in Port Harcourt on 28 May 1939 after suffering for a year from what was diagnosed as laryngitis. Despite his poor health, he continued to write poetry and articles throughout 1938, and the eastern Nigerian newspapers published Odeziaku's increasingly meditative verses, in which he appeared both to predict and to welcome his forthcoming demise. Throughout this period he was cared for in Onitsha by his beloved manservant, Solomon Obike, to whom he willed all of his African properties and several hundred pounds. He was also watched over with rising concern by Nnamdi Azikiwe and other powerful local acquaintances.

In the thirty years of his residence in Onitsha, Stuart-Young had made many male friends in the African community, particularly among newspaper editors and elite anticolonial nationalists. Foremost among these elite men was Azikiwe. Anxious about his friend's declining health in 1938, Zik raised sufficient funds to send him back to England, where he assumed that the sick man would be cared for by his family. Stuart-Young politely refused this money, thanking his donors for their kindness and declaring that he did not wish to undertake the journey in his current state of health.[1] It is doubtful whether he would have found more tender carers in England than Obike in Onitsha.

At no time did his estranged second wife, Nellie Gibson Etheridge Young, make an appearance in Onitsha. Perhaps Stuart-Young chose not to inform her of his illness. More probably, she no longer cared for the man who disclosed his sexual revulsion for women immediately after their honeymoon in 1919 and rejected her when she miscarried their child. After her miscarriage, Nellie returned to her teaching career and remained in Southampton, the place of her birth, until her death at the age of 80 in 1967. Given the exclusively homosocial nature of Stuart-Young's domestic world in West Africa, Nellie's existence must have come as a great surprise to local people in Onitsha when her name was read out in his will as the recipient of £200.[2]

Intense claustrophobia loomed over Stuart-Young throughout his life. His terror of being buried alive was so great that he inserted a clause into his will, insisting that his body be left aboveground for three full days after the certification of death to allow for a possible recovery of consciousness and escape from confinement. Perhaps he had read books such as Alexander Wilder's *Perils of Premature Burial* (1895) and William Tebb and Edward P. Vollum's *Premature Burial and How to Avoid It: With Special Reference to Trance, Catalepsy, and Other Forms of Suspended Animation* (1896). Like many other similar books and journals dedicated to the theme of premature burial in the late nineteenth century, these texts vividly described people's experiences of "suspended life" and offered guidance to readers on how to guard against being taken for dead. They gave practical suggestions, such as that sticks be included at burial for knocking on coffin lids and that breathing tubes be supplied inside the coffin. They also made suggestions about which tools would be suitable to help an entrapped person escape confinement.

Zik publicly demonstrated his respect for Stuart-Young by paying for the corpse to be transported home to Onitsha from the hospital in Port Harcourt where Stuart-Young had been receiving care. At the instigation of Church of England officials, however, the coffin was then taken to the Anglican church in Onitsha, a place Stuart-Young rarely attended in his lifetime. The body was given a Christian burial within two days of his death, a full week before the will was read out with Stuart-Young's request for a three-day "breathing space." This failure to respect his last wishes gave rise to a ghost story that persisted until recently, for it was said that the spirit of Stuart-Young roamed restlessly and discontentedly through the Old Cemetery, terrifying Onitsha residents and causing them to steer clear of the cemetery after dark.

Stuart-Young's intense fear of enclosure was caused in large part by the traumatic memory of his childhood home in Ardwick, where nights were often dominated and disturbed by the movement of his father's body over his mother's body. To the eyes of the powerless boy, the father was suffocating the mother, stifling her cataleptic form. In adult life and in his creative writing, Stuart-Young continually remembered (or reenacted) these sexual scenes from childhood. In life, the reenactment took the form of his claustrophobia, which became so severe that the wearing of a mere hat or a necktie oppressed him. Riding inside motor cars triggered such strong panic attacks that he preferred to walk distances of up to thirty miles, carrying an umbrella for shade.

In his creative writing, the sexual trauma is reenacted again and again as angelic, passive mothers and boy heroes are "buried alive" beneath the physically abusive bodies of the adult male villains.

Stuart-Young's physical and emotional overidentification with the "suffocated" mother and the panic-stricken child help explain his lifelong erotic preference for boys. Physically and sexually, the prepubescent male body represented everything that his father was not. From this perspective, one can start to comprehend Stuart-Young's horror at his own sexual loss of control during his honeymoon with his second wife, where he "went nearly mad with self-loathing—I was like a gluttonous child before a X'mas pudding" (see plate 12 and chapter 5). With Nellie he became a greedy, sexually active adult male just like his father, duplicating the predatory and monstrous heterosexual figure he feared and loathed as a child. At the same time, however, by describing his sexual excesses using the image of the "gluttonous child" with a Christmas pudding, Stuart-Young maintains his primary identification with prepubescent appetites and desires: he refuses to suspend his empathy with the child, even at this moment of uncanny repetition of his father's sexuality.

Viewed from a different vantage point, Stuart-Young's claustrophobia combined with his refusal to live in segregated European quarters to make his body peculiarly open to local inspection by the people of Onitsha. For most of his life in Nigeria, he remained in his Little House of No Regrets on New Market Road, managing several small stores around the town. He built his properties on land leased from Africans in the busy commercial center of town and lived among the Igbos in a way that became increasingly visible and distasteful to the European colonial community as the twentieth century progressed. Here was an Englishman who, from the moment of his first arrival in town, refused to separate himself physically from African society. Defying colonial notions of privacy, he chose to sleep on balconies, and he often sat at his desk in the open air rather than conducting his life within enclosed rooms. He designed his several properties in Onitsha to be as uncramped as possible, preferring to occupy one single expansive multipurpose room with a broad balcony rather than divide his space into functional segments.

The ways in which these domestic and architectural spaces were interpreted in different sectors of colonial society illustrate Richard Parker's comment that "the social and cultural mapping of sexual relations takes place concretely within a world of physical space, of geographical space, in which sexuality is organised and distributed."[3] As I hope I have shown in this book, in a colonial context these physical spaces can rapidly become eroticized, or they can be put under social surveillance.[4] They can also become sites of claustrophobia, institutional interference, and sexual anxiety as power relations shift in the wider community.[5]

Upon hearing of Stuart-Young's death, the Nigerian newspapers filled up with front-page tributes from some of the country's foremost political figures. Zik led the mourning columns with a fortnight of commemorative articles in the *West African Pilot*, remembering this mentor, friend, philosopher, journalist, and poet.[6] These obituaries are intriguing for the manner in which elite intellectuals absorbed Stuart-Young into a Pan-Africanist literary tradition. Since the early 1900s, leading Pan-Africanist thinkers such as Edward W. Blyden and J. E. Casely Hayford had produced heroic biographies and obituaries of leading Africans. Examples of "great men" would be placed before African readers, with eulogies to individuals whose "great deeds and great thoughts are the most glorious legacies to mankind."[7] In the *West African Pilot*, Stuart-Young is positioned within this heroic African discourse. Zik takes charge of producing his friend's memory and reconstructs him as the exemplar of a hoped-for postcoloniality, a leader of "renascent Africa," and a model to Nigerian youths. "I wonder if the people of Onitsha will have the sense of duty and admiration for this white friend of the blacks," he writes, "to erect a monument dedicated to the sacrifice of this hero to the cause of interracial cooperation, and thus make the tomb of 'Odeziaku' a national shrine."[8]

Obituaries by elite Africans in other eastern Nigerian newspapers were equally committed to preserving a positive image of Stuart-Young for posterity. A cluster of praise-names emerged around him at this time, consolidating the image he produced for himself as a literary gentleman. He had certainly persuaded his African acquaintances and readers that he "knew and associated with all those late Victorian writers of note."[9] Many elite obituary writers took their cue from Azikiwe and honored Stuart-Young as a national hero. Hailed as the "father of poetry in West Africa" and the region's "Poet Laureate," Stuart-Young was given full honors as a "poet genius" and buried in Onitsha, described touchingly by one commentator as "the Westminster Abbey of his heart."[10] A wooden statue was erected to him, as Zik had wished, and it remained in place at least until the Biafran War of 1967–70.

In the wake of these formal obituaries, a plethora of young, less-well-educated Onitsha men came forward to celebrate Stuart-Young in the Nigerian newspapers. Among them was the aspiring journalist S. I. Bosah, speaking for the untitled youth of Onitsha in a genre that his mentor would no doubt have applauded. In his "Memoirs of Odeziaku," published in the *West African Pilot*, Bosah writes from an unusual perspective, taking a child's-eye view of the older man. This long article contains a boy's memories of the trader and his homosocial world in the 1920s. Written without sexual innuendo, Bosah describes how Stuart-Young offered him support in his schoolwork, presented him with "Boys' Own" books and other gifts, and encouraged him to embark on a career in journalism.[11] Even in old age, Bosah's memories of Stuart-Young's local names continue to be imbued with the perspective of a prepubescent boy.

The many obituaries to Stuart-Young have a curious life history of their own, developing from the unconditional grief expressed by local elites in the eastern Nigerian press to the cooler tone of obituaries from further afield, particularly in the London-based journal *West Africa*. Immediately after Stuart-Young's death, the Lagosian *Nigerian Daily Times* published tributes to Onitsha's "philosopher and friend," but the editor also acknowledged that "we did not always agree with Mr Stuart-Young in his views and opinions."[12] Meanwhile, in London, much to the distress of Igbo readers, *West Africa* challenged Stuart-Young's academic credibility and called his doctorate into question. Less than a fortnight after his death, editorial staff at *West Africa* contacted the registrar of Durham University, who provided a short statement to the effect that "Mr Stuart-Young does not appear to have received any degree or diploma from this University."[13]

The obituaries to Stuart-Young reveal that in eastern Nigeria he was remembered by the male intelligentsia and their literate sub-elite followers for his generosity and lack of racial prejudice as well as for his literary genius. The flood of obituaries and commemorative articles influenced subsequent recollections of his life by instilling his biography with heroism, making him an anticolonial symbol in preparation for the nationalist 1940s and the future, especially as imagined by Zik.

⇜

The Forger's Tale has revolved around the search for a man whose biography is riddled with anomalies and incongruities. Different sectors of the African community responded to Stuart-Young's rare proximity to them by actively and strategically producing their own man in him, naming and generating the personality called "Odeziaku" or "Odoziaku" over a period of three decades, helping to produce him as a local oral and textual commodity, and making good political use of his receptivity toward their culture. Indeed, the queer openness of Stuart-Young toward these Igbo constructions of his subjectivity has necessitated a different model of biography in this book, one that differs from the "isolated individual" approach to life-writing. It has been necessary to break away from what Judith Okely and Helen Callaway call the "Great White Man tradition" of (auto)biography, in which "the lone achiever has felt compelled to construct and represent his uniqueness, seemingly in defiance of historical conditions, but actually in tune with the dominant power structures which have rewarded him."[14]

Concurring with Okely and Callaway, the feminist scholar Liz Stanley argues that for (auto)biography to be socially and historically accountable, the genre must not describe the lives of individuals in isolation from one another. Such a narrative is "quite unlike life," Stanley notes, "where the lives of even the famous and infamous are densely populated by peers. Only on paper does one person alone occupy a stage."[15] In reaching outward to the lives of others and in highlighting the agency of Africans as contributors to colonial biography, *The Forger's Tale* drew inspiration from this body of feminist biographical theory.

Feminist biographies often seek to retrieve individuals with whole and stable inner lives from history. In this book, however, queer theory has been added to the feminist biographical method in order to preserve an emphasis on the open and shifting nature of Stuart-Young's sexual identities. A "queer" biography recognizes the difficulties and contradictions involved in defining, and seeking to "retrieve," the very human subjects whose repression has made possible the western representation of gender as "masculine" or "feminine." In an effort to write queer history within the genre of biography, I have tried to strike a balance between the presentation of Stuart-Young as an originator of ideas and life choices and a sense of him as a subject enclosed within the lives of others in Britain and West Africa.

Complex international "webs of friendship" held this man's life story in place.[16] As we have seen, Stuart-Young spent a great deal of time attempting to inscribe himself into other people's life stories: he claimed that infamous and scandalous personalities were his close friends in Europe, and in West Africa he cultivated friendships with prominent Africans while nurturing a large fan base of African readers. His status as an open subject, positioned outside mainstream imperial history and infused with others' stories, meant that our search for "Odeziaku" did not have a natural stopping point in theory or interpretation. Here was a character who was entwined in others' lives and who escaped easy theorization. In many ways, Stuart-Young fulfilled Jonathan Dollimore's yearning "for a body that is material in the sense that it is recalcitrant, not malleable to theory; and in particular a body which impedes rather than surrenders to wishful theory."[17]

The imperial encounter between Britain and West Africa produced complicated and subtle cultural tensions between different classes of African and European at different moments in colonial history. As a white palm oil trader in colonial Africa at the turn of the twentieth century, Stuart-Young certainly benefited from racist and Eurocentric models of imperial power, such as the dichotomies of colonizer versus colonized and European versus African that gained increasing currency as the twentieth century progressed. These models structured his homosexual desires and affected the balance of power in his erotic relationships. The "queerness" of Stuart-Young lay, however, in the many ways he unsettled imperialist categories in his writing, in his relationships, and in his boundary-crossing forgeries.

Several unanswered biographical, ethnographic, ethical, and social questions have been raised by this book. What were precolonial and colonial concepts of childhood in Igboland, especially relating to the ways adults distinguished themselves sexually and socially from youths? What social categories of the "pre-adult" or the "not yet adult" existed in Onitsha in the late nineteenth century, and how did these change under the influence of colonialism and Christianity in the early twentieth century? What are the implications of these categories for young people's encounters with the men who sexually desired them? Did the colonies provide "a way out for pedophiles [and pederasts], whose sexual desire was excluded from the realm of respectable homosexuality" in their home cultures, as Rudi Bleys concludes in his survey of homosexuality in colonial ethnographic publications?[18] If we could retrieve the opinions of the market women who led Stuart-Young's funeral in 1939, in what ways would they concur with or differ from the elite men's memories and reminiscences on which this book has largely relied for indigenous accounts of Stuart-Young's life?

Surprisingly, archival material relating to Stuart-Young is also lacking from another, very different quarter: "official" colonial documents make few references to his presence in Onitsha. This man of multiple name changes has no name at all in the British colonial archive. Apart from a series of memos relating to his acquisition of land for property development, Stuart-Young does not figure in the journals, reports, and publications of colonial administrators, missionaries, doctors, or government anthropologists. It is as if members of the colonial regime, in order to erase his identity, collectively refused to acknowledge him. His sole appearance takes the form of the effeminate, eccentric character described by Sylvia Leith-Ross in her memoirs. In all his years in Onitsha, no close friendships developed between Stuart-Young and European officials resident in Onitsha. Barriers of class, sexuality, and politics caused the colonial elite to avoid and exclude him.

A further set of questions relates to Stuart-Young's life. Was he really a passive pederast, as Timothy d'Arch Smith suggests in his study of the Uranian poets, or did he consolidate his Uranian aesthetic with occasional erotic physical encounters with his beloved boys, as his letter to Frank Harris suggests? How did Stuart-Young's two marriages help ease, or exacerbate, these Uranian desires? His first marriage seems easier to comprehend than the second, for in 1909 Stuart-Young was still tortured by the "perversity" of his sexual inclinations and was desperate to escape the anxiety and guilt evoked by his passions. His first marriage can be understood as a brave effort to conform to British social conventions. But what motivated his second marriage? Where did he meet Nellie Gibson Etheridge, and why did he marry her? Did he hope that she would provide a mask behind which he could hide his sexuality, as was the case in the marriages of Richard Burton, Oscar Wilde, André Gide, and many other homosexual men of the nineteenth and twentieth centuries? If so, his letter of 1925 to Frank Harris, written just four years after the disastrous honeymoon, vividly tears off the mask.

In addressing these topics, I have tried to locate Stuart-Young's sexuality in culturally diverse contexts rather than taking for granted a predetermined or global "homosexual identity."[19] Nevertheless, Stuart-Young was one of many men for whom "their homosexual loves, their fear of exposure and experience of marginalization, or their involvement in a gay subculture influenced their work and affected their careers."[20] In Onitsha at the turn of the twentieth century, he entered a sexual culture where same-sex encounters were accommodated within a more expansive "geography of desire" than that of the metropolitan culture.[21] Crucially, in Onitsha, Stuart-Young's passions were filtered through a framework in which his desires were valued for the spiritual and economic benefits they conferred on his love objects, rather than labeled negatively as "sins" or "perversions." He could therefore start to release his desires from their connection with contamination and self-loathing and embark on a creative process of self-renewal. With the slow release of his self-disgust, his public writings filled up with sexual-textual desire, and by the mid-1920s he frequently confessed his sexual preferences without shame.

The common assumption that same-sex desire necessarily generates dissident or resistant identities requires some modification, however, in order to account for Stuart-Young's long residence in Onitsha. On one level, his aesthetic and subcultural identifications did enable him to take up anticolonial and anti-Christian positions in Nigeria, to comment from the social margins, and to be pro-African during a time of intensifying imperial racism. On another level, however, he made use of his African location to seek social integration into English bourgeois society, to express an entitlement to—rather than resistance to—dominant imperial values.

With the birth of "Odeziaku," a splitting of Stuart-Young's identity occurred. While the majority of his political confrontations with colonialism and the Catholic Church occurred through the pen of "Odeziaku," his discussions of English literature and his commentaries on African "backwardness" were usually signed by "J. M. Stuart-Young." The latter gentleman claimed a good education, membership in London clubs, a doctorate, a fine ear for sonnets, and the "natural" authority to comment on matters pertaining to English literature. While "Odeziaku's" writings are often spliced with declarations of working-class solidarity with the racially oppressed colonial masses, the carefully cultivated middle-class identity of "Dr. J. M. Stuart-Young" enabled Stuart-Young to step forward as a public intellectual and fulfill the fantasy of a lifetime. Wearing this mask, he subversively parodied the English class system, but he also conservatively imitated English bourgeois values, "passing" as a middle-class gentleman in order to disguise his other identities. The authoritative demeanor of this "Dr." arose from his enthusiastic endorsement of the dominant values, attitudes, and opportunities of his historical period. Stuart-Young gave up what Gilbert Herdt calls "the secrecy of the closet," but he did so only through the manufacture of a new bourgeois self.[22]

Stuart-Young's expertise in generating new names and identities demonstrates that the practice of forgery involves far more than the existence of an original to be copied or a true self to be hidden away from view. More than a common "liar," he defied the association of forgery with fakery. Indeed, his forged identities often tallied more authentically with his desires, sensibilities, and passions than the identities conferred on him by society. The story of Stuart-Young demonstrates that forgeries are future-oriented rather than imitative of existing objects or configurations: they are acts of persuasion, productions of selves for others, "unending stories, tales that lie awake."[23] The numerous "unrealities" that made up his accounts of his life actually helped constitute the material worlds he occupied, for each of his many truth claims contributed in complex ways to the status and networks he gained in West Africa. Solid social and material structures were generated by Stuart-Young's forgeries. In order to comprehend his phenomenal capacity for self-invention and the important role of others in the production of his identities, it has therefore been necessary to appreciate the inspired "sincerity" of these self-inventions.

The story of Stuart-Young opens doors into some of the most intimate cultural spaces in the British empire. This poorly educated, working-class Englishman sidestepped the British class system and entered the racial hierarchy in Nigeria in the early twentieth century. As a boy-loving man in Onitsha, he negotiated a sexual identity for himself that was taboo in the wake of the Wilde trials in Britain. He thus entered into negotiations with his home and host cultures while living on the West Coast of Africa, especially through his rumored marriage to the mermaid Mami Wata. Here too was a palm oil trader located outside missionary and imperial institutional structures whose passion for adolescent African boys did not go unnoticed by the people of Onitsha. Observing his unconventional behavior, local residents produced a range of different nicknames in which his proclivities were recognized and interpreted. These interpretations were often riddled with ambivalence and warnings, but what they all shared was an impulse to explain Stuart-Young's behavior using social and spiritual categories that furnished alternatives to the more normative gender dichotomies of imperialist discourse.

Today, the only material sign of Stuart-Young's presence in Onitsha is a shabby wooden house situated on New Market Road, surrounded by concrete buildings and petrol stations. Traffic roars past the Little House of No Regrets, and the road is filled with continuous noise (fig. 22). His tombstone in the old cemetery has, like the cemetery itself, disappeared beneath tall grasses and plots of land. The cemetery has been destroyed, replaced by small-scale suburban farms and towering rubbish heaps raked over by hens and goats. Many of the marble slabs from the gravestones have been removed, incorporated into local buildings or used as buttresses for benches in the market stalls nearby (fig. 23).

Material signs of Stuart-Young have almost disappeared, but his cultural traces remain strong in Onitsha in the form of the Odoziaku age-grade of

Fig. 22. The Little House of No Regrets in 2005.

Fig. 23. Contemporary uses for gravestones from the old cemetery, where Stuart-Young was buried.

1909, led by his protégé, Joseph Etukokwo. The saying "He who knows . . . ," still familiar to many Igbos and attributed to Stuart-Young, also preserves the memory of this minor poet and palm oil trader whose story lies buried beneath the grander narratives of imperialism. What remains of Stuart-Young in Onitsha citizens' memories and in the vast body of work he left behind gives us access at the most intimate and personal level to the material and psychological effects of colonialism upon different classes of European and African men. Unique and colorful in its own right, his story also opens up a wider social history of imperialism and homosexuality, revealing much about popular culture, poetry, forgery, and the spirit realm in the sixty-year period between 1880 and 1940. The story of "Odeziaku" provides an unusual glimpse into the aspirations of one "small man" whose life has been passed over by history.

"To the extent . . . that histories of 'sexuality' succeed in concerning themselves with *sexuality*, to just that extent are they doomed to fail as *histories*," writes David Halperin in his analysis of classical sexual cultures; unless, that is, such histories "include as an integral part of their proper enterprise the task of demonstrating the historicity, conditions of emergence, modes of construction, and ideological contingencies of the very categories of analysis that undergird their own practice"[24] (emphasis in original). Much more research is required before Halperin's demanding array of tasks can be met with detailed and contextualized historical studies of West African sexualities. My hope is that the intimate encounters that make up *The Forger's Tale* help us color in one small corner of imperial history and, in so doing, contribute to the broader picture of the cultural encounter between Europe and Africa in the early twentieth century.

Notes

INTRODUCTION

1. Emmanuel Obiechina, *Literature for the Masses: An Analytical Study of Popular Pamphleteering in Nigeria* (Enugu: Nwankwo-Ifejika, 1971), ix.

2. The sources and implications of these names and the persistent misspelling of "Odoziaku" by Stuart Young and his elite acquaintances are discussed in detail in chapter 5.

3. Stuart-Young uses the term "boy lover" to describe his young manservants and protégés. "Boy wife" might be equally appropriate to describe the combination of domestic care, subordination, and erotic companionship offered by the junior male in this type of relationship, which generally ended on his own heterosexual marriage. See E. E. Evans-Pritchard, "Sexual Inversion among the Azande," in *Ethnographic Studies of Homosexuality*, ed. Wayne R. Dynes and Stephen Donaldson (New York: Garland, 1992), 168–74; and Stephen O. Murray and Will Roscoe, eds., *Boy-Wives and Female Husbands: Studies of African Homosexualities* (Basingstoke: Macmillan, 1998). See also chapter 4.

4. See Joseph Thérèse Agbasiere, *Women in Igbo Life and Thought* (London: Routledge, 2000), 39–40.

5. Detailed accounts of the role of women at Igbo funerals and "second burial" ceremonies can be found in Nwando Achebe, "Farmers, Traders, Warriors and Kings: Female Power and Authority in Northern Igboland" (PhD diss., University of California, 2000), 299–306; Agbasiere, *Women in Igbo Life and Thought*, 143; Chigekwu G. Ogbuene, *The Concept of Man in Igbo Myths* (Frankfurt: Peter Lang, 1999); Chidozie Ogbalu, *Igbo Attitude to Sex* (Onitsha: University, ca. 1982).

6. Christopher Chukwuma Ndulue, *Womanhood in Igbo Culture* (Aba: Christopher C. Ndulue, 1995). As demonstrated below in this chapter and in chapter 5, however, Igbo gender codes cannot be regarded as fixed or rigid, especially in the early colonial period, for dual-sex norms were constantly mediated by categories that allowed for gender flexibility. See Ifi Amadiume, *Male Daughters, Female Husbands: Gender and Sex in an African Society* (London: Zed Books, 1987); Achebe, "Farmers, Traders, Warriors and Kings."

7. Between the late nineteenth century and the 1930s, colonial attitudes changed considerably toward Europeans' sexual relationships with local women and miscegenation; by the 1920s, such relationships were intolerable to most European colonial regimes. See Ann Laura Stoler, *Carnal Knowledge and Imperial Power: Race and the Intimate in Colonial Rule* (Berkeley: University of California Press, 2002); Felicity Nussbaum, *Torrid Zones: Maternity, Sexuality, and Empire in Eighteenth-Century English Narratives* (Baltimore, MD: Johns Hopkins University Press, 1995).

8. Chuks Osuji, *Foundation of Igbo Tradition and Culture* (Owerri: Opinion Research and Communications, 1998); S. I. Bosah, *Groundwork of the History and Culture of Onitsha* (Onitsha, 1984).

9. Ndulue, *Womanhood in Igbo Culture*; Achebe, "Farmers, Traders, Warriors and Kings."

10. Agbasiere, *Women in Igbo Life and Thought*. The local connotations of the term "woman-hater" are discussed in chapter 5.

11. Interview with Nwononaku Josephine Ofordile, August 2005; interview with Agnes Okosi, August 2005; Joseph U. Etukokwu, *Life between Two Shrines: An Autobiography* (Onitsha: Etukokwu, ca. 1997); "Natives Decide to Mourn for 4 Days," *West African Pilot*, 3 June 1939, 1.

12. "Natives Decide to Mourn for 4 Days."

13. Agbasiere, *Women in Igbo Life and Thought*, 144.

14. "Natives Decide to Mourn for 4 Days."

15. Ndulue describes the "second burial" as the ceremony in which a person who has lived a "good life" is ensured passage into the land of the ancestors, or the spirit world, where that person will enjoy "peaceful repose and not . . . disturb the living" (*Womanhood in Igbo Culture*, 136). Different categories of person are given different types of second burial, depending on their status and achievements in life. See also Ogbuene, *The Concept of Man in Igbo Myths*, 221–28.

16. Etukokwu, *Life between Two Shrines*, 195.

17. "Africans Bitterly Weep for Odeziaku," *West African Pilot*, 31 May 1939, 1; "Natives Stage Grand Funeral for Late Dr John Stuart-Young," *West African Pilot*, 12 June 1939, 1. The *ogene* is a metal gong traditionally used by town criers to call people's attention to messages or meetings.

18. Etukokwu, *Life between Two Shrines*, 195.

19. See Leith-Ross, *Stepping-Stones: Memoirs of Colonial Nigeria, 1907–1960* (London: Peter Owen, 1983). Elite Igbo men, such as the retired civil servant Akunna John Nworah, also repeatedly described Stuart-Young in these terms: "[Q]ueer is the word," Nworah insisted. Interview with Akunna John Nworah, August 2005.

20. Adiele E. Afigbo, *Ropes of Sand: Studies in Igbo History and Culture* (Ibadan: Ibadan University Press; Oxford: Oxford University Press, 1981); Adiele E. Afigbo, *The Warrant Chiefs: Indirect Rule in Southeastern Nigeria, 1891–1929*

(London: Longman, 1972); Kenneth Onwuka Dike, *Trade and Politics in the Niger Delta, 1830–1885* (Westport, Conn.: Greenwood Press, 1956); Elizabeth Isichei, *A History of the Igbo People* (Basingstoke: Macmillan, 1976).

21. See Samuel Ajayi Crowther and John Christopher Taylor, *The Gospel on the Banks of the Niger: Journals and Notices of the Native Missionaries Accompanying the Niger Expedition of 1857–1859* (1859; London: Dawsons of Pall Mall, 1968); Celestine A. Obi, ed., *A Hundred Years of the Catholic Church in Eastern Nigeria, 1885–1985* (Onitsha: Africana-Fep, 1985).

22. In Onitsha, for example, wealthy merchant queens such as Madame Izadi sponsored and led prominent dance groups. Trained as a girl by Omu Okwei, the merchant queen of Ossomari, Madame Izadi traded directly with the Europeans and became immensely wealthy in the 1920s and 1930s. Her female dance group was called Ejena-Sea, meaning "people who don't go to the water." Its members prided themselves on having servants to fetch water and firewood for their households. Interview with Agnes Okosi, August 2005; see also John C. McCall, *Dancing Histories: Heuristic Ethnography with the Ohafia Igbo* (Ann Arbor: University of Michigan Press, 2000).

23. In the context of this study, "local responses" also refers to responses of members of the working class to political and social affairs in the empire. The first section of this book addresses these issues through the story of Stuart-Young's youth in Manchester.

24. Robert Aldrich, *Colonialism and Homosexuality* (London: Routledge, 2003), 8; italics added.

25. Ibid.

26. See Chandra Talpade Mohanty, "Under Western Eyes: Feminist Scholarship and Colonial Discourses," in *Colonial Discourse and Postcolonial Theory: A Reader*, ed. Patrick Williams and Laura Chrisman (New York: Harvester Wheatsheaf, 1993), 196–220; Amadiume, *Male Daughters, Female Husbands*.

27. Aldrich, *Colonialism and Homosexuality*, 8.

28. Ronald Hyam, *Empire and Sexuality: The British Experience* (Manchester: Manchester University Press, 1991); Joseph Bristow, *Empire Boys: Adventures in a Man's World* (London: HarperCollins, 1991); and Christopher Lane, *The Ruling Passion: British Colonial Allegory and the Paradox of Homosexual Desire* (Durham, NC: Duke University Press, 1995).

29. Hyam, *Empire and Sexuality*, 5–9.

30. Ibid., 1. For detailed critiques of Hyam, see Lane, *Ruling Passion*, 2–6; and Mark T. Berger, "Imperialism and Sexual Exploitation," *Journal of Imperial and Commonwealth History* 17, no. 1 (1988): 83–89.

31. Rudi C. Bleys, *The Geography of Perversion: Male-to-Male Sexual Behaviour outside the West and the Ethnographic Imagination, 1750–1918* (London: Cassell, 1996), 1; see also Gilbert Herdt, *Same Sex, Different Cultures: Gays and Lesbians across Cultures* (Boulder, CO: Westview Press, 1997).

32. Bleys, *Geography of Perversion*, 251.

33. See Jeffrey Weeks and Kevin Porter, *Between the Acts: Lives of Homosexual Men, 1885–1967* (London: Rivers Oram Press, 1998). Many of the interviewees in *Between the Acts* describe feelings of terror and guilt associated with their homosexuality. They feared alienation, isolation, and exclusion from their societies. Several of these men decided leave Britain for the empire. For example, after losing his job as a schoolteacher, "David," a pedophile born in 1904, traveled to Nigeria, where he had a brief relationship with a female prostitute, followed by an intimate, longer-term relationship with a male bodyguard. "Barry," born in 1913, joined the British Council to "escape the intolerance of England"; in the Congo he saw "black boys . . . parading around on the boulevard opposite the big open-air café where all the Europeans went" (50–61, 157–68).

34. Herdt, *Same Sex, Different Cultures*; Murray and Roscoe, *Boy-Wives and Female Husbands*.

35. There are very few studies of lesbian sexuality in Africa and little material in circulation about woman-to-woman desire in the colonial period. For a study of contemporary woman-to-woman erotic relationships, see Kendall, "'When a Woman Loves a Woman' in Lesotho: Love, Sex, and the (Western) Construction of Homophobia," in Murray and Roscoe, *Boy-Wives and Female Husbands*, 223–41.

36. Stoler, *Carnal Knowledge and Imperial Power*; Catherine Hall, *Civilising Subjects: Metropole and Colony in the English Imagination, 1830–1867* (Cambridge: Polity, 2002); Antoinette Burton, *At the Heart of the Empire: Indians and the Colonial Encounter in Late-Victorian Britain* (Berkeley: University of California Press, 1998); Nussbaum, *Torrid Zones*.

37. Hall, *Civilising Subjects*; Mrinalini Sinha, *Colonial Masculinity: The "Manly Englishman" and the "Effeminate Bengali" in the Late Nineteenth Century* (Manchester: Manchester University Press, 1995).

38. Burton, *At the Heart of the Empire*, 6. See Hall, *Civilising Subjects*; Sinha, *Colonial Masculinity*.

39. Ann Laura Stoler and Frederick Cooper, "Between Metropole and Colony: Rethinking a Research Agenda," in *Tensions of Empire: Colonial Cultures in a Bourgeois World*, ed. Frederick Cooper and Ann Laura Stoler (Berkeley: University of California Press, 1997), 1, 5.

40. Hall, *Civilising Subjects*; Burton, *At the Heart of the Empire*. Except for southern Africa, there is a striking absence of material on Sub-Saharan Africa in the "new imperial history." This absence is especially noticeable in the major edited collections, such as Antoinette Burton, *Gender, Sexuality and Colonial Modernities* (London: Routledge, 1999); Catherine Hall, *Cultures of Empire: A Reader* (Manchester: Manchester University Press, 2000); and Cooper and Stoler, *Tensions of Empire*.

41. See Nussbaum, *Torrid Zones*; Ann Laura Stoler, *Race and the Education of Desire: Foucault's History of Sexuality and the Colonial Order of Things* (Durham, NC: Duke University Press, 1995); Stoler, *Carnal Knowledge and Imperial Power*.

42. Foucault, cited in Stoler, *Carnal Knowledge and Imperial Power*, 145.

43. Sexuality and power are key topics in Nussbaum, *Torrid Zones*; Stoler, *Race and the Education of Desire*; Stoler, *Carnal Knowledge and Imperial Power*; Philippa Levine, *Gender and Empire* (Oxford: Oxford University Press, 2004); Anne McClintock, *Imperial Leather: Race, Gender and Sexuality in the Colonial Contest* (London: Routledge, 1995); and Helen Callaway, *Gender, Culture and Empire: European Women in Colonial Nigeria* (Basingstoke: Macmillan, 1987).

44. Hall, *Civilising Subjects*; Stoler, *Carnal Knowledge and Imperial Power*; Cooper and Stoler, *Tensions of Empire*.

45. Amadiume, *Male Daughters, Female Husbands*, 14–16.

46. Ibid. Amadiume also criticizes more recent examples of feminist ethnocentrism, including Maria Rosa Cutrufelli's *Women of Africa: Roots of Oppression*, trans. Nicolas Romano (London: Zed Press, 1983); and Germaine Greer, *Sex and Destiny: The Politics of Human Fertility* (London: Secker and Warburg, 1984); P. Amaury Talbot, *Some Nigerian Fertility Cults* (1927; reprint, London: Frank Cass, 1967); Arthur Glyn Leonard, *The Lower Niger and Its Tribes* (1906; reprint, London: Frank Cass, 1968); G. T. Basden, *Among the Ibos of Nigeria* (1921; reprint, London: Frank Cass, 1966); Sylvia Leith-Ross, *Stepping-Stones: Memoirs of Colonial Nigeria, 1907–1960*, ed. Michael Crowder (London: Peter Owen, 1983).

47. Amadiume, *Male Daughters, Female Husbands*, 15.

48. See also Achebe, "Farmers, Traders, Warriors and Kings."

49. Amadiume, *Male Daughters, Female Husbands*, 15–17; see also Achebe, "Farmers, Traders, Warriors and Kings"; John McCall, "Portrait of a Brave Woman," *American Anthropologist* 98, no. 1 (1996): 127–36.

50. Amadiume, *Male Daughters, Female Husbands*, 9, 15.

51. For a discussion of these issues by queer theorists, see Chris Dunton, "'Wheyting de dat?' The Treatment of Homosexuality in African Literature," *Research in African Literatures* 20, no. 3 (1989): 422–48; Bleys, *Geography of Perversion*; Marc Epprecht, "'Good God Almighty, What's This?': Homosexual 'Crime' in Early Colonial Zimbabwe," in Murray and Roscoe, *Boy-Wives and Female Husbands*, 197–221; Rudolf P. Gaudio, "Male Lesbians and Other Queer Notions in Hausa," in Murray and Roscoe, *Boy-Wives and Female Husbands*, 115–28.

52. Amadiume, *Male Daughters, Female Husbands*, 7.

53. Ibid., 9.

54. Amadiume is not alone in this assertion. Several African cultural nationalist writers insist that homosexuality has its origins elsewhere, that it is part of the continent's history of subjugation by Arab-Islamic invaders and European colonialists. For a discussion of the ways in which homosexuality and imperialism are intertwined for many African nationalists, see Bleys, *Geography of Perversion*; Dunton, "'Wheyting de Dat?'"; Herdt, *Same Sex, Different Cultures*.

55. Marc Epprecht, "The 'Unsaying' of Indigenous Homosexualities in Zimbabwe: Mapping a Blindspot in an African Masculinity," *Journal of Southern African Studies* 24, no. 4 (1998): 633. Amadiume's adoption of the "homosexuality

as alien import" perspective has attracted a degree of criticism that ignores the queer possibilities of her work, explored below: see Gaudio, "Male Lesbians and Other Queer Notions"; Kendall, "'When a Woman Loves a Woman' in Lesotho."

56. Achebe, "Farmers, Traders, Warriors and Kings," 26, 296.

57. Herdt, *Same Sex, Different Cultures*; Bleys, *Geography of Perversion*; Richard Parker, *Beneath the Equator: Cultures of Desire, Male Homosexuality, and Emerging Gay Communities in Brazil* (London: Routledge, 1999).

58. Nii Ajen, "West African Homoeroticism: West African Men Who Have Sex with Men," in Murray and Roscoe, *Boy-Wives and Female Husbands*, 131.

59. Bleys, *Geography of Perversion*, 1–6.

60. Ajen, "West African Homoeroticism."

61. Herdt, *Same Sex, Different Cultures*; Bill Stanford Pincheon, "An Ethnography of Silences: Race, (Homo)Sexualities, and a Discourse of Africa," *African Studies Review* 43, no. 3 (2000): 39–58.

62. Kath Weston, "Lesbian/Gay Studies in the House of Anthropology," *Annual Review of Anthropology* 22 (1993): 339–67.

63. Herdt, *Same Sex, Different Cultures*, 9.

64. David Alderson and Linda Anderson, "Introduction," in *Territories of Desire in Queer Culture: Refiguring Contemporary Boundaries*, ed. David Alderson and Linda Anderson (Manchester: Manchester University Press, 2000), 2; Herdt, *Same Sex, Different Cultures*.

65. Achebe, "Farmers, Traders, Warriors and Kings"; Amadiume, *Male Daughters, Female Husbands*.

66. At the end of his vehement critique of ethnographies of homosexuality in Africa, Bill Stanford Pincheon seems to make space for queer theory without naming it when he calls for the "exploding of rigid conceptions of categories: a blurring of the lines between the fixity and stability of those that are already presumed 'natural,' and thus already taken for granted" ("An Ethnography of Silences," 56). By contrast, Kath Weston's seminal article "Lesbian/Gay Studies in the House of Anthropology" openly rejects "homosexuality" in favor of a "queer studies" model (348).

67. See, e.g., Stephen Ellingson and M. Christian Green, "Introduction," in *Religion and Sexuality in Cross-Cultural Perspective*, ed. Stephen Ellingson and M. Christian Green, 1–18 (London: Routledge, 2002).

68. Weston agrees: "By setting out in advance to look for sexuality," she writes, "the anthropologist cannot help but reify the object of (ethnographic) desire," a move that confirms "western assumptions about the unambiguously binary character of gender" and this endorses the very identity that queer theory seeks to escape. "Lesbian/Gay Studies in the House of Anthropology," 346–47.

69. Amadiume, *Male Daughters, Female Husbands*, 15.

70. Ibid., 89.

71. See Martin Bauml Duberman, Martha Vicinus, and George Chauncey, "Introduction," in *Hidden from History: Reclaiming the Gay and Lesbian Past*, ed.

Martin Bauml Duberman, Martha Vicinus, and George Chauncey, 1–13 (London: Penguin, 1989).

72. Amadiume, *Male Daughters, Female Husbands*, 28, 89; see also Ifi Amadiume, *Reinventing Africa: Matriarchy, Religion and Culture* (London: Zed Books, 1997).

73. E.g., Amadiume, *Male Daughters, Female Husbands*, 42.

74. Duberman, Vicinus, and Chauncey, introduction to *Hidden from History*, 1–13.

75. See Dynes and Donaldson, *Ethnographic Studies of Homosexuality*; Herdt, *Same Sex, Different Cultures*; Gilbert Herdt and Robert J. Stoller, *Intimate Communications: Erotics and the Study of Culture* (New York: Columbia University Press, 1990); David M. Halperin, "Sex before Sexuality: Pederasty, Politics and Power in Classical Athens," in *Hidden from History: Reclaiming the Gay and Lesbian Past*, ed. Martin Bauml Duberman, Martha Vicinus, and George Chauncey, 37–53 (London: Penguin, 1989); Gaudio, "Male Lesbians and Other Queer Notions."

76. Gilbert Herdt and Robert J. Stoller use the term "sexual culture" in their cross-cultural study of (homo)erotics, *Intimate Communications*. Herdt develops the concept in detail in *Same Sex, Different Cultures* in his search for terminology outside the limits of western definitions of sexuality. In both of these texts, the concept of "sexual culture" signifies "a conventionalized and shared system of sexual practices, supported by beliefs and roles" (*Same Sex, Different Cultures*, 11). A sexual culture "suggests a worldview based on specific sexual and gender norms, emotions, beliefs, and symbolic meanings regarding the proper nature and purpose of sexual encounters" (ibid., 17). Herdt thus emphasizes the cultural and ideological spaces that surround a person over an individual's life story in isolation.

77. Amadiume, *Male Daughters, Female Husbands*, 31, 39.

78. Amadiume, *Reinventing Africa*, 112.

79. Herdt, *Same Sex, Different Cultures*, 21; see also Bleys, *The Geography of Perversion*.

80. See Herdt, *Same Sex, Different Cultures*.

81. Such a moment would be the emergence of the strong homosexual subculture of the boy-loving Uranian writers and artists in late-nineteenth-century Britain described in chapter 4. For a critique of the "natural tolerance" of nonwestern cultures for diverse fluid sexualities, see Dennis Altman's "Global Gaze/Global Gays," in *Postcolonial and Queer Theories: Intersections and Essays*, ed. John C. Hawley, 1–18 (Westport, Conn.: Greenwood Press, 2001).

82. See Zachie Achmat, "'Apostles of Civilised Vice': 'Immoral Practices' and 'Unnatural Vice' in South African Prisons and Compounds, 1890–1920," *Social Dynamics* 19, no. 2 (1993): 95. Studies of contemporary African homosexualities include Dunton, "'Wheyting de dat?'"; Dynes and Donaldson *Ethnographic Studies of Homosexuality*; Murray and Roscoe, *Boy-Wives and Female Husbands*.

83. G. T. Basden, *Niger Ibos* (1938; London: Frank Cass, 1966), 38.

84. P. Amaury Talbot, *Some Nigerian Fertility Cults* (1927; London: Frank Cass, 1967), 14–15, 32.

85. Bleys, *Geography of Perversion*, 208.

86. Pincheon, "An Ethnography of Silences," 39.

87. Weston, "Lesbian/Gay Studies in the House of Anthropology," 339.

88. Achebe, "Farmers, Traders, Warriors and Kings," 54.

89. See Stoler, *Carnal Knowledge and Imperial Power*; Nussbaum, *Torrid Zones*.

90. Stoler and Cooper, "Between Metropole and Colony," 27; Stoler, *Carnal Knowledge and Imperial Power*.

91. Stuart-Young, "Changes in Nigerian Life since 1900," *Comet*, 7 December 1935, 7–12.

92. Files at the Nigerian National Archives, Enugu, reveal a considerable degree of suspicion on the part of officials about Stuart-Young's leasing arrangements. They suspected him of property speculation in violation of colonial land laws; see Commissioner of Lands, Lagos, "Application by Mr J. M. Stuart-Young for a site at Onitsha Property of Chief Mba," CSE 2/9/11, no. A1479/1916, Nigerian National Archives, Enugu; "Mr J. M. Stuart-Young: Application for a Site at Old Market Road, Onitsha," CSE 2/11/10, no. A1160/1918, Nigerian National Archives, Enugu; "Requesting Sanction for Crown Prosecution to Prosecute in the Cases vs Messrs Stuart-Young and Bright for Contravention of Native Lands Acquisition Ordinance," CSE 2/9/11, no. A1479/1916, Nigerian National Archives, Enugu.

93. Etukokwu, *Life between Two Shrines*, 43.

94. Ibid.

95. For studies of imperialism and popular literature, see Robert Dixon, *Writing the Colonial Adventure: Race, Gender and Nation in Anglo-Australian Popular Fiction, 1875–1914* (Cambridge: Cambridge University Press, 1995); Mawuena Kossi Logan, *Narrating Africa: George Henty and the Fiction of Empire* (New York: Garland, 1999); Stuart Ward, *British Culture and the Empire* (Manchester: Manchester University Press, 2001).

96. Herdt and Stoller, *Intimate Communications*, 366.

97. Burton, *At the Heart of the Empire*, 13.

98. Stoler and Cooper, "Between Metropole and Colony," 1–56.

99. See also Burton, *At the Heart of the Empire*.

100. See Liz Stanley, "Moments of Writing: Is There a Feminist Auto/biography?" *Gender and History* 2, no. 1 (1990): 58–67.

101. I use the word "scribophile" to suggest the compulsive and prolific nature of Stuart-Young's literary activities and the way that writing permeated all aspects of his identity.

102. Anthony Grafton takes this path in *Forgers and Critics: Creativity and Duplicity in Western Scholarship* (London: Collins and Brown, 1990). Grafton describes forgery as having a "malevolent influence" on society; it is "a sort of crime" committed by "fantasists and liars" who are "infected" with "the desire to forge" (36–37, 41, 48). By contrast, Nick Groom's innovative study of forgers emphasizes

the creativity of forgery as an art form; see *The Forger's Shadow: How Forgery Changed the Course of Literature* (London: Picador, 2002), 55.

103. Alderson and Anderson, "Introduction," 2.

104. Hall, *Civilising Subjects*, 9; see also Sinha, *Colonial Masculinity*; Burton, *At the Heart of the Empire*.

CHAPTER 1

1. "Yesterday's Police Intelligence," *Manchester Courier*, 5 May 1899, 9.
2. J. M. Stuart-Young, *What Does It Matter?* (London: C. W. Daniel Co., 1927), 165.
3. Ibid., 253; see also J. M. Stuart-Young, *Johnny Jones Guttersnipe* (London: C. W. Daniel, 1926), 274. Details of Stuart-Young's clothing have been extrapolated from newspaper reports on the court case and from his two "autobiographical novels," *Johnny Jones Guttersnipe* and *What Does It Matter?*, which are discussed in chapter 7.
4. Records of the Petty Sessional Court are held by the Family History Unit of Manchester Central Library.
5. "Clerk and Spirit Medium," *Manchester Weekly Times*, 5 May 1899, 4.
6. See Paul Thompson, *The Edwardians: The Remaking of British Society* (London: Routledge, 1975; 2nd ed. 1992).
7. Manchester Police Museum records.
8. Ibid.
9. "Embezzlement and Spiritualism: Six Months for the Medium," *Manchester Evening News*, 4 May 1899, 2.
10. "Yesterday's Police Intelligence," 9.
11. "Embezzlement and Spiritualism," 2.
12. "Yesterday's Police Intelligence," 9.
13. Ibid.
14. See Alex Owen, *The Darkened Room: Women, Power, and Spiritualism in Late Nineteenth-Century England* (London: Virago Press, 1989).
15. "Yesterday's Police Intelligence," 9.
16. "Embezzlement and Spiritualism," 2.
17. Ibid.
18. See chapter 3. Nick Groom, *The Forger's Shadow* (London: Picador, 2002) sees forgery as a powerful creative act, in contrast to those who regard forgery as the work of charlatans and frauds.
19. "Yesterday's Police Intelligence," 9; "Embezzlement and Spiritualism," 2.
20. "Yesterday's Police Intelligence," 9.
21. J. M. Stuart-Young, "West African Nights: The Bits I Remember," serialized in the Nigerian *Comet*, 1935. No copies of the *Comet* are available for 1934, when this serial commenced; it ran weekly until 9 February 1935.

22. See Thompson, *Edwardians*; Geoffrey Crossick, ed., *The Lower Middle Class in Britain, 1870–1914* (London: Croom Helm, 1977).

23. Perhaps a struggling, ambitious lower-middle-class writer such as George Gissing, whose own career was ruined in Manchester when he was caught thieving money, would have understood the reasons for Stuart-Young's crimes. The title of Gissing's novel *Born in Exile* (London: Victor Gollancz, 1892) perfectly describes Stuart-Young's mental condition.

24. See Stuart-Young, *Johnny Jones Guttersnipe*; Stuart-Young, *What Does It Matter?*

25. "Yesterday's Police Intelligence," 9.

26. Stuart-Young, *What Does It Matter?*

27. See William Booth, *In Darkest England and the Way Out* (1890; 6th ed., London: Charles Knight, 1970). Citations are to the 1970 edition.

28. Ibid., 13.

29. Charles Booth, *Life and Labour of the People in London* (London: Macmillan 1889); a condensed version is Charles Booth, *Charles Booth's London: A Portrait of the Poor at the Turn of the Century, Drawn from His "Life and Labour of the People in London,"* ed. Albert Fried and Richard M. Elman (1899; London: Hutchinson, 1969); C. F. G. Masterman, ed., *The Heart of the Empire: Discussions of Problems of Modern City Life in England* (1901; Brighton: Harvester Press, 1973).

30. Booth, *Charles Booth's London*.

31. London Congregational Union, *The Bitter Cry of Outcast London* (London: London Congregational Union, 1883); A. Delver [Alfred Alsop], *Ten Years in the Slums* (Manchester: John Heywood, 1879); Arthur Morrison, *A Child of the Jago* (London: Methuen, 1896); Jack London, *The People of the Abyss* (1903; London: Journeyman Press, 1977). Citations are to the 1977 edition.

32. Booth, *Charles Booth's London*, 11; see Robert Colls, "Englishness and the Political Culture," in *Englishness: Politics and Culture, 1880–1920*, ed. Robert Colls and Philip Dodd, 29–61 (London: Croom Helm, 1986).

33. Booth, *In Darkest England*, 9.

34. Booth, *Charles Booth's London*, 60.

35. See David Alderson, *Mansex Fine: Religion, Manliness and Imperialism in Nineteenth-Century British Culture* (Manchester: Manchester University Press, 1998).

36. Booth, *Charles Booth's London*, 12; Masterman, *Heart of the Empire*.

37. Booth, *In Darkest England*.

38. Booth, *Charles Booth's London*.

39. See Robert J. C. Young, *Colonial Desire: Hybridity in Theory, Culture and Race* (London: Routledge, 1995).

40. Stuart-Young was not alone in his subversive mastery of the clothing and writing styles of the bourgeoisie; many of the men on the wanted lists of the Manches-

ter Police Force had committed the crime of posing as gentleman by writing letters falsely petitioning for charitable donations (Manchester Police Museum Archive).

41. See Geoffrey Crossick and Heinz-Gerhard Haupt, *The Petite Bourgeoisie in Europe, 1780–1914: Enterprise, Family, and Independence* (London: Routledge, 1995).

42. See Crossick, *Lower Middle Class in Britain*; Jonathan Wild, *The Rise of the Office Clerk in British Literary Culture* (Basingstoke: Palgrave, 2005).

43. See Hugh McLeod, *Religion and the Working Class in Nineteenth-Century Britain* (London: Macmillan, 1984).

44. Booth, *Charles Booth's London*, 9; Booth, *In Darkest England*, 85.

45. Booth, *Charles Booth's London*, 25.

46. Ibid., 280.

47. Booth, *In Darkest England*, 40.

48. Booth, *Charles Booth's London*, 59.

49. Ibid., 63, 77.

50. See McLeod, *Religion and the Working Class*.

51. See Wild, *Rise of the Office Clerk*.

52. See Ben Brierley, *Home Memories and Out of Work*, ed. Roy Westall (Bramhall, Cheshire: Reword Publishers, 2002).

53. Crossick, *Lower Middle Class in Britain*, 37.

54. See G. L. Anderson, "The Social Economy of Late Victorian Clerks," in Crossick, *Lower Middle Class in Britain*, 113–33.

55. Cited in ibid., 117.

56. Ibid.

57. Stuart-Young, *What Does It Matter?* 275, ellipses in original. See also Gissing, *Born in Exile*.

58. G. L. Anderson, "Social Economy of Late Victorian Clerks," 125.

59. Records held in the Manchester Police Museum. There were different levels of clerks, however, including middle-class men whose networks of patronage and prospects for promotion were good in comparison with those of working-class clerks.

60. It must be noted that before the era of police photography, the portraits obtained by police were often studio portraits that police took from families of wanted men. From the 1870s through to the era of police "mug shots" in the 1890s, the roughest bank robbers can be seen posing with cravats, well-groomed hair, and overcoats.

61. Thompson, *Edwardians*, 168; see Anderson, "Social Economy."

62. See Stuart-Young, *What Does It Matter?* 179.

63. Anderson, "The Social Economy," 125.

64. See Stuart-Young, *What Does It Matter?* 172–75, 210.

65. Ibid.

66. Stuart-Young, *Johnny Jones Guttersnipe*, 287.

CHAPTER 2

1. Ann Laura Stoler, *Carnal Knowledge and Imperial Power: Race and the Intimate in Colonial Rule* (Berkeley: University of California Press, 2002), 42–43.

2. Ibid., 43; Antoinette Burton, *Burdens of History: British Feminists, Indian Women, and Imperial Culture, 1865–1915* (Chapel Hill: University of North Carolina Press, 1994); Catherine Hall, *Civilising Subjects: Metropole and Colony in the English Imagination, 1830–1867* (Cambridge: Polity, 2002); Philippa Levine, introduction to *Gender and Empire*, ed. Philippa Levine, 1–13 (Oxford: Oxford University Press, 2004).

3. Alan Field, "Verb Sap." on Going to West Africa, Northern Nigeria, Southern, and to the Coasts, 3rd ed. (London: Bale, Sons and Danielsson, 1913), 55.

4. For a discussion of the concept of bias history, see Kofi Baku, "An Intellectual in Nationalist Politics: The Contribution of Kobina Sekyi to the Evolution of Ghanaian National Consciousness" (PhD diss., University of Sussex, 1987).

5. See Harry Cottrell, "Reminiscences of One Connected with the West African Trade from 1863 to 1910," in *Trading in West Africa, 1840–1920*, ed. P. N. Davies (London: Croom Helm, 1976), 53.

6. See Margaret Priestley, *West African Trade and Coast Society: A Family Study* (London: Oxford University Press, 1969); Clough, *Oil Rivers Trader: Memories of Iboland* (London: C. Hurst, 1972), 31.

7. William Booth, *In Darkest England and the Way Out* (1890; 6th ed, London: Charles Knight, 1970) (citations are to the 1970 edition); Henry Morton Stanley, *In Darkest Africa* (New York: C. Scribner's Sons, 1890).

8. Booth, *In Darkest England*.

9. Ibid., 11.

10. Philippa Levine, "Sexuality, Gender, and Empire," in *Gender and Empire*, ed. Philippa Levine (Oxford: Oxford University Press, 2004), 134.

11. Samuel Ajayi Crowther and John Christopher Taylor, *The Gospel on the Banks of the Niger* (1859; London: Dawsons of Pall Mall, 1968), ix. "WK" is probably William Knight, the biographer of Henry Venn and a member of the Church Missionary House staff from 1851 to 1862. I am grateful to Brian Stanley for supplying this information via Terry Barringer.

12. Ibid.

13. Field, "Verb Sap," 161.

14. Ibid., 55.

15. Ibid, 57, 164.

16. Warren Henry, *Fantee Carter* (London: Herbert Jenkins, 1931), 24.

17. Timothy Burke, *Lifebuoy Men, Lux Women: Commodification, Consumption and Cleanliness in Modern Zimbabwe* (London: Leicester University Press, 1996).

18. Crowther and Taylor, *Gospel on the Banks of the Niger*, 227.

19. Ibid., 228–29.

20. Ibid., 228.

21. Kathleen Wilson, "Empire, Gender, and Modernity in the Eighteenth Century," in Levine, *Gender and Empire*, 16.

22. "Dirty whites" were looked upon with growing consternation in the early twentieth century, especially when the culprits were colonial officers. An unshaven face, failure to dress for dinner, and dirty flannels were all signs of moral degeneration and a "dirtily kept" station; see Field, *Verb Sap*, 80–81.

23. Mary Kingsley, *Travels in West Africa* (1897; London: Everyman, 1993), 15. Citations are to the (abridged) 1993 edition.

24. Ibid.

25. Ibid., 16.

26. The respect was mutual, although tinged with ambivalence: in *Fantee Carter* (1931), a novel about a white trader, Warren Henry repays the favor, having a "Mary Kingsley" figure turn up in a rugged young trader's remote outpost; the tomboy-heroine, Rhoda K. Marlowe, arrives in West Africa in the manner of Kingsley in search of fetishes and flora. The couple marry and beat a hasty retreat to a cottage with roses around the door in rural England.

27. John Moray Stuart-Young, *The Coaster at Home* (London: Arthur H. Stockwell, 1916), 73. The sequel, *The Iniquitous Coaster* (London: Arthur H. Stockwell, 1917), focuses in detail on the Great War, showing how it brought out a sense of imperial patriotism in the English trader.

28. Crowther and Taylor, *Gospel on the Banks of the Niger*, 4.

29. See Cottrell, "Reminiscences"; Aloysius Horn, *Trader Horn* (1927; Bath: Cedric Chivers, 1974).

30. See Allan McPhee, *The Economic Revolution in British West Africa* (1926; London: Frank Cass, 1971).

31. See David Northrup, *Trade without Rulers: Pre-Colonial Economic Development in South-Eastern Nigeria* (Oxford: Clarendon Press, 1978).

32. G. I. Jones, *From Slaves to Palm Oil: Slave Trade and Palm Oil Trade in the Bight of Biafra* (Cambridge: African Studies Centre, 1989), 46.

33. See Martin Lynn, *Commerce and Economic Change in West Africa: The Palm Oil Trade in the Nineteenth Century* (Cambridge: Cambridge University Press, 1997).

34. For a detailed study of Lever Brothers in West and Central Africa, see D. K. Fieldhouse, *Merchant Capital and Economic Decolonization: The United Africa Company, 1929–1987* (Oxford: Clarendon Press, 1994).

35. Horn, *Trader Horn*, 39.

36. Lynn, *Commerce and Economic Change*, 31.

37. Ibid., 111.

38. Clough, *Oil Rivers Trader*, 16; see also Priestley, *West African Trade*; Kaplow, "African Merchants."

39. See Burke, *Lifebuoy Men, Lux Women*; Thomas Richards, *The Commodity Culture of Victorian England: Advertising and Spectacle, 1851–1914* (Stanford, Calif.: Stanford University Press, 1990).

40. It also symbolized the rise of the cult of domesticity, whereby "femininity" was defined and expressed through personal and household cleanliness.

41. Cited in Richards, *Commodity Culture of Victorian England*, 140.

42. Cited in Anne McClintock, *Imperial Leather: Race, Gender and Sexuality in the Colonial Contest* (London: Routledge, 1995), 207–8.

43. Ibid., 208; Richards, *Commodity Culture of Victorian England*; Burke, *Lifebuoy Men, Lux Women*.

44. Clough, *Oil Rivers Trader*.

45. John Whitford, *Trading Life in Western and Central Africa* (1877; London: Frank Cass, 1967).

46. This work ethic is undermined by the half-hidden confession in several early memoirs that African domestic slaves contributed to the collection and transport of palm products to Britain; see Whitford, *Trading Life*; Cottrell, "Reminiscences." European and African traders thus benefited directly from the continuation of domestic slavery.

47. Whitford, *Trading Life*, 184.

48. McPhee, *The Economic Revolution*, 232.

49. James Deemin, "Autobiography of James Deemin," in *Trading in West Africa, 1840–1920*, ed. P. N. Davies (London: Croom Helm, 1976), 116.

50. Kingsley, *Travels*, 134.

51. Deemin, "Autobiography," 116–17; see also Whitford, *Trading Life*, 148.

52. Kingsley, *Travels*, 132.

53. Ibid.

54. Deemin, "Autobiography," 120.

55. Edward Harrington, "The Letter Book of Captain Edward Harrington," introduction by George E. Brooks, *Transactions of the Historical Society of Ghana* 7 (1962): 76.

56. Whitford, *Trading Life*, 149.

57. See, e.g., McPhee, *Economic Revolution*.

58. Whitford, *Trading Life*, 28.

59. Ibid.

60. Ibid., 71.

61. Ibid.

62. Ibid., 334.

63. Ibid., 142, 316.

64. Ibid., 168, 191.

65. This view characterizes Stuart-Young's engagement with the African environment; see chapter 8.

66. Field, "*Verb Sap*," 36.

67. Clough, *Oil Rivers Trader*, 7.

68. See also Albert Schweitzer, *The Primeval Forest* (1931; Baltimore: Johns Hopkins University Press, 1998). Traders in the nineteenth century concentrated not on the creation of a luxury market but, in the words of G. I. Jones, on the conversion of "former luxuries into necessities"; *From Slaves to Palm Oil*, 56.

69. Clough, *Oil Rivers Trader*, 36.
70. Ibid., 35, 27.
71. See, for example, Whitford, *Trading Life*, 239–40.
72. Ibid., 207.
73. Ibid., 207, 241.
74. Whitford, *Trading Life*, 207.
75. Ibid., 208.
76. Ibid.
77. See Burke, *Lifebuoy Men, Lux Women*, 102.
78. See, for example, Clough, *Oil Rivers Trader*, 11.
79. Whitford, *Trading Life*, 34, 36.
80. Lynn, *Commerce and Economic Change*, 70–75.
81. Clough, *Oil Rivers Trader*, 52.
82. Ibid., 38.
83. Lynn, *Commerce and Economic Change*, 58.
84. Kingsley, *Travels in West Africa*, 136.
85. Stuart-Young composed two "autobiographies" in the voice of his masculine alter ego, the "palm oil trader and ruffian man" Jack O'Dazi. *The Coaster at Home* was published privately by Arthur H. Stockwell in 1916, funded by the author's trade profits. Part two, *The Iniquitous Coaster*, was published by Stockwell the following year. The two books contain a ragbag of items and read like a scrapbook of one man's literary output between 1905 and 1915.
86. See Stoler, *Carnal Knowledge and Imperial Power*; Felicity A. Nussbaum, *Torrid Zones: Maternity, Sexuality, and Empire in Eighteenth-Century English Narratives* (Baltimore: Johns Hopkins University Press, 1995); Antoinette Burton, ed., *Gender, Sexuality and Colonial Modernities* (London: Routledge, 1999).
87. Stoler, *Carnal Knowledge and Imperial Power*, 1.
88. Field, "Verb Sap," 39.
89. Cited in Clough, *Oil Rivers Trader*, 173.
90. Stoler, *Carnal Knowledge and Imperial Power*, 32.
91. Kingsley, *Travels in West Africa*.
92. Ibid., 77; see also Crowther, *Gospel on the Banks of the River Niger*. Missionaries were involved in trade to a greater extent than they let on to their home committees. For example, the contents of the "necessarily large" collecting boxes at mission stations—cloth, heads of tobacco, manillas (copper or brass "bracelets" manufactured in Europe and used as currency in West African transactions from the early sixteenth century to the early twentieth century), and enamelware—required further conversion, through trade and barter, into articles the mission needed (Cottrell, "Reminiscences," 51).
93. Much of what follows is based on interviews I conducted in Onitsha in August 2005 with female market leaders and descendents of prominent merchant queens, including Nwononaku Josephine Ofordile, Cecilia Okwudinka, Agnes Okosi, Enyi Onyeomadiko Helen Onochie, and Emeka Geoffrey Olisa. For more about merchant queens, see Nwando Achebe, "Farmers, Traders, Warriors and

Kings: Female Power and Authority in Northern Igboland, 1900–1960" (PhD diss., University of California, 2000), 245.

94. Felicia Ekejiuba, "Omu Okwei, the Merchant Queen of Ossomari: A Biographical Sketch," *Journal of the Historical Society of Nigeria* 3, no. 4 (1967): 633–46.

95. Ibid., 640.

96. Ibid., 641–43.

97. Ibid., 646, quoting Stuart-Young, letter to Mr. Gill, September 10, 1918.

98. Clough, *Oil Rivers Trader*, 36–37; see also Ekejiuba, "Omu Okwei"; Whitford, *Trading Life*, 254.

99. Drawn from my interviews with Nwononaku Josephine Ofordile, Cecilia Okwudinka, and Agnes Okosi in August 2005.

100. Nussbaum, *Torrid Zones*; Stoler, *Carnal Knowledge and Imperial Power*, 1–8.

101. Clough, *Oil Rivers Trader*, 97–112.

102. Ibid., 112–15.

103. Ibid., 100; see Susan Martin, *Palm Oil and Protest: An Economic History of the Ngwa Region, South-East Nigeria, 1800–1980* (Cambridge: Cambridge University Press, 1988).

104. Harrington, "Letter Book," 74.

105. Ibid.

106. See Stoler, *Carnal Knowledge and Imperial Power*; Felicity Nussbaum, *Torrid Zones: Maternity, Sexuality, and Empire in Eighteenth Century English Narratives* (Baltimore: Johns Hopkins University Press, 1995).

107. Harrington, "Letter Book," 75.

108. Ibid., 76.

109. Lynn, *Commerce and Economic Change*, 78; Martin, *Palm Oil and Protest*, 87–88; Northrup, *Trade without Rulers*; Sandys Sherwood, *It's Been a Pleasure* (Washington: Minerva Press, 1994), 37.

110. Ekejiuba, "Omu Okwei," 637. A photograph of Omu Okwei surrounded by her team of beautiful trainees can be found in Emeka Geoffrey Olisa's *Between Three Worlds: An Autobiography* (Toronto: Epic Press, 2002), 140.

111. Robert Young, *Colonial Desire: Hybridity in Theory, Culture, and Race* (London: Routledge, 1995), 142–58.

112. See Stephanie Newell, *Literary Culture in Colonial Ghana: "How to Play the Game of Life"* (Manchester: Manchester University Press; Bloomington: Indiana University Press, 2002).

113. Stoler, *Carnal Knowledge and Imperial Power*, 39.

114. In moral terms, the degenerate promiscuous "mulatto" is herself regarded as a visible symbol of such liaisons.

115. Stuart-Young, *Coaster at Home*, 75.

116. J. M. Stuart-Young, *Merely a Negress: A West African Story* (London: John Long, 1904).

117. Stuart-Young, *Merely a Negress*.
118. Ibid., 14.
119. Ibid., 15.
120. Ibid., 49.
121. Ibid., 234–35.
122. Ibid., 83–84.
123. Ibid., 338.
124. Ibid., 340.
125. Ibid.
126. Warren Henry, *The Confessions of a Tenderfoot "Coaster": A Trader's Chronicle of life on the West African Coast* (London: H. F. and G. Witherby, 1927), 150.
127. Ibid., 159–60.
128. Henry, *Fantee Carter*, 41.
129. Ibid., 12; see Joseph Bristow, *Empire Boys: Adventures in a Man's World* (London: HarperCollins, 1991).
130. Henry, *Fantee Carter*, 42.
131. Burke, *Lifebuoy Men, Lux Women*, 32.
132. Whitford, *Trading Life*, 251.
133. Northrup, *Trade without Rulers*; Lynn, *Commerce and Economic Change*, 7.

CHAPTER 3

1. See "Angling for Autographs," *African Messenger*, 16 June 1922, 3, 6.
2. See J. M. Stuart-Young, *Merely a Negress: A West African Story* (London: John Long, 1904); J. M. Stuart-Young, *Osrac, the Self-Sufficient and Other Poems with a Memoir of the Late Oscar Wilde* (London: The Hermes Press, 1905); J. M. Stuart-Young, *Passion's Peril: A Romance* (London: The Hermes Press, 1906).
3. Odeziaku, "35 Years Ago: My First Tour on the West Coast," African Advertiser, 24 December 1936, 5, 15.
4. See Martin Lynn, *Commerce and Economic Change in West Africa: The Palm Oil Trade in the Nineteenth Century* (Cambridge: Cambridge University Press, 1997). A "dash" is a small additional gift to accompany a transaction and serve as an incentive for future transactions.
5. Stuart-Young, *Osrac*, 2.
6. Ibid., 5.
7. Ibid., 8.
8. Ibid., 9, 8.
9. Ibid., 15.
10. See Hesketh Pearson, *The Life of Oscar Wilde* (1946; Middlesex: Penguin, 1985).
11. Stuart-Young, *Osrac*, 30.

12. Ibid., 5. Several critics, however, believe the date and dedication on this photograph to be false, including Timothy d'Arch Smith in *Love in Earnest: Some Notes on the Lives and Writings of English "Uranian" Poets from 1889 to 1930* (London: Routledge, 1970); and Regina Gagnier, *Idylls of the Marketplace: Oscar Wilde and the Victorian Public* (England: Scolar Press, 1986).

13. Samples of Stuart-Young's and Wilde's handwriting were submitted for forensic analysis to Mrs. K. Thorndycraft of Forensic Handwriting and Document Investigation, Aberdeen, along with the facsimile letters purported to be from Wilde. No carbon dating of the paper was possible as the original letters were unavailable, but analysis of the samples revealed many differences between Wilde's and Stuart-Young's styles and between Stuart-Young's handwriting and the facsimile letters. Advice was also generously given by Karen Chiarodit.

14. Stuart-Young, *Osrac*, 9.

15. Ibid., 10.

16. Ibid., 22.

17. Ibid., 10.

18. Ibid., 2.

19. Pearson, *The Life of Oscar Wilde*, 263.

20. Ibid.

21. Ibid.

22. Stuart-Young, *Osrac*, 27.

23. Cited in G. D. Killam, "John Moray Stuart-Young: The Iniquitous Coaster of Onitsha (Nigeria)," *Black Academy Review* 2, no. 3 (1971): 29–30.

24. Stuart-Young's letter to Robert Ross is cited in d'Arch-Smith, *Love in Earnest*, 210. See also Stuart-Young, "The Truth about Oscar Wilde," *NDT*, 18 June 1931, 9.

25. Rupert Croft-Cooke, *The Unrecorded Life of Oscar Wilde* (London: W. H. Allen, 1972), 12, 14.

26. Ibid. The African boy referred to here, "Ibrahim the Unkissed," was a young servant brought to Britain by Stuart-Young in 1905; their relationship is discussed in chapter 4.

27. Gagnier, *Idylls of the Marketplace*, 43.

28. Stuart-Young, *Osrac*, 5.

29. Ibid., 22.

30. Eve Kosofsky Sedgwick, *Tendencies* (London: Routledge, 1994), 1. For Sedgwick, "queer" is a boundary-crossing term that defies social and sexual identities and challenges normative categories. This leaves queer teenagers peculiarly vulnerable to anxiety, depression, and suicide. In their urgent search for "resources for survival," modern queer teenagers form attachments to strange, oblique, and fascinating cultural objects which mirror the teenagers' own unstable subject-positions.

31. Ibid., 1–4.

32. Cited in Alan Sinfield, *The Wilde Century* (London: Cassell, 1994), 125–26.

33. Joseph Bristow, *Effeminate England: Homoerotic Writing after 1885* (Buckingham: Open University Press, 1995), 11.

34. Stuart-Young, *Osrac*, 15.
35. Ibid., 2, 13.
36. Ibid., 10.
37. Ibid., 1; see also chapter 7.
38. Ibid., 14.
39. See Sinfield, *Wilde Century*; Jeffrey Weeks, *Sex, Politics, and Society: The Regulation of Sexuality since 1800* (London: Longman, 1989).
40. Stuart-Young, *Osrac*, 3.
41. Ibid., 10.
42. Ibid., 11.
43. Ibid., 25–26.
44. Ibid., 27. Faced with the problem of representing the inimitable Wilde in his novel *Passion's Peril*, Stuart-Young adopts a more effective technique, plundering Wilde's published works, especially *The Picture of Dorian Gray*, for material that he quotes intertextually. References to *Dorian Gray* also appear in the facsimile letters. The letter reproduced in fig. 5, for example, reads, "They tell me I look younger every day: how delightful this is: you grow older Jack, whilst I become younger."
45. See Ed Cohen, *Talk on the Wilde Side: Towards a Genealogy of a Discourse on Male Sexuality* (London and New York: Routledge, 1993).
46. Ibid., 1.
47. Stuart-Young, *Passion's Peril*, 250.
48. Ibid., 249.
49. Croft-Cooke, *The Unrecorded Life*, 2, 10.
50. Stuart-Young, *Osrac*, 1.
51. Ibid., 2.
52. Ibid., Stanza ix, ibid., 52.
53. Stanza xvii, ibid., 60.
54. Stanza xxvi, ibid., 69.
55. Weeks, *Sex, Politics, and Society*, 49.
56. Sinfield, *Wilde Century*, 3; Sedgwick, *Tendencies*.
57. Sinfield, *Wilde Century*, 91.
58. Sedgwick, *Tendencies*.
59. Ibid., 8, 117.
60. See Sinfield, *Wilde Century*, 16.
61. Stuart-Young, *Osrac*, 5.
62. See Weeks, *Sex, Politics, and Society*; Alan Sinfield, *Cultural Politics—Queer Reading* (London: Routledge, 1994); Cohen, *Talk on the Wilde Side*.
63. Josephine Butler, *The Hour Before Dawn: An Appeal to Men* (London: Trubner, 1876), 1.
64. Ibid., 26. With this pamphlet in mind, it is one of the most astonishing ironies of history that Mrs. Josephine Butler, arch-purity campaigner, wished to marry the homosexual writer John Addington Symonds, whose autobiography (which was not published until 1984) discloses numerous sexual encounters with

male prostitutes. See John Addington Symonds, *The Memoirs of John Addington Symonds*, ed. Phyllis Grosskurth (London: Hutchinson, 1984), 135.

65. See Bristow, *Effeminate England*.

66. Ibid., 135–37. Symonds also worked with Havelock Ellis, offering himself as a case study to members of the medical establishment.

67. See Stuart-Young, *The Coaster at Home* (London: Arthur H. Stockwell, 1916); Stuart-Young, *The Iniquitous Coaster* (London: Arthur H. Stockwell, 1917).

68. Symonds, *Memoirs*, 17.

69. Sinfield, *Wilde Century*; Bristow, *Effeminate England*.

70. Sinfield, *Wilde Century*, 12. Each item in this chain has multiple meanings with numerous links to parallel belief systems, such as the Victorian bourgeois rejection of "aristocratic" decadence, which coexisted with the rise of British imperialism as an ideology in the popular press.

71. See Bristow, *Effeminate England*.

72. Edward Carpenter, *Homogenic Love* (1894; London: Redundancy Press, 1980).

73. See Bristow, *Effeminate England*.

74. Sylvia Leith-Ross, *Stepping-Stones: Memoirs of Colonial Nigeria, 1907–1960* (London and Boston: Peter Owen, 1983), 75, 105.

75. d'Arch Smith, *Love in Earnest*, 202.

76. Sinfield, *Cultural Politics—Queer Reading*, 10.

77. Sedgwick, *Tendencies*, 8.

78. Ibid.

79. Symonds, *Memoirs*, 96.

80. Ibid., 81.

81. Ibid., 100, 117.

82. Ibid., 166, 168; see Bristow, *Effeminate England*, 137.

83. Killam, "John Moray Stuart-Young"; see also J. Ayodele Langley, *Pan-Africanism and Nationalism in West Africa, 1900–1945* (Oxford: Clarendon Press, 1973).

84. Leith-Ross, *Stepping-Stones*, 105.

85. Langley, *Pan-Africanism*.

86. Leith-Ross, *Stepping-Stones*, 75.

87. Ibid.

88. Joseph Bristow, *Empire Boys: Adventures in a Man's World* (London: Harper Collins, 1992); John M. MacKenzie, ed., *Imperialism and Popular Culture* (Manchester: Manchester University Press, 1986).

CHAPTER 4

1. J. M. Stuart-Young, "West African Nights: The Bits I Remember," *Comet*, 26 January 1935, 11.

2. C. A. J. Onwuegbuzia, "'Odeziaku' of Onitsha: A Reminiscence," *Comet*, 31 May 1941, 14–15.
3. See chapter 6 for more about Stuart-Young's writings for African newspapers.
4. J. M. Stuart-Young, "George Bernard Shaw at Eighty-Two," *African Advertiser*, 8 April 1938, 4. For a detailed discussion of Stuart-Young's poetry and its readership, see chapter 8.
5. See Timothy d'Arch Smith, *Love in Earnest: Some Notes on the Lives and Writings of English "Uranian" Poets from 1889 to 1930* (London: Routledge and Keegan Paul, 1970).
6. Ibid., 2.
7. Paul John Eakin, *How Our Lives Become Stories: Making Selves* (Ithaca, NY: Cornell University Press, 1999), 58.
8. Stuart-Young, "West African Nights," 13.
9. Ibid.
10. Ibid.
11. See Alex Hughes, *Heterographies: Sexual Difference in French Autobiography* (Oxford: Berg, 1999).
12. Not everything is encoded or masked in the memoirs. Stuart-Young's writings also contain moments of explicit Uranian desire. For instance, in "West African Nights," he rails against a commemorative statue of Rupert Brooke, insisting that this statue *"libels* him. It will not do!" (11). For evidence of the libel, he offers the fact that "I have bathed several times with him and if there was one thing about his beautiful torso it was the grace and almost effeminacy of the hip contours. . . . I remember him best at the bathing pool—supple, boyish and very frankly paidophilic" (ibid.).
13. Alan Sinfield (*The Wilde Century* [London: Cassell, 1994]) and Eve Kosofsky Sedgwick (*Tendencies* [London: Routledge, 1994]) argue that the binary division between homosexuality and heterosexuality arose as a consequence of the Wilde trials in 1895. After the Wilde case, they suggest, what had been plural sexual identities in Britain slowly polarized into the clear-cut homo/hetero division that dominates twentieth-century discourse (see chapter 3).
14. Ronald Hyam, *Empire and Sexuality: The British Experience* (Manchester: Manchester University Press, 1991); Joseph Bristow, *Empire Boys: Adventures in a Man's World* (London: HarperCollins, 1991); Robert Aldrich, *Colonialism and Homosexuality* (London: Routledge, 2003). See introduction above.
15. Aldrich, *Colonialism and Homosexuality*, 2.
16. Ibid.
17. André Gide's autobiography, *Si le grain ne meurt* (1926), describes a wide variety of homoerotic events initiated by Europeans between 1869 and 1895, ranging from mutual masturbation to pederastic rape. See Hughes, *Heterographies*, 75–85.
18. Aldrich, *Colonialism and Homosexuality*, 43.
19. Geoffrey Crossick and Heinz-Gerhard Haupt, eds., *The Petite Bourgeoisie in Europe, 1780–1914: Enterprise, Family, and Independence* (London: Routledge, 1995).

20. d'Arch Smith, *Love in Earnest*, xx.

21. Sedgwick, *Tendencies*, 80.

22. Sinfield, *Wilde Century*, 89.

23. Interviews with Akunne Alfred Bosah, July 2002 and August 2005; interview with Agnes Okosi, August 2005.

24. Interview with S. I. Bosah, July 2002; Chike Akosa, *Heroes and Heroines of Onitsha* (Onitsha: Etukokwu, 1987), 70. S. I. Bosah is no relation of Alfred Bosah and Onwuije Hayford Bosah.

25. Akosa, *Heroes and Heroines of Onitsha*, 70.

26. Interview with Akunne Alfred Bosah, July 2002.

27. Interview with Akunne Alfred Bosah, August 2005.

28. Joseph U. Etukokwu, *Life between Two Shrines: An Autobiography* (Onitsha: Etukokwu Publishers, ca. 1997), 193.

29. Ibid.

30. Ibid.

31. Interview with S. I. Bosah, July 2002.

32. Ibid.

33. Etukokwu, *Life between Two Shrines*, 194.

34. Interview with Emeka Geoffrey Olisa, August 2005.

35. "Odeziaku's Will Benefits Servant," *West African Pilot*, 14 June 1939, 1.

36. Interview with Akunne Alfred Bosah, August 2005.

37. d'Arch Smith, *Love in Earnest*.

38. See David Alderson, *Mansex Fine: Religion, Manliness and Imperialism in Nineteenth-Century British Culture* (Manchester: Manchester University Press, 1998).

39. J. M. Stuart-Young, *Through Veiled Eyes: Being the Story of a Dead Lad's Love* (London: John Ouseley, 1908), 20–23; see also d'Arch Smith, *Love in Earnest*.

40. Stuart-Young, *Through Veiled Eyes*.

41. Ibid., 37.

42. Ibid., 31.

43. Ibid., 23.

44. Ibid., 39.

45. Ibid., 58.

46. d'Arch Smith, *Love in Earnest*, 174.

47. Ibid., 208. In 1905, Thomas Olman Todd published the first edition of *Osrac, the Self-Sufficient*, and it is likely that their friendship developed at this time.

48. See chapter 5 for a discussion of Stuart-Young's Uranian identity.

49. See Anne McClintock, *Imperial Leather: Race, Gender and Sexuality in the Colonial Contest* (London: Routledge, 1995); Antoinette Burton, *At the Heart of the Empire: Indians and the Colonial Encounter in Late Victorian Britain* (Berkeley: University of California Press, 1998).

50. d'Arch Smith, *Love in Earnest*.

51. Stuart-Young, *Through Veiled Eyes*, 23.

CHAPTER 5

1. J. M. Stuart-Young, "Tribute to Tom," *NDT*, 1 September 1936, 2, 9.
2. Major Arthur Glyn Leonard, *The Lower Niger and Its Tribes* (1906; London: Frank Cass, 1968), 548.
3. Ibid.
4. Joseph Thérèse Agbasiere, *Women in Igbo Life and Thought* (London: Routledge, 2000), 72.
5. Nwando Achebe, "Farmers, Traders, Warriors and Kings: Female Power and Authority in Northern Igboland" (PhD diss., University of California, 2000), 256.
6. Leonard, *The Lower Niger and Its Tribes*, 558.
7. S. I. Bosah, "Memoirs of Odeziaku," *West African Pilot*, 15 June 1939, 4.
8. Ibid.
9. C. A. J. Onwuegbuzia, "'Odeziaku' of Onitsha: A Reminiscence," *Comet*, 31 May 1941, 14.
10. Bosah, "Memoirs of Odeziaku," *West African Pilot*, 15 June 1939, 4.
11. "Letters: Mr Stuart-Young and 'Odeziaku,'" *West Africa*, 10 June 1933, 564. The obituary in *West Africa* put it rather differently, remarking curtly that "[a] few years ago he constructed for himself the pen name 'Odeziaku'"; 3 June 1939, 733.
12. Agbasiere, *Women in Igbo Life and Thought*, 173.
13. S. I. Bosah, *Groundwork of the History and Culture of Onitsha* (Onitsha, 1984), 138.
14. Agbasiere, *Women in Igbo Life and Thought*, 59, 173.
15. "An Early Love Affair Related by Odeziaku in an Hour's Interview," *African Advertiser*, 30 April 1937, 5.
16. See Ifi Amadiume, *Male Daughters, Female Husbands: Gender and Sex in an African Society* (London: Zed Books, 1987); Achebe, "Farmers, Traders, Warriors and Kings."
17. Patricia Hayes, "'Cocky' Hahn and the 'Black Venus': The Making of a Native Commissioner in South West Africa, 1915–1946," in *Cultures of Empire: A Reader*, ed. Catherine Hall (Manchester: Manchester University Press, 2000), 349.
18. Onwuegbuzia, "'Odeziaku' of Onitsha: A Reminiscence," 14.
19. Interview with Akunne John Nworah, August 2005.
20. Chike Akosa, *Heroes and Heroines of Onitsha* (Onitsha: Etukokwu Press, 1987).
21. See Antoinette Burton, *Gender, Sexuality and Colonial Modernities* (London: Routledge, 1999); Felicity A. Nussbaum, *Torrid Zones: Maternity, Sexuality, and Empire in Eighteenth-Century English Narratives* (Baltimore: Johns Hopkins University Press, 1995); Ann Laura Stoler, *Carnal Knowledge and Imperial Power: Race and the Intimate in Colonial Rule* (Berkeley: University of California Press, 2002).
22. Agbasiere, *Women in Igbo Life and Thought*, 94.

23. Richard N. Henderson, *The King in Every Man: Evolutionary Trends in Onitsha Ibo Society and Culture* (New Haven: Yale University Press, 1972), 106.

24. Ibid.

25. Interview with Chike Akosa, July 2002; interview with Akunne John Nwora, August 2005.

26. Paul Gordon Schalow, "Male Love in Early Modern Japan: A Literary Depiction of the 'Youth,'" in *Hidden from History: Reclaiming the Gay and Lesbian Past*, ed. Martin Bauml Duberman, Martha Vicinus, and George Chauncey (London: Penguin, 1989), 120.

27. Gilbert Herdt and Robert J. Stoller, *Intimate Communications: Erotics and the Study of Culture* (New York: Columbia University Press, 1990), 279–84.

28. Ibid., 284.

29. *Urninge* was the term coined by the German sexologist Carl Henry Ulrichs to explain same-sex desire in scientific rather than social terms in an effort to avoid the discourse of "sin" and "perversion." According to Ulrichs's theory, same-sex desire was a natural instinct located in the human brain that was formed at the fetal stage and thus beyond individual or social control. Ulrichs' theory that the homosexual man had a woman's soul trapped in his male body was "quintessential to the late-nineteenth-century emancipatory movement of homosexual men and women in Europe"; Bleys, *The Geography of Perversion*, 157. See chapter 3 for a discussion of different terminology and labels for same-sex passion in the late nineteenth century.

30. See Frank Harris's four-volume autobiography, *My Life and Loves*, published on private presses in the late 1920s and early 1930s. See also Frank Harris, *Oscar Wilde: His Life and Confessions* (1916; New York: Frank Harris, 1918); Frank Harris, *Frank Harris: His Life and Adventures: An Autobiography* (1942; London: Richards Press, 1952).

31. Even had she wished to accompany her husband to West Africa, Annie's lung disease would have prevented her from traveling to the tropics. Tuberculosis and lung disease were the curse of the slums, decimating numerous families in working-class districts of Manchester in the Victorian and Edwardian eras. Several members of Stuart-Young's family succumbed, including his sister, Margaret Gibson Young (1879–94), and his mother, Mary Gibson Young (1845–1912).

32. See Jeffrey Weeks and Kevin Porter, *Between the Acts: Lives of Homosexual Men, 1885–1967* (London: Rivers Oram Press, 1998).

33. For a discussion of similar negotiations of sexual identity from lesbian women's point of view, see Kendall, "'When a Woman Loves a Woman' in Lesotho: Love, Sex, and the (Western) Construction of Homophobia," in *Boy-Wives and Female Husbands: Studies of African Homosexualities*, ed. Stephen O. Murray and Will Roscoe (Basingstoke: Macmillan, 1998), 233.

34. For studies of cross-dressing in West Africa and discourses of effeminacy, see Michael Davidson, "A 1958 Visit to a Dakar Boy Brothel," in Murray and Roscoe, *Boy-Wives and Female Husbands*, 111–13; see also Rudolf P. Gaudio,

"Male Lesbians and Other Queer Notions in Hausa," in Murray and Roscoe, *Boy-Wives and Female Husbands*, 115–28.

35. See Bosah, *Groundwork*.

36. Interview with Patrick Ekwerekwu, July 2002. Akunne John Nworah, born in 1911, has vivid childhood memories of Boxing Day outside Stuart-Young's shop in Old Market Road. He and his friends would take turns peeping through the window to look at Stuart-Young, who sat stock still, reading and writing, his tall body curled in a chair. After some time, the trader would suddenly jump to his feet, rush to a box, and take packets of biscuits from it. Without speaking a word, he would throw the biscuits out of the door and watch excitedly through his spectacles as the boys fought for these treats. Interview with Akunne John Nworah, August 2005.

37. Igbo is a tonal language and, depending on intonation, "eke" may also mean "market day," "the Creator," "to create," "to share," "to tie." In the accounts of Stuart-Young given by interviewees, "Eke" refers to the sacred python or, on two occasions, the boa constrictor.

38. P. Amaury Talbot, *Tribes of the Niger Delta: Their Religions and Customs* (London: The Sheldon Press, 1932), 35.

39. Eke pythons are not revered in other parts of the region, such as Enugu State.

40. Akachi Ezeigbo, personal communication.

41. Agbasiere, *Women in Igbo Life and Thought*, 59; Amadiume, *Male Daughters, Female Husbands*, 54.

42. Leonard, *The Lower Niger and Its Tribes*, 330.

43. Misty Bastian, personal communication.

44. Onwuegbuzia, "'Odeziaku' of Onitsha: A Reminiscence," *Comet*, 14.

45. Ibid.

46. Bosah, "Memoirs of Odeziaku," *West African Pilot*, 15 June 1939, 4.

47. Ibid.

48. Interview with Akunne John Nworah, August 2005.

49. Akosa, *Heroes and Heroines of Onitsha*, 70.

50. Ibid., 65.

51. See Onwuegbuzia, "'Odeziaku' of Onitsha," *Comet*, 31 May 1941, 14–15.

52. See Henry John Drewel, "Interpretation, Invention and Re-Presentation in the Worship of Mami Wata," *Journal of Folklore Research* 25, nos. 1–2 (1988): 101–139; Misty Bastian, "Mami Wata, Mr White, and the Sirens of Bar Beach: Spirits and Dangerous Consumption in the Nigerian Popular Press," in *Afrika und das Andere: Alteritat und Innovation*, ed. Heike Schmidt and Albert Wirz (Hamburg: Lit. Verlag, 1998), 21–31.

53. Charles Gore and Joseph Nevadomsky, "Practice and Agency in Mammy Wata Worship in Southern Nigeria," *African Arts* 3, no. 30 (1997): 60–95.

54. Interview with Patrick Ekwerekwu, July 2002.

55. Interview with Chike Akosa, July 2002.

56. Interview with Isaac I. Ekwerekwu, July 2002.
57. Interview with S. I. Bosah, July 2002.
58. Interview with Akunne John Nworah, August 2005.
59. Talbot, *Tribes of the Niger Delta*, 39–42.
60. Chinua Achebe, *Morning Yet on Creation Day: Essays* (London: Heinemann, 1975).
61. Akosa, *Heroes and Heroines of Onitsha*, 65.
62. Onwuegbuzia, "'Odeziaku' of Onitsha," 14. Interviews with market women from the 1930s and with the descendants of Onitsha's powerful merchant queens produced an array of accounts of trading life in the 1920s and 1930s but failed to produce material about Stuart-Young. Even though the market women named him "Odoziaku" and led his funeral, it seems that Stuart-Young has greater significance for the history of elite males than for the history of market women. For an outline of his relationship with one powerful market queen, see chapter 2, above, and Felicia Ekejiuba, "Omu Okwei, the Merchant Queen of Ossomari: A Biographical Sketch," *Journal of the Historical Society of Nigeria* 3, no. 4 (1967): 633–46.
63. Etukokwu, *Life between Two Shrines*, 193.
64. Ibid., 196; italics in the original.
65. As recently as the late 1980s, homosexuality was considered to be one of the signs that Mami Wata was "disturbing" a person. Misty Bastian, personal communication.
66. Drewal, "Interpretation, Invention and Re-Presentation," 103.
67. Many of the most prominent Igbo merchant queens also remained childless. Josephine Ofordile, the daughter of Onitsha businesswoman Eunice Nnoruka, reported that the most wealthy female traders of Onitsha were often said by their neighbors to "drink water from the River Niger"; that is, to have a connection with Mami Wata in which they exchanged their fertility for other forms of wealth. Onlookers would say of such women, "her children are gold and silver." Interview with Josephine Ofordile, August 2005.
68. Chinua Achebe, "Uncle Ben's Choice," in Chinua Achebe, *Girls at War and Other Stories* (London: Heinemann, 1972), 83–89. I am indebted to Lyn Innes for alerting me to this story.
69. Ibid., 89. See also Chinua Achebe, *Morning Yet on Creation Day*, 92.
70. Drewal, "Interpretation, Invention and Re-Presentation," 103.
71. Bosah, *Groundwork*, 95.
72. See Ekejiuba, "Omu Okwei, the Merchant Queen of Ossomari."
73. Bosah, "Memoirs of Odeziaku," 4.
74. Ibid.
75. Ibid.
76. Drewal, "Interpretation, Invention and Re-Presentation," 105.
77. Ibid.
78. Ibid.

79. Onwuegbuzia, "'Odeziaku' of Onitsha," 14–15.
80. Interview with Akunne John Nworah, August 2005.
81. Drewal, "Interpretation, Invention and Re-Presentation," 122.
82. Ibid. See also Bastian, "Mami Wata, Mr. White, and the Sirens."
83. Drewal, "Interpretation, Invention and Re-Presentation," 109, 135.
84. Ibid., 135. It is rumored in Onitsha that in the 1920s one of Stuart-Young's servants attempted to verify the trader's connection to Mami Wata and hid underneath his bed one night, hoping to witness any intercourse with the water spirit. The servant was discovered, however, and while he was not physically punished, he was spiritually reprimanded by Stuart-Young, who summoned powerful occult forces against him. Such stories feed into the mythical framework that informs people's memories of Stuart-Young.
85. Simon Gikandi, *Maps of Englishness: Writing Identity in the Culture of Colonialism* (New York: Columbia University Press, 1996), 19.
86. Ibid.
87. Ann Laura Stoler and Frederick Cooper, "Between Metropole and Colony: Rethinking a Research Agenda," in *Tensions of Empire: Colonial Cultures in a Bourgeois World*, ed. Frederick Cooper and Ann Laura Stoler (Berkeley: University of California Press, 1997), 3–4.

CHAPTER 6

1. Stuart-Young wrote two regular columns for the *Nigerian Daily Times* in the 1930s: "Looking at Lagos" and "Nigerian Notabilities."
2. J. M. Stuart-Young, "Interest, Inspiration and Insomnia," *Gold Coast Leader*, 30 May 1925, Supplement, i.
3. See, e.g., "Our Mail Bag: 'War or Peace This Year?' from J. M. Stuart-Young," *Nigerian Eastern Mail*, 6 March 1937, 3.
4. "Our Mail Bag: 'Woman Versus Lady' from Odeziaku," *Nigerian Eastern Mail*, 1 May 1937, 7.
5. J. M. Stuart-Young, "I Love the Forest," *Gold Coast Leader*, 28 August 1920, 5.
6. Odeziaku, "Educating the African," *Nigerian Eastern Mail*, 18 September 1937, 11.
7. Stuart-Young, *The Seductive Coast: Poems Lyrical and Descriptive from West Africa* (London: John Ouseley, 1909), 2.
8. Ibid.
9. Ibid., 76; see also Stuart-Young, *Who Buys My Dreams? Poems and Lyrics* (London: Cecil Palmer, 1923), 279.
10. Stuart-Young, *Seductive Coast*, 2.
11. "On Native Administration: An Informal Chat with Odeziaku," *Nigerian Eastern Mail*, 4 September 1937: 11; J. M. Stuart-Young, "The Negro at Home," *Gold Coast Leader*, 1 August 1922, 5.

12. J. M. Stuart-Young, "Will Our Empire Dissolve?" *Nigerian Daily Times*, 21 April 1931, 8.

13. J. M. Stuart-Young, "The Negro at Home," *Gold Coast Leader*, 1 August 1922, 5.

14. Stuart-Young, "The Negro at Home," *Gold Coast Leader*, 29 July 1922, 5.

15. Ibid., 6.

16. Stuart-Young, "The Negro at Home," *Gold Coast Leader*, 16 September 1922, 6.

17. "Letter to the Editor' from 'Reform,'" *African Messenger*, 14 January 1926, 7.

18. Ibid.

19. For detailed studies of educational changes in colonial West Africa, particularly as they affected policies regarding the teaching of African languages, see David Kimble, *A Political History of Ghana: The Rise of Gold Coast Nationalism, 1850–1928* (Oxford: Clarendon Press, 1965); Gareth Griffiths, *African Literatures in English: East and West* (Harlow: Longman, 2000); Stephanie Newell, *Literary Culture in Colonial Ghana: How to Play the Game of Life* (Manchester: Manchester University Press; Bloomington: Indiana University Press, 2002).

20. J. M. Stuart-Young, "To Make Better Provision . . . ?" *African Messenger*, 27 March 1926, 5.

21. Ibid.

22. Ibid.

23. "Letters to the Editor: 'Agents Be Careful,' from 'O.E.O,'" *Nigerian Eastern Mail*, 18 December 1937, 8.

24. See "Correspondence: 'Why I Should Read the Nigerian Observer' from 'Interested Reader,'" *Nigerian Observer*, 14 November 1931, 8.

25. Ibid.

26. "Correspondence: From 'Jack Never Fear,'" *Nigerian Observer*, 18 October 1930, 8.

27. "'Observations' by Observer," *Nigerian Observer*, 25 July 1931, 5.

28. "Correspondence: 'Why I Should Read the Nigerian Observer' from 'Interested Reader,'" *Nigerian Observer*, 14 November 1931, 8. It is, of course, possible that some, or all, of these letters were composed by a member of staff at the *Observer*; the newspaper was experiencing financial difficulties as a consequence of the Great Depression and appealed continually for readers to become regular subscribers.

29. See Ann Laura Stoler, *Carnal Knowledge and Imperial Power: Race and the Intimate in Colonial Rule* (Berkeley: University of California Press, 2002); and Felicity Nussbaum, *Torrid Zones: Maternity, Sexuality, and Empire in Eighteenth-Century English Narratives* (Baltimore: Johns Hopkins University Press, 1995).

30. See, e.g., J. M. Stuart-Young, "Humanity as One Family," *Gold Coast Leader*, 7 October 1922, Supplement, ii; italics in original.

31. See, for example, J. M. Stuart-Young, "Why West Africa Is Suffering," *African Messenger*, 24 January 1924, 4–5.

32. Stuart-Young, "Humanity as One Family," Supplement, ii.

33. "To J. M. Stuart-Young, Esquire, Poet and Author," *Gold Coast Leader*, 19 December 1925, 7.

34. J. M. Stuart-Young, "From Spiritualism to Freethought," *Gold Coast Leader*, 20 March 1929, 11.

35. Odeziaku, "Church Marriage for the African: A Reply to Critics," *African Advertiser*, 15 October 1937, 5.

36. "Odeziaku and the Catholic Church: Fr. Brolly Replies," *African Advertiser*, 24 December 1937, 6. Father Brolly is remembered by Rev. Father N. C. Tagbo of Onitsha as a charming man with a fierce temper who kept his students in a "jittery" state. "He would not disturb you if you did not disturb the peace," Tagbo commented, "but once you disturb the peace you are in for it." Interview with N. C. Tagbo, August 2005.

37. Odeziaku, "Marriage and Roman Catholicism," *African Advertiser*, 3 December 1937, 6.

38. Ibid., 11.

39. Ibid., 6.

40. "Letters to the Editor: 'Science and Religion,' from 'Veritas,'" *Nigerian Eastern Mail*, 27 March 1937, 6. Stuart-Young did not initiate the debate about monogamy in Nigeria; heated debates about the benefits and limitations of Christian marriage and polygyny were ubiquitous in West African newspapers from the time of their inception in the 1880s.

41. Ofidendewah, "An Opinion on the Man J. M. Stuart-Young and Truth," *Gold Coast Leader*, 1 January 1927, 7.

42. Ibid.

43. J. M. Stuart-Young, "Miscellaneous Unions," *Gold Coast Leader*, 29 April 1922, 5, italics in original.

44. Chas Ndaguba, "Mr J. M. Stuart-Young on Christian Marriage," *African Advertiser*, 25 February 1938, 13.

45. In the *Gold Coast Leader* in 1922, Stuart-Young wrote in praise of Sekyi's lengthy serial "Our White Friends," which criticized British colonial rule in West Africa. In this piece, Stuart-Young petitioned Sekyi to write on the topic of "women's suffrage" (*Gold Coast Leader*, 4 March 1922, 5). "I have always held," he commented, "that the women of the West African littoral are singularly 'free' and most gratifyingly happy," showing "an instinctive willingness to bear healthy children to their husbands" (ibid.). He contrasted such happiness and health with the degenerate state of urban western women, who lived with "weary wombs" in slums devoid of "laughter and sunshine and joy" (ibid.). Sekyi did not respond.

46. Kobina Sekyi, "To Albion," *Gold Coast Leader*, 19 November 1921, 3.

47. "A Winter Love Song" and many other poems by Stuart-Young were reprinted from his volumes of poetry.

48. Zik, "My Friend 'Odeziaku,'" *West African Pilot*, 3 January 1938, 4–5.

49. "The Educated African: Mr Stuart-Young Derides—Philosophers Investigate!" *Gold Coast Times*, 18 March 1933, 11.

50. Ibid.
51. Ibid.
52. J. M. Stuart-Young, "The Negro at Home," *Gold Coast Leader*, 29 July 1922, 6.
53. Stuart-Young, "The Negro at Home," *Gold Coast Leader*, 16 September 1922, 6.
54. Sir Harry Johnston, "Why a Nigger Republic Must Fail: Growing Menace from Millions of Embittered Aframericans," *Gold Coast Leader*, 23 October 1920, 5.
55. "Correspondence: 'Mr Stuart-Young and the Big Combine,' from 'Manu,'" *Nigerian Observer*, 22 November 1930, 8.
56. Ibid.

CHAPTER 7

1. William Booth, *In Darkest England and the Way Out* (1890; 6th ed., London: Charles Knight and Co., 1970), 79–80. Citations are to the 1970 edition.
2. Stuart-Young was criticized by several contributors to *West Africa*, including E. D. Morel, for his overromanticized construction of the continent.
3. The street is thinly disguised as "Bank Hey Street, Aldwick Green, Walkden" in *The Coaster at Home* (London: Arthur H. Stockwell, 1916). The street is not disguised in other novels and articles, where Stuart-Young names it as Back Kay Street, Ardwick.
4. These reviewers' comments are published on the final two pages of Stuart-Young's *What Does It Matter?* (London: C. W. Daniel, 1927).
5. Ibid., 8.
6. Ibid., 160.
7. J. M. Stuart-Young, *Johnny Jones Guttersnipe* (London: C. W. Daniel, 1926), 140.
8. J. M. Stuart-Young, *The Coaster at Home* (London: Arthur H. Stockwell, 1916), 329.
9. Ibid.
10. Stuart-Young wrote a passionate denial that the material in the Johnny Jones novels was autobiographical in a letter to the editor of the *Gold Coast Leader*, 25 Feb–3 March 1928, 7. However, the novels are the only published source of some of the details of his biography. For example, were it not for *What Does It Matter?* I would never have learned about Stuart-Young's court case and imprisonment in 1899.
11. Timothy d'Arch Smith, *Love in Earnest: Some Notes on the Lives and Writings of English "Uranian" Poets from 1889 to 1930* (London: Routledge and Kegan Paul, 1970); see also Killam, "John Moray Stuart-Young: The Iniquitous Coaster of Onitsha (Nigeria)," *Black Academy Review* 2, no. 3 (1971): 22–41.

12. Killam, "John Moray Stuart-Young," 27–28.
13. *Daily Herald*, cited in Stuart-Young, *What Does It Matter?*
14. *Merthyr Express*, cited in Stuart-Young, *What Does It Matter?*
15. Stuart-Young, "Johnny Jones Guttersnipe," *TLS*, 10 June 1926, 396. I am grateful to Jonathan Wild for providing this reference.
16. "Factual fiction" is Lennard Davis's term for sixteenth- and seventeenth-century didactic news stories that are also filled with details of current affairs. See Lennard J. Davis, *Factual Fictions: The Origins of the English Novel* (New York: Columbia University Press, 1983).
17. See Stuart-Young, *What Does It Matter?* 170.
18. See Stuart-Young, *Johnny Jones Guttersnipe*.
19. Stuart-Young, *What Does It Matter?* 165.
20. Ibid., 169.
21. Stuart-Young, *Johnny Jones Guttersnipe*, 117.
22. Oscar Wilde, *De Profundis* (1905; 2nd ed., London: Methuen, 1909).
23. See Stuart-Young, *What Does It Matter?* 190.
24. Ibid.
25. Ibid., 163. In one scene, the prisoner in cell C32 taps a friendly greeting in Morse code on the walls of Johnny's cell, to which the reply is "I do not know you. I do not wish to know you" (*What Does It Matter?* 199). Consciously or unconsciously, Stuart-Young here quotes directly from Lord Alfred Douglas's letter repudiating his friendly correspondence regarding *Osrac, the Self-Sufficient* (see chapter 3). Bosie's vehement dismissal did not prevent Stuart-Young from sending further letters and enclosing complimentary copies of subsequent publications. In fact, on receiving *Johnny Jones Guttersnipe*, Lord Alfred apparently replied in a far more amenable tone: "A charming book. You must really write a sequel" (cited in Stuart-Young, *What Does It Matter?*).
26. Stuart-Young, *Johnny Jones Guttersnipe*, 320.
27. Ibid.
28. Ibid.
29. Peter Hitchcock, "They Must Be Represented? Problems in Theories of Working-Class Representation," *PMLA* 115, nos. 20–32 (2000): 23.
30. Stuart-Young, *What Does It Matter?* 200.
31. Stuart-Young, *Johnny Jones Guttersnipe*, 62.
32. Stuart-Young, *The Soul-Slayer* (London: Arthur H. Stockwell, 1920), 355.
33. Stuart-Young, *What Does It Matter?* 227.
34. Ibid., 82.
35. Stuart-Young, *Johnny Jones Guttersnipe*, 92, 124.
36. Stuart-Young, *What Does It Matter?* 226.
37. Ibid., 227.
38. Ibid., 234.
39. *Johnny Jones Guttersnipe*, 114.
40. Ibid.

41. *What Does It Matter?* 184. The *TLS* review of *What Does It Matter?* describes these regeneration-in-prison scenes as unconvincing; 29 December 1927.
42. Stuart-Young, *What Does It Matter?* 185.
43. Ibid., 185, 208.
44. Ibid., 201, 219.
45. Stuart-Young, *Johnny Jones Guttersnipe,* 222.
46. Stuart-Young, *What Does It Matter?* 224.
47. William Greenslade, *Degeneration, Culture and the Novel, 1880–1940* (Cambridge: Cambridge University Press, 1994), 17–21.
48. See Joseph Bristow, *Effeminate England: Homoerotic Writing after 1885* (Buckingham: Open University Press, 1995); David Alderson, *Mansex Fine: Religion, Manliness and Imperialism in Nineteenth-Century British Culture* (Manchester: Manchester University Press, 1998).
49. Stuart-Young, *Johnny Jones Guttersnipe,* 118, 283.
50. Ibid., 117.
51. Ibid., 44.
52. Ibid., 58, 119, 221, 283.
53. Ibid., 117.
54. Ibid., 43–44.
55. Ibid., 10.
56. Ibid., 37–38.
57. Stuart-Young, *What Does It Matter?* 165.
58. Stuart-Young, *Johnny Jones Guttersnipe,* 167.
59. Ibid., 36.
60. Ibid., 45.
61. Ibid., 317.
62. Ibid.
63. Stuart-Young, *Johnny Jones Guttersnipe,* 229–30.
64. Stuart-Young, *What Does it It Matter?* 231; see also Stuart-Young, *The Soul-Slayer.*
65. Stuart-Young, *The Coaster at Home,* 69; Stuart-Young, *The Soul-Slayer,* 354. As explained in chapter 4, in Stuart-Young's time, "pederast" and "paidophil" had different connotations from today, referring less to physically and sexually active interference with children than to an aesthetic appreciation of pubescent male bodies in art. However, the sheer physicality of these adult-boy beatings in Stuart-Young's writing problematizes the "paidophil" aesthetic by introducing a sadomasochistic element.
66. See Joseph Bristow, *Effeminate England.*
67. See Stuart-Young, *Johnny Jones Guttersnipe,* 281.
68. Ibid., 305.
69. Ibid., 88, 91.
70. Ibid., 91.
71. Stuart-Young, *What Does It Matter?* 17.

72. Ibid., 221.
73. Ibid., 222.
74. Ibid., 223.
75. Ibid.
76. Ibid., 223.
77. Ibid. This ethical myopia echoes Oscar Wilde's essay "Pen, Pencil and Poison: A Study in Green," in *The Works of Oscar Wilde* (London: Spring Books, 1963), 844–56, which also fails to account for violence toward women.
78. Stuart-Young, *What Does It Matter?* 263.
79. Ibid., 266.
80. *What Does It Matter?* contains an extensive debate about the moral wrongs of British intervention in South Africa and a critique of newspaper jingoism at the time. The novel develops a theory of "willing Empire," describing Stuart-Young's "glorious dream" whereby the vanquished retain their freedom and political integrity within the unity of the British Empire; see *What Does It Matter?* 303–309.
81. See Jonathan Rose, *The Intellectual Life of the British Working Classes* (New Haven and London: Yale University Press, 2001).
82. Stuart-Young, *What Does It Matter?* 267; see Booth, *In Darkest England*.
83. Stuart-Young, *What Does It Matter?* 278.
84. Ibid., 272.
85. See Booth, *In Darkest England*.
86. Stuart-Young, *What Does It Matter?* 336.

CHAPTER 8

1. Robert Graves, *On English Poetry: Being an Irregular Approach to the Psychology of this Art, from Evidence Mainly Subjective* (London: William Heinemann, 1922), 98.
2. *Authors' and Artists' Who's Who* (London: Shaw, 1934). The information in this volume was provided by Stuart-Young.
3. Ibid., 533.
4. Ibid. Stuart-Young mistakenly conferred a royal blessing on the Society of Authors.
5. In 1936 he also claimed an eminent ancestor, Edward Young, who famously wrote that "procrastination is the thief of time." *African Advertiser*, 24 December 1926, 5.
6. Cited in David Perkins, *A History of Modern Poetry: From the 1890s to the High Modernist Mode* (Cambridge, Mass: Harvard University Press, 1976), 167. Robert Bridges (1844–1930) received the laureateship in 1913.
7. See J. M. Stuart-Young, "More about Poetry," *West African Pilot*, 9 March 1939, 5.
8. Ibid.

9. Odeziaku, "Dreaming True," *West African Pilot*, 15 February 1939, 5.

10. Such sentiments can be located in the platonic tradition, after Walter Pater, whose notion of the connection between beauty and goodness, developed in books such as *Plato and Platonism* (1893) and *The Renaissance* (1913), was so strongly held that it affected the material texture of his books. For example, *Plato and Platonism* was a work of art that was filled with beautiful fonts, colors, and decorations.

11. See Peter Nicholls, *Modernisms: A Literary Guide* (Basingstoke: Macmillan, 1995).

12. J. M. Stuart-Young, "To Make Better Provision . . . ?" *African Messenger*, 27 March 1926, 5.

13. See "Editorial: R.I.P. J. M. Stuart-Young, D.Ph.," *Nigerian Daily Times*, 30 May 1939, 6; C. A. J. Onwuegbuzie, "'Odeziaku' of Onitsha: A Reminiscence," *Comet*, 31 May 1941, 14–15.

14. O. Dazi Aku, "A Canadian Poet," *Nigerian Pioneer*, 6 November 1914, 9.

15. Ibid.

16. See J. M. Stuart-Young, "West African Nights: The Bits I Remember," *Comet*, 9 February 1935, 11–12; J. M. Stuart-Young, "The Pliable Years," *Gold Coast Leader*, 13 September 1924, 7.

17. M. O. Kodit Onwuli, "A Brief Tribute to Our Friend Mr. J. M. Stuart-Young," *African Messenger*, 24 December 1925, 7.

18. "J. M. Stuart-Young, Poet and Man of Letters," *Gold Coast Leader*, 20 February 1929, 7–8. Possibly written by the prominent lawyer, political leader, and newspaperman J. E. Casely Hayford (1866–1930), who was no parochial, unworldly man and who knew about the "world" throughout which Stuart-Young was supposedly famous.

19. "Comment on Stuart-Young," *West Africa*, 4 August 1917, 567. This praise was uncommon in *West Africa*, however, and within three months Stuart-Young had his knuckles firmly rapped by the editors for criticizing the Niger Company's river tariffs and the British government's complicity with the exploitation of local traders (*West Africa*, 10 November 1917, 593). By the early 1930s, although his articles on West African witchcraft and supernaturalism continued to appear in the journal, he was regularly caricatured by correspondents as an ill-informed reactionary when he commented on global trade or politics (see, e.g., "Competition and Sweated Labour: Letter to the Editor." J. Isherwood, *West Africa*, 10 June 1933, 564–65). An ambivalent obituary summed up his political views as "picturesquely denunciatory of Governments" (*West Africa*, 3 June 1939, 733).

20. "Editorial: The Passing of Dr J. M. Stuart-Young, PhD," *Gold Coast Times*, 17 June 1939, 8. The *Gold Coast Times* listed Stuart-Young's successful prophecies, mythologizing and accepting his forecasts of imminent war that appeared in the *Nigerian Eastern Mail* throughout 1937 and 1938. "We shall be at war on 5th of October this year. The conflict will start between Russia and Japan. Germany will aid Japan," Odeziaku prophesied in March 1937. More accurately, he

added that "hostilities will not end for five years"; *Nigerian Eastern Mail*, 6 March 1937, 3.

21. Onwuegbuzia, "'Odeziaku' of Onitsha," *Comet*, 31 May 1941, 14–15.

22. "Editorial: Exit Stuart-Young," *West African Pilot*, 30 May 1939, 5. "Dr. Azikiwe" was not altogether innocent of artificially inflating his own academic qualifications, for he claimed a PhD many years before receiving the honorary doctorates American universities conferred on him in the 1960s. Emeka Okeke-Ezeigbo writes, "The truth, of course, is that Zik did not earn an academic doctorate degree but rather disingenuously assumed the honorific 'Doctor'" ("Anu Solu nwa-enwe omajie aka: Ogbuefi Nramdi Azikiwe as an Igbo Folk Hero," in *The Hero in Igbo Life and Literature*, ed. Donatus Nwoga and Chukwuma Azuonye (Enugu: Fourth Dimension, 2002), 158.

23. Interview with Patrick Ekwerekwu, July 2002.

24. S. I. Bosah, *Groundwork of the History and Culture of Onitsha* (Onitsha, 1984), 95.

25. Olomu, "Onitsha Notes," *Nigerian Pioneer*, 16 November 1917, 8.

26. "Editorial: J. M. Stuart-Young at His 58th Birthday," *West African Pilot*, 4 March 1939, 4.

27. Ibid.

28. J. M. Stuart-Young, "Teaching the Novice to Know," *Gold Coast Leader*, 21 June 1924, 5.

29. His surname, Coker, locates him as a Sierra Leonean, although he may have resided in any town along the West African littoral among the many migrant "Saro" families who set up businesses in the region.

30. Stuart-Young, "Teaching the Novice to Know," *Gold Coast Leader*, 21 June 1924, 5.

31. Ibid.; italics in original.

32. Ibid.

33. Ibid.

34. Ibid.

35. J. M. Stuart-Young, "How to Speak in Public," *Gold Coast Leader*, 15 November 1924, 8; also J. M. Stuart-Young, "How to Speak in Public," *African Messenger*, 9 October 1924, 3. Igbo readers would have paid close attention to this material, for Stuart-Young gave regular public lectures in Onitsha and is said to have set up a literary and debating society in the town.

36. "Tuition by Post: Mr J. M. Stuart-Young," *African Messenger*, 16 April 1925, 9. Several local poets were directly inspired by Stuart-Young's verse. For example, in the poem "Farewell Stuart-Young," by a regular contributor to the eastern Nigerian press, "Osadenis," Stuart-Young is honored immediately after his death. *Nigerian Daily Times*, 30 May 1939, 5. The poem for the Lagos-based *Daily Times* is written in the style of Stuart-Young's own nature poetry: "O Lordly Niger, weep and overflow, / And let thy rippling rapids turn and go; / The poet that loved and lived by thee is dead, / His form in dust has found eternal bed" (ibid.). Besides

these inspired amateurs, several other talented young poets found their first platform in the newspapers. Most prominent among them were Gladys May Casely Hayford, whose experiments with Creole-language poetry are a great deal more successful than Stuart-Young's Pidgin English verses, and Kobina Sekyi, whose mythological vision of African nature represents a strikingly new mode of West African nature poetry. "Hail! Lord of Light," opens Sekyi's poem "To the Sun." "To thee all Nature Cries, / When thou, for long, in thy parental love, / Yield'st to the clouds they sway o'er Heav'n above . . . / These are your children: mighty seas and streams, / And all the things wherewith the forest teems; / And last, and least, / Comes Man. . . ." *Gold Coast Leader*, 8 October 1921, 3. Both Sekyi and Casely Hayford are talented, complex writers whose place in West African newspaper culture merits further study.

37. Cited in J. M. Stuart-Young, "Genius, Talent or Mediocrity?" *Gold Coast Leader*, 9 February 1924, 6.

38. "Mr J. M. Stuart-Young," *West Africa*, 3 June 1939, 733.

39. J. M. Stuart-Young, *The Seductive Coast: Poems Lyrical and Descriptive from West Africa* (London: John Ouseley, 1909), 42.

40. J. M. Stuart-Young, *Minor Melodies: Lyrics and Songs* (Edinburgh: T. and A. Constable, 1921), 141.

41. J. M. Stuart-Young, *Who Buys My Dreams? Poems and Lyrics* (London: Cecil Palmer, 1923), 13.

42. Edmund Gosse, *The Collected Poems* (London: William Heinemann, 1911), vii.

43. See Stuart-Young, *Who Buys My Dreams?* ix.

44. See J. M. Stuart-Young, "What Is Poetry?" *West African Pilot*, 4 February 1939, 5.

45. Stuart-Young, *Minor Melodies*, vii–viii; italics in original.

46. Stuart-Young, *Who Buys My Dreams?* 107. Across the cultural board, from music hall audiences to the Aesthetes, musicality was regarded as integral to a poem's success in the late nineteenth century. The principle of musicality also became a significant feature of avant-garde English criticism in the 1890s, when Arthur Symons developed his theory that the interface between music and poetry provided an arena for the development of Symbolist language. For Symons and his peers, musical rhythms and forms (and later dance) allowed for the achievement of poems-beyond-words and the transcendence of rigid meanings. Elite and popular cultural spheres are not therefore necessarily opposed; indeed, Symons adored the music hall and attended performances with compulsive regularity. While Stuart-Young makes a very literal reading of these principles, writing actual lyrics, copying music hall stars, and inviting readers to set his work to music, nevertheless he can be situated firmly within these fin-de-siècle literary currents that swelled through his verse and informed his aesthetic.

47. In Alfred H. Miles, ed., *Robert Bridges and Contemporary Poets*, vol. 7 of *The Poets and the Poetry of the Nineteenth Century* (1892; London: Routledge, 1906), 537. Citations are to the 1906 edition.

48. Richard Le Gallienne, *Retrospective Reviews: A Literary Log*, vol. 1, 1891–93 (London: John Lane, 1896), 175.

49. Peter Brooker and Peter Widdowson, "A Literature for England," in *Englishness: Politics and Culture, 1880–1920*, ed. Robert Colls and Philip Dodd (London: Croom Helm, 1986), 131. It must be noted, however, that *A Shropshire Lad* is not simply a nostalgic text: it contains many disturbing and experimental passages that disrupt the pastoral flow.

50. Brooker and Widdowson, "A Literature for England," 129–33; see also Kenneth Millard, *Edwardian Poetry* (Oxford: Clarendon Press, 1991).

51. David Perkins, *A History of Modern Poetry from the 1890s to the High Modernist Mode* (Cambridge, Mass: Harvard University Press, 1976), 166–72; see Millard, *Edwardian Poetry*.

52. There are many links between these poets and the "slum writing" discussed in chapter 1, for sociologists such as William Booth and Charles Masterman were also heavily invested in an English pastoral ideal.

53. Robert Bridges, *A Choice of Bridges's Verse* (London and Boston: Faber and Faber, 1987), 11–12.

54. Stuart-Young does not mention Walt Whitman in his essays, or Edward Carpenter's developments of Whitman's ideas of comradeship, perhaps because of the potential for a homosexual reading of both men's work. However, he was almost certainly influenced by Whitman's conception of rugged, healthy "outdoors" masculinities.

55. Stuart-Young, *Minor Melodies*, xvi.

56. In an article for the *West African Pilot* in 1939 he criticized Swinburne's "cold-hearted cynicism" ("What Is Poetry?" *West African Pilot*, 3 February 1939, 5 [this was one of a series of articles]).

57. Watson, cited in Stuart-Young, *Minor Melodies*, xvi, xix.

58. Throughout his life, Stuart-Young remained troubled by the "shameful" response Oscar Wilde and John Addington Symonds triggered in him. Symonds's *In the Key of Blue* caused him to be "revolted, even while I was allured," creating a remarkably similar response to his fascinated horror for Wilde's writing, discussed in chapter 1; Stuart-Young, "The Pliable Years," 7.

59. J. M. Stuart-Young, "West African Nights: The Bits I Remember," *Comet*, 5 January 1935, 13.

60. Rictor Norton, "Pastoral Homoeroticism and Barnfield, the Affectionate Shepherd," in *The Affectionate Shepherd: Celebrating Richard Barnfield*, ed. Kenneth Borris and George Klawitter (Selinsgrove, PA: Susquehanna University Press and Associated University Press, 2001), 117.

61. See, e.g., Stuart-Young, "I Cannot Tell," *Minor Melodies*, 83.

62. Stuart-Young, "West African Nights," 13.

63. Stuart-Young, *The Seductive Coast*, 127.

64. Stuart-Young, *Who Buys My Dreams?* 215. Christopher Robinson suggests that in the face of homophobia, homosexual writers tend to operate within the dominant sexual codes, substituting female for male lovers when describing

scenes of passion. See *Scandal in the Ink: Male and Female Homosexuality in Twentieth-Century French Literature* (London: Cassell, 1995), 50–53.

65. J. M. Stuart-Young, "The Feline Sex: A Glimpse of the Late W. L. George, Novelist and Novice," *Gold Coast Leader*, 2 October 1926, 9.

66. Ibid. This point, it seems, could not be repeated often enough: see also Stuart-Young, *Minor Melodies*, 26; *Who Buys My Dreams?* 172, 183, 301.

67. J. M. Stuart-Young, "Companionate Marriage: An Impression of Havelock Ellis," *African Advertiser*, 31 December 1937, 7. In this same article, Stuart-Young claims to have corresponded with Ellis; the psychologist explained to him his idea of the "companionate" marriage, suited to those "to whom the thought of parenthood is repugnant" (7).

68. Ibid., 13.

69. J. M. Stuart-Young, "What Is Poetry?" *West African Pilot*, 3 February 1939, 5.

70. Ibid. Jonathan Wild comments that the editors at *John O'London's Weekly* were anything but "egregious moderns" at this time (personal communication). It is more likely that Stuart-Young's poetry was rejected because of changing English tastes in verse.

71. Stuart-Young, "What Is Poetry?" *West African Pilot*, 3 February 1939, 5.

72. J. M. Stuart-Young, "Music Hall Garbage," *African Messenger*, 18 September 1924, 5; J. M. Stuart-Young, "More about Poetry," 5.

73. Interview with Akunne John Nworah, August 2005.

74. Stuart-Young, "More about Poetry," 5.

75. Ibid.

76. Stuart-Young, *The Seductive Coast*, 121.

77. See Stephanie Newell, *Ghanaian Popular Fiction: 'Thrilling Discoveries in Conjugal Life' and Other Tales* (Oxford: James Currey; Athens: Ohio University Press, 2000).

78. Ibid.

79. Joyce Penfield, *Communicating with Quotes* (Westport, CT: Greenwood Press, 1983); Kwesi Yankah, *The Proverb in the Context of Akan Rhetoric: A Theory of Proverb Praxis* (Bern: Peter Lang, 1989).

80. See *Nigerian Eastern Mail*, 1936–37.

81. "Sayings of Yesterday and Today: Of the Trade Relations Between White and Black on the Coast," *Nigerian Eastern Mail*, 25 December 1937, 16.

82. "Ex Ore Infantium: Some Sayings of Odeziaku," *Nigerian Eastern Mail*, 4 September 1937, 10.

83. Stuart-Young, "What Is Poetry?" *West African Pilot*, 4 February 1939, 5.

84. J. M. Stuart-Young, "Genius, Talent or Mediocrity?" *Gold Coast Leader*, 9 February 1924, 5.

85. Ibid.

86. "Poet's Nook: 'The Man Who Knows,'" *West African Pilot*, 17 March 1938, 5.

87. Stuart-Young, *The Seductive Coast*, 20.

88. See Steve Connor, *Dumbstruck: A Cultural History of Ventriloquism* (Oxford: Oxford University Press, 2000).

89. J. M. Stuart-Young, "From Spiritualism to Free Thought," *Gold Coast Leader*, 27 February 1929: 11.

90. Stuart-Young, *The Seductive Coast*, 151.

91. Timothy d'Arch Smith, *Love in Earnest: Some Notes on the Lives and Writings of English "Uranian" Poets from 1889 to 1930* (London: Routledge and Kegan Paul, 1970).

92. See Edward Cracroft Lefroy, "A Football-Player" and "A Cricket-Bowler," Miles, *Robert Bridges and Contemporary Poets*, 444.

93. See Connor, *Dumbstruck*.

94. Stuart-Young, *Who Buys My Dreams?* 238.

95. In the mid-1930s Stuart-Young reported having a vision in which Wilde appeared and spoke to him in a clear voice, taking possession of his mind.

96. Stuart-Young, *Who Buys My Dreams?* 238.

97. Ibid.

98. Ibid.

99. Swinburne became increasingly defensive and anxious in the face of reviewers' remarks about his poetic influences. When he was described by Matthew Arnold as a "pseudo-Shelley," he retaliated by labeling Arnold a "pseudo-Wordsworth." See *Influence and Resistance in Nineteenth Century English Poetry*, ed. G. Kim Blank and K. Louis (Basingstoke: Macmillan, 1993), 2.

100. Material objects also feature in the encoded vocabulary, taking on a metonymic value. Thus, the green carnation became a code among gay men for Wilde's homosexuality, especially once his sexuality was "discovered" by mainstream culture. Many other symbols were shared by Uranian poets and artists. See Joseph Bristow, *Effeminate England: Homoerotic Writing after 1885* (Buckingham: Open University Press, 1995).

101. Stuart-Young, "Genius, Talent or Mediocrity?" 6. Many of Stuart-Young's African poems are addressed to young children, celebrating their innocence and purifying effect on the poet; for example, "I love to hold you thus, my consolation: / May our love's stream run ever undefiled, / That I may carry 'mid Life's desolation / The trusting spirit of a Little Child!" Stuart-Young, *Who Buys My Dreams?* 56; see also Stuart-Young, *Minor Melodies*, 78, 96, 104, 128.

102. A useful contrast for Stuart-Young's poetry in the English lyrical tradition is the poetry of Arthur Cripps set in central and eastern Africa. While Cripps recognized the beauty of the African countryside, he continually juxtaposed it with nostalgic memories of rural England in order to enhance his feelings of "exile." See, for example, "The End of the Rains," in *Lake and War: African Land and Water Verses* (Oxford: Blackwell, 1917), 17.

103. Stuart-Young, *The Seductive Coast*, 5; See Alfred Hayes, Richard Le Gallienne, and Norman Gale, *A Fellowship in Song* (Rugby: George E. Over, 1893).

104. See, e.g., Stuart-Young, *Minor Melodies*, 25; Stuart-Young, *Who Buys My Dreams?* 8.

105. Other early European explorers looked for points of similarity with England in their descriptions of "exotic" foreign landscapes such as Australia.

106. Stuart-Young, *The Seductive Coast*, 157; italics in original.

107. Stuart-Young, *Who Buys My Dreams?* 250, 252.

108. Brooker and Widdowson, "A Literature for England," 129.

109. Stuart-Young, *The Seductive Coast*, 27.

110. Ibid.

111. Ibid, 163.

112. Stephen Phillips, *Lyrics and Dramas* (London: John Lane, the Bodley Head, 1913), 67.

113. Ibid.

114. Adisa Williams, "The Poems of Odeziaku," *West African Pilot*, 2 December 1938, 5.

115. Ibid.

116. Stuart-Young, *The Seductive Coast*, 52.

117. J. M. Stuart-Young, "The Lure of the Forest," *Gold Coast Leader*, 6 January 1923, Supplement, ii; see also J. M. Stuart-Young, "Time in the Tropics," *Gold Coast Leader*, 4 July 1925, 9.

118. Stuart-Young, *Minor Melodies*, 74; see also Stuart-Young, *Who Buys My Dreams?* 156.

119. "Editorial: 'JMSY,'" *West African Pilot*, 4 March 1939, 4. Not everyone wanted to emulate Stuart-Young, however. Onitsha elder Akunne John Nworah said vehemently that Stuart-Young was too much "akin to a spirit" to be regarded as a role model by the youths of Onitsha in the 1930s. Interview with Akunne John Nworah, August 2005.

120. The term "renascent Africa" was formulated by Azikiwe and appeared regularly in the *West African Pilot* in the 1930s.

121. Stuart-Young, *Who Buys My Dreams?* 80.

CONCLUSION

1. Nnamdi Azikiwe, "'Odeziaku' as I Knew Him," *West African Pilot*, 30 May 1939, 3–4.

2. See "Odeziaku's Will Benefits Servant," *West African Pilot*, 14 June 1939, 1; also "Dr John Murray Stuart-Young Dies at the Age of 58 Years," *West African Pilot*, 29 May 1939, 1. Nellie is named as "my wife, Ethel Etheridge" in Stuart-Young's will ("Odeziaku's Will Benefits Servant," 1).

3. Richard Parker, *Beneath the Equator: Cultures of Desire, Male Homosexuality, and Emerging Gay Communities in Brazil* (London: Routledge, 1999), 54.

4. Ibid., 55.

5. See Ann Laura Stoler, *Carnal Knowledge and Imperial Power: Race and the Intimate in Colonial Rule* (Berkeley: University of California Press, 2002).

6. "Dr John Murray Stuart-Young Dies at the Age of 58 Years"; "Big Crowd Watches Burial of Odeziaku," *West African Pilot*, 30 May 1939, 1; "Editorial: Exit Stuart-Young," *West African Pilot*, 30 May 1939, 3–4. I was denied access to Zik's archive at his home in Enugu, preventing a fuller examination of the two men's correspondence over many years.

7. Magnus J. Sampson, *Gold Coast Men of Affairs (Past and Present)* (London: Arthur H. Stockwell, 1937), 44–45. See Stephanie Newell, *Literary Culture in Colonial Ghana: "How to Play the Game of Life"* (Manchester: Manchester University Press; Bloomington: Indiana University Press), 142–45.

8. Azikiwe, "'Odeziaku' as I Knew Him," 4–5.

9. Duse Mohamed Ali, "Lest We Forget," *Comet*, 25 May 1940, 23.

10. C. A. J. Onwuegbuzia, "'Odeziaku' of Onitsha: A Reminiscence," *Comet*, 31 May 1941, 14–15.

11. S. I. Bosah, "Memoirs of Odeziaku," *West African Pilot*, 15 June 1939, 4.

12. "Editorial: R.I.P. J. M. Stuart-Young, D.Ph.," *Nigerian Daily Times*, 30 May 1939, 6.

13. "Mr J. M. Stuart-Young," *West Africa*, 10 June 1939, 768. One Onitsha elder, Emeka Geoffrey Olisa, suggested that Stuart-Young's doctorate was in botany from the University of Bristol; interview with Emeka Geoffrey Olisa, August 2005. Again, however, no evidence can be found for this qualification.

14. Judith Okely and Helen Callaway, "Anthropology and Autobiography: Participatory Experience and Embodied Knowledge," in *Anthropology and Autobiography*, ed. Judith Okely and Helen Callaway (London: Routledge, 1992), 7.

15. Liz Stanley, "Moments of Writing: Is There a Feminist Auto/biography?" *Gender & History* 2, no. 1 (1990): 61. See also Okely and Callaway, "Anthropology and Autobiography," 1–28.

16. Stanley, "Moments of Writing," 61.

17. Jonathan Dollimore, *Sex, Literature, and Censorship* (Cambridge: Polity Press, 2001), 51.

18. Rudi C. Bleys, *The Geography of Perversion: Male-to-Male Sexual Behaviour Outside the West and the Ethnographic Imagination, 1750–1918* (London: Cassell, 1996), 252.

19. Gilbert Herdt, *Same Sex, Different Cultures: Gays and Lesbians across Cultures* (Boulder, Colo.: Westview Press, 1997).

20. Martin Bauml Duberman, Martha Vicinus, and George Chauncey, "Introduction," in *Hidden from History: Reclaiming the Gay and Lesbian Past*, ed. Martin Bauml Duberman, Martha Vicinus, and George Chauncey (London: Penguin, 1989), 3.

21. See Bleys, *Geography of Perversion*.

22. See Herdt, *Same Sex, Different Cultures*, 126.

23. Nick Groom, *The Forger's Shadow: How Forgery Changed the Course of Literature* (London: Picador, 2002), 51.

24. David Halperin, "Sex before Sexuality: Pederasty, Politics, and Power in Classical Athens," in *Hidden from History*, ed. Martin Bauml Duberman, Martha Vicinus, and George Chauncey (London: Penguin, 1989), 52.

Bibliography

Achebe, Chinua. "Onitsha, Gift of the Niger." In *Morning Yet on Creation Day*. London and Ibadan: Heinemann, 1975.
———. "Uncle Ben's Choice." In *Girls at War and Other Stories*. London and Ibadan: Heinemann, 1972.
Achebe, Nwando. "Farmers, Traders, Warriors and Kings: Female Power and Authority in Northern Igboland." PhD diss., University of California, 2000.
Achmat, Zachie. "'Apostles of Civilised Vice': 'Immoral Practices' and 'Unnatural Vice' in South African Prisons and Compounds, 1890–1920." *Social Dynamics* 19, no. 2 (1993): 95.
Afigbo, Adiele E. *Ropes of Sand: Studies in Igbo History and Culture*. Ibadan: Ibadan University Press; Oxford: Oxford University Press, 1981.
———. *The Warrant Chiefs: Indirect Rule in Southeastern Nigeria, 1891–1929*. London: Longman, 1972.
Agbasiere, Joseph Thérèse. *Women in Igbo Life and Thought*. London: Routledge, 2000.
Ajen, Nii. "West African Homoeroticism: West African Men Who Have Sex with Men." In Murray and Roscoe, *Boy-Wives and Female Husbands*.
Akosa, Chike. *Heroes and Heroines of Onitsha*. Onitsha: Etukokwu Press, 1987.
———. Interview with the author, July 2002.
Alderson, David. *Mansex Fine: Religion, Manliness and Imperialism in Nineteenth-Century British Culture*. Manchester: Manchester University Press, 1998.
———, and Linda Anderson, ed. *Territories of Desire in Queer Culture: Refiguring Contemporary Boundaries*. Manchester: Manchester University Press, 2000.
Aldrich, Robert. *Colonialism and Homosexuality*. London: Routledge, 2003.
Alsop, A. *Ten Years in the Slums*. Manchester: John Heywood, 1879.
Altman, Dennis. "Global Gaze/Global Gays." In *Postcolonial and Queer Theories: Intersections and Essays*, edited by John C. Hawley. Westport, CT: Greenwood Press, 2001.
Amadiume, Ifi. *Male Daughters, Female Husbands: Gender and Sex in an African Society*. London: Zed Books, 1987.
———. *Reinventing Africa: Matriarchy, Religion and Culture*. London: Zed Books, 1997.

Anderson, G. L. "The Social Economy of Late Victorian Clerks." In *The Lower Middle Class in Britain, 1870–1914*, edited by Geoffrey Crossick, 113–33. London: Croom Helm, 1977.

Anderson, Gregory. *Victorian Clerks*. Manchester: Manchester University Press, 1979.

Application for Lease of Land by Mr J. M. Stuart-Young from Mr Joseph Ekwerekwu. OP 226/1925, On. Dist. 11/12/7. Nigerian National Archives, Enugu.

Author's and Writer's Who's Who. London: Shaw, 1934.

Azikiwe, Nnamdi. *My Odyssey: An Autobiography*. London: C. Hurst and Co., 1970.

Baku, Kofi. "An Intellectual in Nationalist Politics: The Contribution of Kobina Sekyi to the Evolution of Ghanaian National Consciousness." PhD diss., University of Sussex, 1987.

Bamford, Samuel. *Passages in the Life of a Radical*. 1844. London: Frank Cass, 1967.

Barrow, Logie. *Independent Spirits: Spiritualism and English Plebians, 1850–1910*. London: Routledge and Kegan Paul, 1986.

Bartlett, Neil. *Who Was That Man? A Present for Mr. Oscar Wilde*. London: Penguin, 1993.

Basden, G. T. *Among the Ibos of Nigeria*. 1921; reprint, London: Frank Cass, 1966.

——. *Niger Ibos*. 1938; reprint, London: Frank Cass, 1966.

Bastian, Misty. "Mami Wata, Mr. White, and the Sirens Off Bar Beach: Spirits and Dangerous Consumption in the Nigerian Popular Press." In *Afrika und das Andere*, edited by Heike Schmidt and Albert Wirz, 21–31. Hamburg: Lit Verlag, 1998.

——. "Married in the Water: Spirit Kin and Other Afflictions of Modernity in Southeastern Nigeria." *Journal of Religion in Africa* 27, no. 2 (1997): 116–34.

Baudelaire, Charles. *Les Fleurs du Mal*. Translated by Arthur Symons. London: Casanova Society, 1925.

Benson, John. *The Working Class in Britain, 1850–1930*. London: Longman, 1989.

Berger, Mark T. "Imperialism and Sexual Exploitation." *Journal of Imperial and Commonwealth History* 17, no. 1 (1988): 83–89.

Blank, G. Kim, and K. Louis Blank, eds. *Influence and Resistance in Nineteenth-Century English Poetry*. Basingstoke: Macmillan, 1993.

Bleys, Rudi C. *The Geography of Perversion: Male-to-Male Sexual Behaviour Outside the West and the Ethnographic Imagination, 1750–1918*. London: Cassell, 1996.

Booth, Charles. *Charles Booth's London: A Portrait of the Poor at the Turn of the Century, Drawn from his "Life and Labour of the People in London."* Edited by Albert Fried and Richard M. Elman. 1889. London: Hutchinson, 1969.

Booth, William. *In Darkest England and the Way Out*. 1890. London: Charles Knight and Co., 1970.

Bosah, Akunne Alfred. Interview, July 2002.

———. Interview, August 2005.
Bosah, S. I. *Groundwork of the History and Culture of Onitsha.* Onitsha: n.p., 1984.
———. Interview with the author, July 2002.
Breach of Native Lands Acquisition Ordinance by Messrs Nottidge and Stuart-Young. CSE 2/7/8, No. A1417/1916. Nigerian National Archives, Enugu.
Bridges, Robert. *A Choice of Bridges's Verse.* Edited by David Cecil. London: Faber and Faber, 1987.
———. *Selected Poems.* Cheshire: Carcanet Press, 1974.
Brierley, Ben. *Home Memories and Out of Work.* Edited by Roy Westall. Cheshire: Reword, 2002.
Bristow, Joseph. *Effeminate England: Homoerotic Writing after 1885.* Buckingham: Open University Press, 1995.
———. *Empire Boys: Adventures in a Man's World.* London: HarperCollins, 1991.
Brooker, Peter, and Peter Widdowson. "A Literature for England." In *Englishness: Politics and Culture, 1880–1920,* edited by Robert Colls and Philip Dodd, 116–63. London: Croom Helm, 1986.
Brooks, George E. "The Letter Book of Captain Edward Harrington." *Transactions of the Historical Society of Ghana* 6 (1962): 71–77.
Burke, Timothy. *Lifebuoy Men, Lux Women: Commodification, Consumption and Cleanliness in Modern Zimbabwe.* London: Leicester University Press, 1996.
Burton, Antoinette. *At the Heart of the Empire: Indians and the Colonial Encounter in Late-Victorian Britain.* Berkeley: University of California Press, 1998.
———, ed. *Gender, Sexuality, and Colonial Modernities.* London: Routledge, 1999.
Butler, Josephine. *The Hour before Dawn: An Appeal to Men.* London: Trubner and Co., 1876.
Callaway, Helen. *Gender, Culture, and Empire: European Women in Colonial Nigeria.* Basingstoke: Macmillan, 1987.
Carpenter, Edward. *Homogenic Love.* 1894. London: Redundancy Press, 1980.
———. *Selected Writings.* Vol. 1, *Sex.* London: Gay Modern Classics, 1984.
Church, Richard. *Over the Bridge: An Essay in Autobiography.* London: Heinemann Educational Books, 1966.
Clough, Raymond Gore. *Oil Rivers Trader: Memories of Iboland.* London: C. Hurst, 1972.
Coaster [possibly John Moray Stuart-Young]. *Coast and Bush Life in West Africa: A Book for the Potential Coaster,* edited by William Holt-Jackson London: Gay and Hancock, n.d.
Cohen, Ed. *Talk on the Wilde Side: Towards a Genealogy of a Discourse on Male Sexualities.* London: Routledge, 1993.
Coker, D. D. Africanus. "D. D. Africanus Coker." In *Trading in West Africa, 1840–1920,* ed. P. N. Davies, 155–72. London: Croom Helm, 1976.

Cole, Patrick. *Modern and Traditional Elites in the Politics of Lagos.* Cambridge: Cambridge University Press, 1975.
Colls, Robert, and Philip Dodd, eds. *Englishness: Politics and Culture, 1880–1920.* London: Croom Helm, 1986.
Commissioner of Lands, Lagos. Application by Mr J. M. Stuart-Young for a Site at Onitsha Property of Chief Mba. CSE 2/6/12. No. A2659/1913. Nigerian National Archives, Enugu.
Connor, Steven. *Dumbstruck: A Cultural History of Ventriloquism.* Oxford: Oxford University Press, 2000.
Cooper, Frederick, and Ann Laura Stoler, eds. *Tensions of Empire: Colonial Cultures in a Bourgeois World.* Berkeley: University of California Press, 1997.
Cottrell, Harry. "Reminiscences of One Connected with the West African Trade from 1863 to 1910." In *Trading in West Africa, 1840–1920,* ed. P. N. Davies, 13–92 London: Croom Helm, 1976.
Cripps, Arthur S. *Lake and War: African Land and Water Verses.* Oxford: Blackwell, 1917.
Croft-Cooke, Rupert. *The Unrecorded Life of Oscar Wilde.* London: W. H. Allen, 1972.
Crossick, Geoffrey, ed. *The Lower Middle Class in Britain, 1870–1914.* London: Croom Helm, 1977.
Crossick, Geoffrey, and Heinz-Gerhard Haupt, eds. *The Petite Bourgeoisie in Europe, 1780–1914: Enterprise, Family, and Independence.* London and New York: Routledge, 1995.
Crowther, Samuel Ajayi, and John Christopher Taylor. *The Gospel on the Banks of the Niger: Journals and Notices of the Native Missionaries Accompanying the Niger Expedition of 1857–1859.* 1859; reprint, London: Dawsons of Pall Mall, 1968.
d'Arch Smith, Timothy. *Love in Earnest: Some Notes on the Lives and Writings of English "Uranian" Poets from 1889 to 1930.* London: Routledge and Kegan Paul, 1970.
Davies, Andrew, and Steven Fielding, eds. *Workers' Worlds: Cultures and Communities in Manchester and Salford, 1880–1939.* Manchester: Manchester University Press, 1992.
Davies, P. N., ed. *Trading in West Africa, 1840–1920.* London: Croom Helm, 1976.
Davis, Lennard J. *Factual Fictions: The Origins of the English Novel.* New York: Columbia University Press, 1983.
Deemin, James. "Autobiography of James Deemin." In *Trading in West Africa, 1840–1920,* edited by P. N. Davies, 93–136. London: Croom Helm, 1976.
Dike, Kenneth Onwuka. *Trade and Politics in the Niger Delta, 1830–1885.* Westport, Conn.: Greenwood Press, 1956.
Dixon, Robert. *Writing the Colonial Adventure: Race, Gender and Nation in Anglo-Australian Popular Fiction, 1875–1914.* Cambridge: Cambridge University Press, 1995.

Dodd, Philip. "Englishness and National Culture." In *Englishness: Politics and Culture, 1880–1920*, edited by Robert Colls and Philip Dodd, 1–28. London: Croom Helm, 1986.

Dowling, Linda. *Hellenism and Homosexuality*. Ithaca, NY: Cornell University Press, 1994.

Drewal, Henry John. "Interpretation, Invention, and Re-Presentation in the Worship of Mami Wata." *Journal of Folklore Research* 25, no. 1–2 (1988): 101–39.

———. "Mami Wata Shrines: Exotica and the Construction of Self." In *African Material Culture*, edited by Mary Jo Arnoldi, Christraud M. Geary, and Kris L. Hardin. Bloomington: Indiana University Press, 1996.

Duberman, Martin Bauml, Martha Vicinus, and George Chauncey, eds. *Hidden from History: Reclaiming the Gay and Lesbian Past*. London: Penguin, 1989.

Duffield, Ian. "The Business Activities of Duse Mohamed Ali: An Example of the Economic Dimension of Pan-Africanism, 1912–1945." Paper presented to the University of Ibadan Department of History Postgraduate Seminar, 28 April 1967.

Dunton, Chris. "'Wheyting de dat?' The Treatment of Homosexuality in African Literature." *Research in African Literatures* 20, no. 3 (1989): 422–48.

Eakin, Paul John. *How Our Lives Become Stories: Making Selves*. Ithaca, NY: Cornell University Press, 1999.

Ekejiuba, Felicia. "Omu Okwei, the Merchant Queen of Ossomari: A Biographical Sketch." *Journal of the Historical Society of Nigeria* 3, no. 4 (1967): 633–46.

Ekwerekwu, Isaac I. Interview, July 2002.

Ekwerekwu, Patrick. Interview, July 2002.

Ellingson, Stephen, and M. Christian Green, eds. *Religion and Sexuality in Cross-Cultural Perspective*. London: Routledge, 2002.

Ellis, Havelock. *Studies in the Psychology of Sex*. Vol. 6, *Sex in Relation to Society*. 1910. Philadelphia: F. A. Davis, 1929.

Epprecht, Marc. "'Good God Almighty, What's This?' Homosexual 'Crime' in Early Colonial Zimbabwe." In Murray and Roscoe, *Boy-Wives and Female Husbands*, 197–221.

———. "The 'Unsaying' of Indigenous Homosexualities in Zimbabwe: Mapping a Blindspot in an African Masculinity." *Journal of Southern African Studies* 24, no. 4 (1998): 631–51.

Etukokwu, Joseph U. *Life between Two Shrines: An Autobiography*. Onitsha: Etukokwu, ca. 1997.

Evans-Pritchard, E. E. "Sexual Inversion among the Azande." In *Ethnographic Studies of Homosexuality*, edited by Wayne R. Dynes and Stephen Donaldson, 168–74. New York: Garland, 1992.

Field, Alan. *"Verb Sap." on Going to West Africa, to Northern, Southern Nigeria and to the Coasts*. 3rd ed. London: Bale, Sons and Danielsson, 1913.

Fieldhouse, D. K. *Merchant Capital and Economic Decolonization: The United Africa Company, 1929–1987*. Oxford: Clarendon Press, 1994.

Gagnier, Regina. *Idylls of the Marketplace: Oscar Wilde and the Victorian Public.* London: Scolar Press, 1986.

Gaudio, Rudolf P. "Male Lesbians and Other Queer Notions in Hausa." In Murray and Roscoe, *Boy-Wives and Female Husbands,* 115–28.

Gikandi, Simon. *Maps of Englishness: Writing Identity in the Culture of Colonialism.* New York: Columbia University Press, 1996.

Gissing, George. *Born in Exile.* 1892. London: Victor Gollancz, 1970.

Gore, Charles, and Joseph Nevadomsky. "Practice and Agency in Mammy Wata Worship in Southern Nigeria." *African Arts* 3, no. 30 (1997): 60–95.

Gosse, Edmund. *The Collected Poems.* London: William Heinemann, 1911.

———. *Gossip in a Library: Collected Essays.* Vol. 2. 1891; reprint, London: William Heinemann, 1913.

Grafton, Anthony. *Forgers and Critics: Creativity and Duplicity in Western Scholarship.* London: Collins and Brown, 1990.

Graves, Robert. *On English Poetry: Being an Irregular Approach to the Psychology of this Art, from Evidence Mainly Subjective.* London: William Heinemann, 1922.

Greenslade, William. *Degeneration, Culture, and the Novel, 1880–1940.* Cambridge: Cambridge University Press, 1994.

Griffiths, Gareth. *African Literatures in English: East and West.* Harlow: Longman, 2000.

Groom, Nick. *The Forger's Shadow: How Forgery Changed the Course of Literature.* London: Picador, 2002.

Hall, Catherine. *Civilising Subjects: Metropole and Colony in the English Imagination, 1830–1867.* Cambridge: Polity, 2002.

———. *Cultures of Empire:* A Reader. Manchester: Manchester University Press, 2000.

Halperin, David M. "Sex before Sexuality: Pederasty, Politics and Power in Classical Athens." In *Hidden from History: Reclaiming the Gay and Lesbian Past,* edited by Martin Bauml Duberman, Martha Vicinus, and George Chauncey, 37–53. London: Penguin, 1989.

Harrington, Edward. "The Letter Book of Captain Edward Harrington." *Transactions of the Historical Society of Ghana* 6 (1962): 71–77.

Harrison, Anthony H. *Victorian Poets and Romantic Poems: Intertextuality and Ideology.* Charlottesville: University of Virginia Press, 1990.

Hayes, Alfred, Richard Le Gallienne, and Norman Gale. *A Fellowship in Song.* Rugby: George E. Over, 1893.

Henderson, Richard N. *The King in Every Man: Evolutionary Trends in Onitsha Ibo Society and Culture.* New Haven, CT: Yale University Press, 1972.

Henry, Warren. *The Confessions of a Tenderfoot "Coaster": A Trader's Chronicle of Life on the West Coast of Africa.* London: H. F. and G. Witherby, 1927.

———. *Fantee Carter.* London: Herbert Jenkins, 1931.

Herdt, Gilbert. *Same Sex, Different Cultures: Gays and Lesbians across Cultures.* Boulder, CO: Westview Press, 1997.

———, and Robert J. Stoller. *Intimate Communications: Erotics and the Study of Culture*. New York: Columbia University Press, 1990.
Hitchcock, Peter. "They Must Be Represented? Problems in Theories of Working-Class Representation." *PMLA* 115 (2000): 20–32.
Horn, Aloysius. *Trader Horn.* 1927; Bath: Cedric Chivers, 1974.
Housman, A. E. *A Shropshire Lad.* 1896.London: Grant Richards, 1907.
Hughes, Alex. *Heterographies: Sexual Difference in French Autobiography.* Oxford: Berg, 1999.
Hyam, Ronald. *Empire and Sexuality: The British Experience.* Manchester: Manchester University Press, 1991.
Isichei, Elizabeth. *A History of the Igbo People.* Basingstoke: Macmillan, 1976.
Jackson, Holbrook. *The 1890s: A Review of Art and Ideas at the Close of the Nineteenth Century.* 1913. London: Cresset Library, 1988.
Jell-Bahlsen, Sabine. "The Concept of Mammywater in Flora Nwapa's Novels." *Research in African Literatures* 2, no. 26 (1995): 30–39.
Jones, Alfred Lewis. "Alfred Lewis Jones." In *Trading in West Africa, 1840–1920*, edited by P. N. Davies, 180–202. London: Croom Helm,1976.
Jones, G. I. *From Slaves to Palm Oil: Slave Trade and Palm Oil Trade in the Bight of Biafra.* African Monographs No. 13. Cambridge: African Studies Centre, 1989.
J. M. Stuart-Young: Transfer of His Premises in the Onitsha Province to the Niger Company Limited, 26-2-1936. OP 340, On. Dist. 12/1/1885. Nigerian National Archives Enugu.
Kaplow, Susan Beth. "African Merchants of the Nineteenth-Century Gold Coast." PhD diss., Columbia University, 1971.
Kendall. "'When a Woman Loves a Woman' in Lesotho: Love, Sex, and the Western Construction of Homophobia." In Murray and Roscoe, *Boy-Wives and Female Husbands*, 223–41.
Kerr, Howard. *Mediums, and Spirit-Rappers, and Roaring Radicals: Spiritualism in American Literature, 1850–1900.* Chicago: University of Illinois Press, 1972.
Kidd, Alan J., and K. W. Roberts, eds.. *City, Class and Culture: Studies in Social Policy and Cultural Production in Victorian Manchester.* Manchester: Manchester University Press, 1985.
Killam, G. D. "John Moray Stuart-Young: The Iniquitous Coaster of Onitsha (Nigeria)." *Black Academy Review* 2, no. 3 (1971): 22–41.
Kimble, David. *A Political History of Ghana: The Rise of Gold Coast Nationalism, 1850–1928.* Oxford: Clarendon Press, 1963.
Kingsley, Mary. *Travels in West Africa.* 1897. London: Everyman, 1993.
Lane, Christopher. *The Ruling Passion: British Colonial Allegory and the Paradox of Homosexual Desire.* Durham, NC: Duke University Press, 1995.
Langley, J. Ayodele. *Pan-Africanism and Nationalism in West Africa, 1900–1945.* Oxford: Clarendon Press, 1973.

Le Gallienne, Richard. *Retrospective Reviews: A Literary Log.* Vol 1, 1891–93. London: John Lane, 1896.
———. *The Romantic '90s.* 1926. London: Putnam, 1951.
Leith-Ross, Sylvia. "Memories of Nigeria." Unpublished manuscript in the possession of G. D. Killam, 1964.
———. *Stepping-Stones: Memoirs of Colonial Nigeria, 1907–1960.* Edited by Michael Crowder. London: Peter Owen, 1983.
Leonard, Arthur Glyn. *The Lower Niger and Its Tribes.* 1906. Reprint,c London: Frank Cass, 1968.
Lerner, Laurence. *The Uses of Nostalgia.* London: Chatto and Windus, 1972.
Levine, Philippa. "Sexuality, Gender, and Empire." In *Gender and Empire,* edited by Philippa Levine, 134–55. Oxford: Oxford University Press, 2004.
———. *Victorian Feminism, 1850–1900.* London: Hutchinson, 1987.
Logan, Mawuena Kossi. *Narrating Africa: George Henty and the Fiction of Empire.* New York: Garland, 1999.
London, Jack. *The People of the Abyss.* 1903. London: The Journeyman Press, 1977.
Lynn, Martin. *Commerce and Economic Change in West Africa.* Cambridge: Cambridge University Press, 1997.
MacKenzie, John M. *Propaganda and Empire: The Manipulation of British Public Opinion, 1880–1960.* Manchester: Manchester University Press, 1984.
———, ed. *Imperialism and Popular Culture.* Manchester: Manchester University Press, 1986.
Maidment, B. E. "Class and Cultural Production in the Industrial City: Poetry in Victorian Manchester." In *City, Class and Culture,* edited by Alan J. Kidd and K. W. Roberts, 148–66. Manchester: Manchester University Press, 1985.
Manchester Grammar School—Old Mancunians Association's 21st Annual Report and Register of Members, 1925. MC: M267/3/8. Manchester Archives and Local Studies Unit, Manchester Central Library, Manchester, UK.
Martin, Susan. *Palm Oil and Protest: An Economic History of the Ngwa Region, South-Eastern Nigeria, 1800–1980.* Cambridge: Cambridge University Press, 1988.
Masterman, Charles F. G., ed. *The Heart of the Empire: Discussions of Problems of Modern City Life in England.* 1901; reprint, Brighton: Harvester Press, 1973.
McCall, John C. *Dancing Histories: Heuristic Ethnography with the Ohafia Igbo.* Ann Arbor: University of Michigan Press, 2000.
———. "Portrait of a Brave Woman." *American Anthropologist* 98, no. 1 (1996): 127–36.
McClintock, Anne. *Imperial Leather: Race, Gender and Sexuality in the Colonial Contest.* London: Routledge, 1995.
McLeod, Hugh. *Religion and the Working Class in Nineteenth-Century Britain* London: Macmillan, 1984.
McPhee, Allan. *The Economic Revolution in British West Africa.* 1926. London: Frank Cass, 1971.

Miles, Alfred H., ed. *The Poets and the Poetry of the Nineteenth Century: Robert Bridges and Contemporary Poets.* 1891. London: Routledge, 1906.

Millard, Kenneth. *Edwardian Poetry.* Oxford: Clarendon Press, 1991.

Mitchell, Angus, ed. *The Amazon Journal of Roger Casement.* London: Anaconda Editions, 1997.

Mohanty, Chandra Talpade. "Under Western Eyes: Feminist Scholarship and Colonial Discourses." In *Colonial Discourse and Postcolonial Theory: A Reader,* edited by Patrick Williams and Laura Chrisman. New York: Harvester Wheatsheaf, 1993.

Mr J. M. Stuart-Young: Application for Land at Atani from Chief Chukumma for Trading Purposes. OP 289/1914, On. Dist. 11/1/12. Nigerian National Archives, Enugu.

Mr J. M. Stuart-Young: Application for a Site at Old Market Road, Onitsha. CSE 2/11/10, No. A1160/1918. Nigerian National Archives, Enugu.

Murray, Stephen O., and Will Roscoe, eds. *Boy-Wives and Female Husbands: Studies of African Homosexualities.* Basingstoke: Macmillan, 1998.

Ndulue, Christopher Chukwuma. *Womanhood in Igbo Culture.* Aba: Christopher C. Ndulue, 1995.

Newell, Stephanie. *Ghanaian Popular Fiction: "Thrilling Discoveries in Conjugal Life" and Other Tales.* Oxford: James Currey; Athens: Ohio University Press, 2000.

———. *Literary Culture in Colonial Ghana: "How To Play the Game of Life."* Manchester: Manchester University Press; Bloomington: Indiana University Press, 2002.

Nicholls, Peter. *Modernisms: A Literary Guide.* Basingstoke: Macmillan, 1995.

Nicholson, John Gambril. *In the Dreamy Afternoon.* London: Gay Men's Press, 1989.

Northrup, David. *Trade without Rulers: Pre-Colonial Economic Development in South-Eastern Nigeria.* Oxford: Clarendon Press, 1978.

Norton, Rictor. "Pastoral Homoeroticism and Barnfield, the Affectionate Shepherd." In *The Affectionate Shepherd: Celebrating Richard Barnfield,* edited by Kenneth Borris and George Klawitter, 117–29. Selinsgrove, PA:: Susquehanna University Press; London: Associated University Press, 2001.

Noyes, Alfred. *The Accusing Ghost, or Justice for Casement.* London: Victor Gollancz, 1957.

Nussbaum, Felicity. *Torrid Zones: Maternity, Sexuality, and Empire in Eighteenth-Century English Narratives.* Baltimore: Johns Hopkins University Press, 1995.

Nworah, Akunne John. Interview with the author, August 2005.

Obi, Celestine. *A Hundred Years of the Catholic Church in Eastern Nigeria, 1885–1985.* Onitsha: Africana-Fep, 1985).

Obi, Chike. Interview, July 2002.

Obiechina, Emmanuel N. *Literature for the Masses: An Analytical Study of Popular Pamphleteering in Nigeria.* Enugu: Nwankwo-Ifejika, 1971.

———. *Onitsha Market Literature*. London: Heinemann, 1972.
Ofordile, Nwononaku Josephine. Interview, August 2005.
Ogbalu, Chidozie. *Igbo Attitudes to Sex*. Onitsha: University, ca. 1982.
Ogbuene, Chigekwu G. *The Concept of Man in Igbo Myths*. Frankfurt: Peter Lang, 1999.
Okeke-Ezigbo, Emeka. "Anu Solu Nwa-Enwe O Majie Aka: Ogbuefi Nnamdi Azikiwe as an Igbo Folk Hero." In *The Hero in Igbo Life and Literature*, edited by Donatus Nwoga and Chukwuma Azuonye, 157–72. Enugu: Fourth Dimension, 2002.
Okonkwo, Rita. *Protest Movements in Lagos, 1908–1930*. Lampeter: Edwin Mellon Press, 1995.
Okosi, Agnes. Interview, August 2005.
Okwudinka, Cecilia. Interview, August 2005.
Olisa, Emeka Geoffrey. Interview, August 2005.
Onochie, Enyi Onyeomadiko Helen. Interview, August 2005.
Osuji, Chuks. *Foundation of Igbo Tradition and Culture*. Owerri: Opinion Research and Communications, 1998.
Owen, Alex. *The Darkened Room: Women, Power, and Spiritualism in Late Nineteenth-Century England*. London: Virago Press, 1989.
Parker, Richard. *Beneath the Equator: Cultures of Desire, Male Homosexuality, and Emerging Gay Communities in Brazil*. London: Routledge, 1999.
Pater, Walter. *Appreciations, with an Essay on Style*. London: Macmillan, 1897.
Pearson, Hesketh. *The Life of Oscar Wilde*. 1946. Middlesex: Penguin, 1985.
Penfield, Joyce. *Communicating with Quotes*. Westport, CT: Greenwood Press, 1983.
Perkins, David. *A History of Modern Poetry: From the 1890s to the High Modernist Mode*. Cambridge, MA: Harvard University Press, 1976.
Phillips, Stephen. *Lyrics and Dramas*. London: John Lane, the Bodley Head, 1913.
Pincheon, Bill Stanford. "An Ethnography of Silences: Race, (Homo)Sexualities, and a Discourse of Africa." *African Studies Review* 43, no. 3 (2000): 39–58.
Priestley, Margaret. *West African Trade and Coast Society: A Family Study*. London: Oxford University Press, 1969.
Records of the Manchester City Sessions. M116/2/4/333–371 and M117/1/2/41–43. Manchester Archives and Local Studies Unit, Manchester Central Library, Manchester, UK.
Requesting Sanction for Crown Prosecution to Prosecute in the Cases vs Messrs Stuart-Young and Bright for Contravention of Native Lands Acquisition Ordinance. CSE 2/9/11, No. A1479/1916. Nigerian National Archives, Enugu.
Richards, Thomas. *The Commodity Culture of Victorian England: Advertising and Spectacle, 1851–1914*. Stanford, CA: Stanford University Press, 1990.
Roberts, Robert. *The Classic Slum*. Manchester: Manchester University Press, 1971.

Robinson, Christopher. *Scandal in the Ink: Male and Female Homosexuality in Twentieth-Century French Literature*. London: Cassell, 1995.
Rose, Jonathan. *The Edwardian Temperament, 1895–1919*. Athens, OH: Ohio University Press, 1986.
———. *The Intellectual Life of the British Working Classes*. New Haven, CT: Yale University Press, 2001.
Schur, Owen. *Victorian Pastoral: Tennyson, Hardy, and the Subversion of Forms*. Columbus: Ohio State University Press, 1989.
Schweitzer, Albert. *The Primeval Forest*. 1931. Baltimore: Johns Hopkins University Press, 1998.
Sedgwick, Eve Kosofsky. *Epistemology of the Closet*. London: Penguin, 1990.
———. *Tendencies*. London: Routledge, 1994.
Service, Robert. *Rhymes of a Rolling Stone*. Toronto: William Briggs, 1912.
———. *Songs of a Sour-Dough*. Toronto: William Briggs, 1911.
Sherwood, Sandys. *It's Been a Pleasure*. Washington: Minerva Press, 1994.
Sinfield, Alan. *Cultural Politics—Queer Reading*. London: Routledge, 1994.
———. *The Wilde Century*. London: Cassell, 1994.
Sinha, Mrinalini. *Colonial Masculinity: The "Manly Englishman" and the "Effeminate Bengali" in the Late Nineteenth Century*. Manchester: Manchester University Press, 1995.
"Special Report of Meritorious Conduct: Chief Inspector Hargreaves and Inspector Corden." 29 June 1899. Greater Manchester Police Museum Archives.
Stallybrass, Peter and Allon White. *The Politics and Poetics of Transgression*. London: Methuen, 1986.
Stanley, Henry Morton. *In Darkest Africa*. New York: C. Scribner's Sons, 1890.
Stanley, Liz. "Moments of Writing: Is There a Feminist Auto/biography?" *Gender and History* 2, no. 1 (1990): 58–67.
Stokes, John. *Oscar Wilde: Myths, Miracles and Imitations*. Cambridge: Cambridge University Press, 1996.
Stoler, Ann Laura. *Carnal Knowledge and Imperial Power: Race and the Intimate in Colonial Rule*. Berkeley: University of California Press, 2002.
———. *Race and the Education of Desire: Foucault's History of Sexuality and the Colonial Order of Things*. Durham, NC: Duke University Press, 1995.
Stuart-Young, John Moray. *The After-Life: A Poetic Service of Song*. Sunderland: Keystone Press, 1905.
———. *The Antinomian: An Elegaic Poem. Also a Prose Trifle in Memory of "Sebastian."* London: Hermes Press, 1909.
———. *Candles in Sunshine: Poems*. Edited by Charles Kains Jackson. London: Arthur H. Stockwell, 1919.
———. *Chits from West Africa: Stories and Sketches*. London: Arthur H. Stockwell, 1923.
———. *A Calabash of Kola Nuts: West African Rhymes by O. Dazi Ako*. London: Lynwood, 1911.

———. *The Coaster at Home*. London: Arthur H. Stockwell, 1916.
———. *A Cupful of Kernels: Stories, Studies and Sketches Mainly from the West African Coast*. London: John Ouseley, 1909.
———. *Dreaming True*. London: C. W. Daniel, 1934.
———. *Faery Gold: A Poem and Prose Allegories*. Manchester: John Heywood, 1904.
———. *The Immortal Nine: An Introduction to the Poetry of Last Century*. London: Fowler and Wright, 1928.
———. *Impressions: Being Casual Jottings from the Note-Book of a Journalist in Western Africa*. Sunderland: Keystone Press, 1904.
———. *The Iniquitous Coaster*. London: Arthur H. Stockwell, 1917.
———. Introduction to *The Almighty Power of Love*, by Alfred Stringer. London: Arthur H. Stockwell, 1927.
———. *Johnny Jones Guttersnipe*. London: C. W. Daniel, 1926.
———. Letter to West African Co-Operative Producers, Ltd., Lagos, 11 March 1930. In *Macaulay Papers, General Correspondence* III, 9, 1930. In the possession of G. D. Killam.
———. *Merely a Negress: A West African Story*. London: John Long, 1904.
———. *Minor Melodies*. London: Kegan Paul, 1904.
———. *Minor Melodies: Lyrics and Songs*. Edinburgh: T. and A. Constable, 1921.
———. *Osrac, the Self-Sufficient and Other Poems with a Memoir of the Late Oscar Wilde*. London: Hermes Press, 1905.
———. "Oscar Wilde: A Memoir." *English Illustrated Magazine* 33 (1905): 573–76.
———. *Out of Hours: Poems, Lyrics, Sonnets*. London: A. H. Stockwell, 1909.
———. *Passion's Peril: A Romance*. London: Hermes Press, 1906.
———. *The Seductive Coast: Poems Lyrical and Descriptive from West Africa*. London: John Ouseley, 1909.
———. *The Soul-Slayer*. London: Arthur H. Stockwell, 1920.
———. *Through Veiled Eyes: Being the Story of a Dead Lad's Love*. London: John Ouseley, 1908.
———. *An Urning's Love, Being a Poetic Study of Morbidity*. London: Hermes Press, 1905.
———. *What Does It Matter?* London: C. W. Daniel, 1927.
———. *Who Buys My Dreams? Poems and Lyrics*. London: Cecil Palmer, 1923.
Sutton, Les. *Mainly about Ardwick*. 3 vols. Manchester: Les Sutton, 1975–81.
Swinburne, Algernon Charles. *Collected Poetical Works*, vol. 1. 1924; London: William Heinemann, 1927.
Symons, A. J. A. *The Quest for Corvo: An Experiment in Biography*. 1934; reprint, Middlesex: Penguin Books, 1950.
Symons, Arthur. *Confessions: A Study in Pathology*. New York: Jonathan Cape and Harrison Smith, 1930.
———. *The Romantic Movement in English Poetry*. London: Archibald Constable, 1909.

Symons, Julian. *A. J. A. Symons: His Life and Speculations.* Oxford: Oxford University Press, 1986.
Symonds, John Addington. *Essays Speculative and Suggestive,* vol. 1. London: Chapman and Hall, 1890.
——. *The Memoirs of John Addington Symonds.* Edited by Phyllis Grosskurth. London: Hutchinson, 1984.
——. *Walt Whitman: A Study.* London: George Routledge, 1893.
Tagbo, N. C. Interview, August 2005.
Talbot, P. Amaury. *Some Nigerian Fertility Cults.* 1927.;London: Frank Cass, 1967.
Tebb, William, and Edward Perry Vollum. *Premature Burial and How to Avoid It: With Special Reference to Trance, Catalepsy, and Other Forms of Suspended Animation.* London: Swann, Sonnenschein and Co., 1896.
Thomas, T. "Representation of the Manchester Working-Class in Fiction, 1850–1900." In *City, Class and Culture: Studies in Social Policy and Cultural Production in Victorian Manchester,* edited by Alan J. Kidd and K. W. Roberts, 193–216. Manchester: Manchester University Press, 1985.
Thompson, Andrew S. *Imperial Britain: The Empire in British Politics, c. 1880–1932.* Harlow: Pearson Education, 2000.
Thompson, Paul. *The Edwardians: The Remaking of British Society.* London: Routledge, 1992.
Thurschwell, Pamela. *Literature, Technology and Magical Thinking, 1880–1920.* Cambridge: Cambridge University Press, 2001.
Ward, Stuart. *British Culture and the Empire.* Manchester: Manchester University Press, 2001.
Watson, William. *Collected Poems.* London: John Lane, 1899.
——. *The Poems of Sir William Watson, 1878–1935.* London: George G. Harrap, 1936.
Weeks, Jeffrey. *Sex, Politics and Society: The Regulation of Sexuality since 1800.* London: Longman, 1989.
——, and Kevin Porter. *Between the Acts: Lives of Homosexual Men, 1885–1967.* London: Rivers Oram Press, 1998.
Weston, Kath. "Lesbian/Gay Studies in the House of Anthropology." *Annual Review of Anthropology* 22 (1993): 339–67.
Whitford, John. *Trading Life in Western and Central Africa.* 1877. London: Frank Cass, 1967.
Wild, Jonathan. *The Rise of the Office Clerk in British Literary Culture.* Basingstoke: Palgrave, 2005.
Wilde, Oscar. *De Profundis.* 1905. London: Methuen, 1909.
——. "Pen, Pencil and Poison: A Study in Green." In *Essays by Oscar Wilde,* edited by Hesketh Pearson, 73–99. 1889. London: Methuen, 1950.
Wilder, Alexander. *Perils of Premature Burial.* London: E. W. Allen, 1895.
Yankah, Kwesi. *The Proverb in the Context of Akan Rhetoric: A Theory of Proverb Praxis.* Bern: Peter Lang, 1989.

Young, J. M. D. [possibly J. M. Stuart-Young]. *The Fallen Angel.* Poppy's Library Series 98 London: Amalgamated Press, 1932.
Young, Robert J. C. *Colonial Desire: Hybridity in Theory, Culture and Race.* London: Routledge, 1995.
Young, T. Rex. *West African Agent: A British Coaster's Anglo-French Log.* London: Heath Cranton, 1943.

Index

Aba, 111
Accra, 16
Achebe, Chinua, 102, 103
Achebe, Nwando, 9, 10, 12
adolescence, 65
Aesthetic Movement, 80
African clubs, 115
African nationalism, 74, 75, 151, 157, 159, 163
age-grades, 82, 168
agriculture, African, 42
Ahebe Ugbabe, 10
Ajen, Nii, 10
Akosa, Chike, 93, 100, 101, 102
Aku, O.Dazi (pseud. J. M. Stuart-Young), 90, 141
Ala (earth goddess), 98
Alderson, David, 11
Aldrich, Robert, 5, 6
Algiers, 77
Ali, Duse Mohamed, 75, 110
Amadiume, Ifi, 8–9, 10, 12; *Male Daughters, Female Husbands*, 8, 12
Anderson, Linda, 11
Anglican Church (Onitsha), 4
anthropology. *See* ethnography
anticolonialism, 108, 116, 151, 158, 163, 166
Arabian oral tradition, 151
architecture, 4
Ardwick (Manchester), 22, 31, 118, 160
Ardwick Green, 121
athleticism, 135
avant garde, 148, 149, 158
Azikiwe, Nnamdi (Zik), 3, 75, 101, 110, 116, 140, 150, 152, 159, 160, 162, 163

Back Kay Street (Manchester), 25, 32, 73, 119, 121, 123, 130, 132

Basden, G. T., 8
Bastian, Misty, 98
Biafran War, 162
binary oppositions, 6, 12, 13, 14, 18, 69
Binyon, Lawrence, 144
biography, 3, 13, 14, 17–20
blackmail, 57
Bleys, Rudi, 6, 10, 14, 165
Blyden, Edward W., 162
Boer War, 33, 136
Booth, Charles, 26, 28, 29, 129
Booth, William, 26, 35, 120, 137
Bosah, Akunne Alfred, 80
Bosah, Onwuije Hayford, 80, 83, 98, 99, 100, 147
Bosah, S. I., 91, 92, 98, 99, 101, 103, 104, 162–63
Bosie. *See* Douglas, Lord Alfred
bourgeoisie, 7, 15, 38, 40, 50, 52, 54, 76, 77, 83, 96, 106, 166, 167
Bridges, Robert, 130, 139, 140, 144, 145, 153, 155
Bristow, Joseph, 5, 6, 7, 65, 71
British Empire, 3, 15–16, 136, 109, 141, 165, 167. *See also* imperialism
British Supernaturalists' Lyceum Union, 86
Brolly, William L., 113, 114, 118
Brooke, Rupert, 76
Brooker, Peter, 145
Budapest, 77
Burke, Timothy, 36, 54
Burton, Antoinette, 7, 9, 17, 33
Burton, Richard, 166
Butler, Josephine, 70

Caine, Hall, 150
Calabar, 16

Callaway, Helen, 163
Cambridge Senior Examinations, 141
Carpenter, Edward, 25, 71, 76, 77, 135, 147
Casely Hayford, J. E., 162
Casement, Roger, 76, 78
celibacy, 135, 139, 147
chiefs, 3, 4, 15, 34, 99
Chorlton-on-Medlock (Manchester), 96
Christ the King College (Onitsha), 113
Christian Spiritual Hall, 23
Christianity, 14, 23, 40, 100, 165; Anglican, 160; Evangelical, 70; Nonconformist, 23, 127; Roman Catholic, 112, 113, 114, 166
Church Missionary House, 35
class system (British), 7, 24–33, 72, 106, 114, 115, 118, 128–30, 165; and empire, 35, 37, 51; and gender, 132; middle-class values, 23–5, 26, 29, 32, 35, 51, 53, 70, 79, 126, 130–2, 167; "poor whites," 33, 36, 38, 51, 55; white-collar crime, 22, 30; white-collar workers, 110; working-class autobiography, 128–29, 131; working-class life, 3–4, 15–17, 18, 19, 20, 25–9, 31–32, 34, 47, 57, 78, 119, 120, 126–28, 131, 137, 167; working-class respectability, 28, 132. *See also* clerks; slum life; slum writing
claustrophobia, 160, 161
clerks: African, 3, 15, 103; British, 16, 22, 25, 28–30, 33, 52
Clinton family (Calabar), 75
Clough, Raymond Gore, 44, 47, 48, 49
Coker, Percy Bysshe Shelley, 141–2
colonial officials, 3, 4, 12, 33, 75, 78, 90, 112, 113, 117, 161, 165
colonial rule, 4, 13–15, 37, 44, 49, 50, 53, 74, 76, 78, 87, 107, 110, 155, 157, 165, 169; and archives, 13, 14, 165; and education policy, 110, 111, 112, 115; protest against, 49; and settlers, 7, 120, 137; and taxation, 49, 113
commodities, 4; and African consumers, 4, 38–45, 46, 47, 55, 100, 113; and British consumers, 28–29, 34, 40; and British traders in West Africa, 38–45; imported trade goods, 38, 41, 44–5, 56, 92, 99, 103, 104, 109
Conakry (French Guinea), 56, 57, 87
Conrad, Joseph, 43, 155

consumers. *See* commodities
Cook, Thomas, 77
Cooper, Frederick, 7, 17, 18
Corelli, Marie, 150
Corvo, Baron (pseud. Frederick Rolfe), 81
Cottrell, Harry, 37
credit, 56
Croft-Cooke, Rupert, 64, 68
Crossick, Geoffrey, 29
Crowther, Samuel Ajayi, 35, 36, 37–8
cultural nationalism, 109, 110, 116, 120

d'Arch Smith, Timothy, 72, 80, 126
Decadent Movement, 76, 129, 131, 145, 146, 148, 154
Deemin, James, 37, 41
degeneration, theories of, 35, 51, 52, 53, 70, 110, 120, 127, 129–32, 137. *See also* miscegenation
dirt, 35, 36, 38, 135; and empire, 29, 37, 40, 42, 51. *See also* soap
Dixcove (Ghana), 50
Dollimore, Jonathan, 164
domesticity, 7, 78
Dominica, 113
Douglas, Alfred, 63, 64, 76, 80
Drewal, Henry John, 103, 104
DuBois, W. E. B., 112, 117
Durham University, 138, 163
Dutch East Indies, 51

Eakin, Paul John, 76
Edwardian society, 67, 72, 129, 145, 155–56
effeminacy, 71, 74, 97, 148, 165
Eke (or Ekke) python, 97–102, 105, 106
Ekwerekwu, I. I., 101
Ekwerekwu, Patrick, 100
Elgar, Edward, 76
elites: European colonial, 14, 35; African, 1, 3, 14, 75, 90, 98, 100, 101, 140, 159, 162–65; and nonelites, 3, 18, 104
Ellis, Havelock, 65, 76
embezzlement, 21, 22, 24–27, 30, 124, 127, 132, 139
English language, 110, 117
English literature, 17, 28, 63, 139, 152, 166
Englishness, 105, 139, 145, 155
Epprecht, Marc, 9
ethnography, 5, 6, 7, 8, 13–14, 53, 117, 165

Etukokwu, Joseph U., 3, 81, 89, 102, 169
eurocentrism, 8
Europe, 77, 78
evolutionary theory, 131

fan mail, 62, 137, 141
femininity, 40, 164
feminism, 164
fin-de-siècle, 27, 28, 69
First World War, 5, 35, 99, 139, 145, 148
forgery: as conferring status, 16, 17, 18, 25, 27, 64; as creative expression, 24; degrees of, 28; as dissidence, 11; endemic among clerks, 30; history of, 19; as production of self, 167; as ritual of queer expression, 20; Stuart-Young's reputation for, 3; Stuart-Young charged with, 21, 139; Wilde's fascination with, 62. *See also* embezzlement
Forster, E. M., 77–78
French Guinea, 78
Freud, Sigmund, 131
funerals, Igbo, 1–3, 17, 98; "second burial," 3

Gagnier, Regina, 64
Gale, Norman, 144, 145
Garvey, Marcus, 117
gender, 7, 8, 18, 33–34, 37, 92, 98, 100, 129, 131, 153, 164, 168; ambiguity, 14; Igbo dual-sex system, 12; Igbo flexibility of, 9, 10, 12–13, 146. *See also* femininity; masculinity
General Register Office (England), 94
Georgian society, 129
Germany, 105
Gide, André, 77, 166
Gikandi, Simon, 105
globalization, 41, 46
Gold Coast (Ghana), 16, 114, 116, 143
Gone Native, 53
Gordon, Leon, *White Cargo*, 51, 52, 53
Gosse, Edmund, 143, 145
Grand Bassa (Liberia), 56
Great Depression, 49, 76, 101, 106, 138, 148

Haggard, H. Rider, 43
Hall, Catherine, 7, 9, 20
Halperin, David, 169–70
Hargreaves (police inspector), 22, 23, 26
Harrington, Edward, 42, 50

Harris, Frank, 76, 94, 96, 165, 166
Hayes, Alfred, 144, 145, 155, 156
Hayes, Patricia, 92
Hellenism, 154
Henry, Warren, 51, 53
Herdt, Gilbert, 13, 93, 97, 167
Hermes Press (London), 57
heterosexuality, 5, 94, 97, 133, 135, 147, 148
Hindu, 105
Hitchcock, Peter, 128
Hitchins, Robert Smythe, 57
Hollings, James, 21
Holt, John, 29
homophobia, 11
homosexuality: in British popular imagination, 67; construction of, 69–71; Decadent literature and, 148; denial of in Africa, 9–10, 12; and empire, 3, 78, 135; history of, 71, 169; in Igboland, 88; in imperial history, 5–7; indigenous, 7, 9; and Mami Wata, 102; and masturbation, 70, 130; natural, 97; and the pastoral, 146; as product of urban modern living, 131; as "spoiled identity," 19–20; stereotype of, 74; Stuart-Young's, 3, 77, 94, 97, 120, 160, 166; and travel, 77, 78; Wilde's, 18, 65, 67, 70, 96; and writing, 106, 154. *See also* pederasty; Uranian
Housman, A. E., 144–45
Howara, Henry Newman, 144
Hyam, Ronald, 5–6, 7
hygiene, 36, 40, 51. *See also* soap

Ibibio, 98
"Ibrahim the Unkissed," 64, 78, 86, 87
idealism, 136
imperial history, 5, 13, 14, 17, 18, 164, 169, 170. *See also* new imperial history
imperialism (British), 5, 6, 7, 15, 17, 18, 27, 35, 38, 40, 46, 50, 53, 54, 71, 74, 110, 112, 116, 157, 166
India, 17, 105
individualism, 113
industrialization, 46, 120, 129, 131, 157
infertility, 103, 104
ivory, 45, 46

Japan, 93
Johnston, Harry, 117

Index ↩ 229

Joyce, James, 148
Kalulu, 78
Kay Street (Manchester), 121
Killam, G. D., 126
Kingsley, Mary, 37, 41–42, 47, 48, 54
Kipling, Rudyard, 25, 76, 126, 140, 145, 149, 153
Knight, Annie, 96
Krafft-Ebing, Richard von, 71
Kwaansa, Kobina, 116, 117

Lagos, 16, 110
Lamarr, Hedy, 51
Lane, Christopher, 5
Lauder, Harry, 144
Lawrence, D. H., 148
Lawrence, T. E., 5, 6, 77
Lefroy, Edward Cracroft, 83, 153
Le Gallienne, Richard, 156
Leith-Ross, Sylvia, 8, 72, 74, 165
Leonard, Arthur Glyn, 8, 89, 98
Liberia, 32, 52
libraries: in Britain, 129, 130; personal, 25, 32; in West Africa, 117
Lincoln's Inn Fields, 63
Little College Street (London), 57, 63
Little House of No Regrets (Onitsha), 1, 2, 16, 80, 81, 82, 96, 102, 138, 148, 149, 161
Liverpool, 30, 44, 48
Livingstone, David, 40
local cultures, African, 5, 6, 7, 8, 15, 17, 41, 46, 55, 87, 88, 92, 103, 112, 143, 149, 161, 166
London, 29, 52, 57, 68, 147, 148
Long, John, 52
Longfellow, Henry Wadsworth, 147

Mami Wata, 6, 100, 101–5, 139, 167; shrines to, 104
Manchester, 3, 17, 20, 30, 32, 45, 48, 65, 74, 78, 80, 118, 119, 128, 130, 136
Manchester City Police Force, 22
Manchester Grammar School, 138
Manchester Petty Sessional Court, 21
marriage, 2, 10, 34, 54, 78, 92–4, 96, 102, 112, 114, 115, 165–66; monogamous, 18, 112, 114; in the spirit world, 100, 105, 106, 167
masculinity, 34, 38, 47, 70, 71, 97, 120, 130, 135, 136, 158, 164; and empire, 35, 48, 51, 52, 54

Masterman, C. F. G., 26
masturbation, 57, 66, 68–9, 70, 120, 130, 132, 135
Mbari shrines, 14
McClintock, Anne, 40
memoirs, 15, 16, 18, 56, 57, 62, 65, 67, 68, 76, 77, 82, 94, 98, 102, 106, 119, 124, 126, 127, 162, 165
Mersey River, 43
metropolitan culture, 7, 8, 40, 75, 88, 105, 106, 149, 166
Miller Brothers (Manchester), 32, 56
Milton, John, 153
miscegenation, 7, 16, 42, 50, 51, 52, 53, 54, 134
misogyny. *See* Stuart-Young as "woman-hater"
mission schools, 101
missionaries, 4, 8, 14, 18, 26, 33, 35, 37, 48, 50, 54, 78, 113, 165, 167
Modernism, 144, 145, 147, 148, 149, 155; and counter-Modernism, 144–5, 149
modernity, 100
Moore, George, 67
morbidity, 135, 146
mulatto. *See* miscegenation
music: accordion, 144; organ, 24; piano, 24
music hall, 29, 143–44, 146, 153

Ndaguba, Charles, 116
Nelson Street (Manchester), 23–25, 32, 127
new imperial history, 7, 9, 17, 33, 112. *See also* imperial history
New Market Road (Onistha), 1, 81, 149, 161, 168
newspapers: African-owned, 3, 4, 14, 16–18, 57, 75, 76, 90, 101, 107, 108, 110, 111, 112, 114, 115, 118, 139, 141, 144, 145, 149, 158, 159, 162–63; as archive, 117; British, 23, 33, 56, 57, 64–65, 66–68; and nationalism, 16
Nicholson, John Gambril, 76, 83, 153
Niger Company, 103
Niger Delta, 48, 49
Nigeria, 34, 98, 114, 139, 140, 143, 144
Niger River, 3, 4, 15, 38, 56, 102, 106
Nordau, Max, 131
North America, 77, 78
Norton, Rictor, 146
novels, 16, 56, 57, 83, 112, 119, 127; autobiographical, 94

Noyes, Alfred, 144
Nsukka Division, 10
Nupe, 36
Nussbaum, Felicity, 7
Nwora, Akunne John, 93, 99, 101, 148

obi (king), 3
Obike, Solomon I., 1, 82, 83, 159
obituaries, 162–63
O'Dazi, Jack (pseud. J. M. Stuart-Young), 90, 119, 120, 129, 132, 134
Odeziaku (pseud. J. M. Stuart-Young), 1, 3, 6, 8, 19, 76, 82, 90, 91, 92, 97, 98, 99, 102, 105, 108, 139, 150, 162, 163
Odoziaku. *See* Odeziaku
Okely, Judith, 163-4
Okwei, Omu, 48, 50
Old Cemetery (Onitsha), 160
Olisa, Emeka Geoffrey, 82
Olomo, 49
Omvaro, Madame, 49
Onitsha, 1, 56, 74, 75, 77, 78, 90, 91, 155; history of, 15, 92; intellectual culture in, 7, 15, 116, 141, 149; market and commerce, 2, 82; people of, 91, 98, 104, 106; senior men of, 80
Onitsha Province, 4
Onwuegbuzia, C. A. J., 93, 98, 99, 102
Onwuh, M. O. Kodit, 140
orality: Igbo, 4, 14, 151; naming, 4, 6, 7, 19, 88, 89, 92, 97, 99, 101, 105, 106, 168; praise-names, 82, 90, 92, 103, 139, 162; praise-songs, 2; songs of abuse, 2; storytelling, 81
orientalism, 43
orthography, 90
Osika, Madame, 49
Ouseley, John, 83

palm oil and kernels, 4–5, 15, 92, 138; African middlemen, 15, 34, 56; African traders, 3, 4, 34, 88, 105, 113; European middlemen, 16; European trade combines, 5, 39, 117, 118, 150; European traders, 1, 4, 14, 15, 16, 17, 29–30, 33, 34–41, 44, 49, 50, 56, 75, 77, 78, 82, 90, 91, 92, 96, 98, 99, 101, 102, 103, 105, 108, 109, 119, 139, 150, 155, 157, 164; merchant princes, 39; products made from, 38, 40, 42, 47, 103; trade routes, 34, 39, 92, 100. *See also* trade currencies; traders' writings; women

Pan-Africanism, 75, 110, 112, 115, 117, 157, 162
Paris, 57, 67, 77
Park, Mungo, 54, 55
Parker, Richard, 161
Pater, Walter, 76
patronage, European, 2, 3, 78, 82, 83, 97, 98, 99
Pears soap, 40, 135
Pearson, Hesketh, 62, 63
pederasty, 17, 19, 66, 76, 80, 82, 83, 86, 87, 97, 133, 134, 135, 165
Perkins, David, 145
Peter Pan, 109, 110
Phillips, Stephen, 144, 156, 157
photography, 56, 57, 64, 73, 78, 83, 84, 87
Pincheon, Bill Stanford, 14
poetry, 1, 16, 56–8, 83, 90, 106, 109, 110, 119, 130, 139, 147, 159, 169; pastoral, 43, 84, 87, 145, 146, 155–8; sonnets, 142, 144, 147, 154, 167
police "wanted" lists, 30
popular literature, 15, 33; and empire, 35, 50, 52. *See also* slum writing
Port Harcourt, 1, 16, 111, 159, 160
postcolonial literature, 16
poststructuralism, 11, 72, 151
precolonial cultures, 4, 12, 34, 38, 41, 89, 109, 165
python. *See* Eke

queer theory, 10–11, 12, 13, 17, 19, 65, 66, 69, 73, 164
quoting techniques, 150, 151, 152

race, 3, 7, 18, 35, 36, 72, 115, 167; and colonialism, 32, 83; and sexuality, 50, 51, 93
racism, 8, 94, 108, 109, 110, 116, 156, 164, 166
rape, 134
readers: British, 65, 67, 129, 136; West African, 16, 17, 75, 76, 110, 111, 112, 118, 141–43, 148–50, 162, 164
realism, 128, 129
Remington Typewriter Company, 25
Roman Catholic Mission (Onitsha), 3, 15, 113
Romanticism, 141, 142, 158
Ross, Robert, 64

sadomasochism, 134, 135
Sambia (Papua New Guinea), 93

Savoy Hotel (London), 62, 63
Schalow, Paul Gordon, 93
séances, 11, 99, 101, 105, 153. *See also* spiritualism
secretaries, African, 82
Sedgwick, Eve Kosofsky, 65, 72, 80
Sekyi, Kobina, 116, 117
sexology, 10, 65, 71
sexuality, 2, 5–8, 10, 57, 65, 66, 69, 71, 72, 74, 77, 86, 110, 113, 118, 126, 129, 131, 132, 134, 136, 139, 154, 165–6, 170; and desire, 10, 34, 66, 69, 73, 80, 83, 93, 134, 146, 166, 167; and empire, 4, 5, 6, 8, 92, 93, 98, 106; and forgery, 20; and identity, 68, 71, 73, 77, 94, 106, 164; and power, 12–13; history of, 10, 12, 14. *See also* gender; heterosexuality; homosexuality; queer theory
Shakespeare, William, 62, 75, 140, 147, 149, 150, 153, 155
Shaw, George Bernard, 76
Sheik, The, 53
Shelley, Percy Bysshe, 130, 142
Shirley (Southampton), 94
Simonton, Ida Vera, 51, 52
Sinfield, Alan, 71, 72
slavery, 4, 27, 38, 43, 100
slum life, 26–27, 29, 38, 40, 120, 124, 127, 131, 132
slum writing, 26, 29, 35, 119, 120, 128, 129, 132, 134, 157
soap, 27, 36, 38, 40
Society of Authors, 138
South Africa, 30, 33, 136, 137
Southampton, 96, 159
Southampton West Hotel, 96
Southern Africa, 36
spiritualism, 4, 23, 24, 99, 101, 104, 139, 153, 154, 169
St. Thomas's School (Ardwick), 123
Stanley, Henry Morton, 5, 35, 78, 119
Stanley, Liz, 164
status, Igbo, 2. *See also* title-taking
Stead, W. T., 76
Stockwell, Arthur, 78
Stoler, Ann Laura, 7, 9, 17, 18, 33, 47, 51, 112
Stoller, Robert J., 93, 97
Strangeways Prison (Manchester), 21, 31, 124, 129, 130, 135, 136
Stuart-Young, John Moray: as trader, 33, 44, 48, 90, 103, 104, 149, 169; doctorate, 101, 108, 138, 139, 140, 148, 163, 167; funeral of, 1–3, 165; illness and death of, 82, 83, 91, 105, 159, 160; *Johnny Jones Guttersnipe,* 94, 119, 121, 126, 128, 129, 131, 133–35; marriage of, 93, 94, 96, 165–66; *Merely a Negress,* 51–53; *Osrac, the Self-Sufficient,* 57–68, 75, 86, 118, 130, 138, 139; *Passion's Peril,* 68; property owned by, 83, 161, 165; *The Seductive Coast,* 156; *Soul-Slayer,* 78, 128, 134–35; *Through Veiled Eyes,* 83–87, 153; trial and imprisonment of, 22–33, 30–31, 127; *What Does it Matter?* 94, 119, 120, 126, 133, 135; as "woman hater," 13, 49, 50, 93, 94, 97, 136
Sunderland, 57, 86
Swanzy, 50
Swinburne, Algernon, 146, 153
Symonds, John Addington, 71, 73, 76, 77
Symons, Arthur, 67, 130

Talbot, P. Amaury, 8, 14, 98
Taylor, Alfred, 57, 63
Taylor, Walter (Liverpool), 75
Tebb, William, 160
theology, 114
Tinubu, Madame, 48
Tinubu Square (Lagos), 108
title-taking, Igbo, 2, 4, 34, 102
Todd, Thomas Olman, 57, 86
Todd, Tommy ("T.O.T. Junior"), 84, 86, 87
tourism, 78, 83
trade currencies, 44, 48
traders' writings, 33, 34, 38, 40, 46, 50, 52, 53, 55
tuberculosis, 96, 124

Ulrichs, Karl, 71
Umuahia, 82
Unilever, 40
United States of America, 16, 117, 152
Unuka, Madame, 49
Uranian, 76, 77, 78, 80, 81, 83, 86, 87, 89, 96, 102, 106, 110, 134, 135, 136, 146, 147, 153, 154, 165
Urning, 71

Venice, 77
vernacular languages, 110, 115

Victorian culture, 13, 17, 28–29, 40, 42, 67–70, 77, 110, 126, 129, 130, 131, 137, 143, 144, 154
Vollum, Edward P., 160

Walker, Frederick, 83
Wallace, Edgar, 156
Watson, William, 130, 142, 144, 145, 146, 153
Webb, Beatrice, 26
Weston, Kath, 14
Whitford, John, 37, 40, 42–4, 45, 46, 55
White Cargo (film), 51
Widdowson, Peter, 145
Wilde, Oscar, 11, 18, 25, 57–74, 76, 77, 78, 80, 86, 96, 97, 126, 130, 131, 153, 154, 166; *Ballad of Reading Gaol*, 127–28; death of, 65; *De Profundis*, 57, 128; letters from, 57, 60, 62; "A Portrait of Mr WH," 62; sexuality of, 60–62, 69; trials and imprisonment of, 57, 65, 68, 89, 167
Wilder, Alexander, 160
Williams, Adisa, 157
women, European, 47, 48
women, Igbo, 1–3, 8, 9–10, 38, 50; as farmers, 49; as "female husbands," 9, 13; as merchant queens, 3, 15, 48, 49, 102; as traders and brokers, 1, 2, 3, 4, 34, 44, 48, 49, 56, 88, 90, 92, 101, 103, 165. *See also* Women's War
Women's War, 49
Wordsworth, William, 130

Young, John Pultney, 21, 26, 96
Young, Nellie Gibson Etheridge, 94, 96, 97, 159, 166
Young, Robert, 51

Zik. *See* Azikiwe, Nnamdi
Zola, Émile, 67

www.ingramcontent.com/pod-product-compliance
Lightning Source LLC
Chambersburg PA
CBHW031241290426
44109CB00012B/394